THE ADVENTURES OF THE MOSS

The Men Of Sixty Something

By

Gasper A. Chifici

ISBN: 978-1-916770-71-3 (Paperback)

ISBN: 978-1-916770-72-0 (Hardcover)

Dedication

This book is dedicated to all of us men over 60 years old who have so much wisdom and advice to offer but are disappointed to find that there's so little demand for it. Our children and grandchildren insist on wanting to make their own mistakes, or else how will they ever learn? They may just learn a lot, seeing as how prolific they are at the mistake part. We can rest assured that if they fail to come to us for advice, they will most certainly come to us for money to fix things.

This book is more specifically dedicated to those men over sixty who were, and are still (whether they like it or not) members of the MOSS, and especially those who are charter members, having joined during that first year of 2011. Over the years, some members have moved away, presumably to start new chapters of the MOSS. We miss them and applaud them for their attempts at keeping the spirit of the MOSS alive. To those men, I say, you still owe a franchise fee, so cough it up.

Others of our original members have passed on to their heavenly reward and so have better things to do than to hang around with a bunch of geezers. Nick, Hickley, C.J., we miss you guys, and since most of us are in our late sixties now (I'm sixty-twelve), we'll no doubt be passing on relatively soon unless the Rapture happens first. Now that would be something to write about!

Disclaimer

This book is a work of friction because it will no doubt rub some people the wrong way. It is also mostly a work of fiction. Most of the names in this book are fictitious, along with some of the places. The events that take place are mostly fictitious, and the ones that actually happened should have been fictitious. Any similarity between certain fictional characters in this book and real people, living or dead, is unintentional. Any similarity between certain other fictional characters in this book and real people, living or dead, is intentional. You know who you are.

Acknowledgment

To my wife Denise, who has put up with my nonsense for more than 51 years of marriage and encourages me in everything I do. She is the best, and I thank God for her every day.

To my daughters Amy and Ellen, two wonderful and accomplished women of whom I couldn't be prouder and who encouraged me to write this book as long as they weren't in it.

To fellow members of the MOSS, whose friendships, personalities, and quirks offered tons of fodder for this book.

To my Uncle Charles, who bears only a passing resemblance to Uncle Joe in this book. I had the most fun with this character. I hope he doesn't seek revenge.

To my friend, author, and fellow Civil Engineer Stephen Estopinal, who, in addition to several technical books on surveying, has written ten wonderful novels of historical fiction. His advice to me on attempting to write a book was to 'discipline yourself to set aside time every day to write.' His inspiration, advice, and encouragement are very much appreciated.

To my Christian friend and author Janice Boekhoff, who has written at least eight books, including the Earth Hunters Trilogy. She gave me suggestions on helpful tools with which to write and encouragement to keep the faith – that authoring a book and leading a Christian life can be completely compatible.

To growing up in Donaldsonville, Louisiana, an experience appreciated only in hindsight. Being poor, living in the government housing project – twice – and in too many rental houses to count forced me to be more self-reliant than I otherwise might have been and led me to take very little for granted in life. Not a bad way at all to grow up.

To a valuable lesson learned. Writing a book isn't rocket science. Rocket science is easier.

Table Of Contents

About the Author

Gasper Chifici was born on Father's Day on June 18, 1950, in the small but bustling little town of Donaldsonville, Louisiana. As the first grandchild of his paternal Italian and maternal French grandparents, his birth was much celebrated. His 18-year-old mother, Peggy, and his often-unemployed father, Henry, unable to pay the hospital bill, succumbed to the bribery of Gasper's grandmother Chifici who agreed to pay the bill if the boy was named after his grandfather Gasper. Some 16 years later, when applying for social security, grandfather Gasper discovered two things: he was one year younger than he supposed he was, and his actual name was Andrew Gasparo Chifici. It was too late for young Gasper to change his name, having suffered through childhood when Casper the Friendly Ghost was inexplicably popular. His mother apologized for naming him Gasper to her dying day.

Gasper was fortunate to meet his future wife at a mutual cousin's wedding reception at the Royal Orleans in New Orleans during the summer prior to beginning his studies at LSU in Baton Rouge. He and Denise were married on January 8, 1972, during his junior year in Civil Engineering, and began married life in an apartment near campus before being accepted into married student housing. Upon his graduation in May of 1973, and having accepted a job with the State of Louisiana Office of Public Works, he and Denise lived in Baton Rouge, then in Lafayette, Thibodaux (where their daughters were born), Metairie, and Kenner. Through several career changes, they set up residence in Baton Rouge again, then in Miami, Florida, followed by Carlsbad, California, and finally back to Ascension Parish 6 months after Hurricane Katrina in 2006.

Gasper is semi-retired now but is busier than ever. He is President of his one-man project management consulting firm, and is a board member of the Ascension Parish Tourism Commission and the Greater Ascension Rotary Club, on the Advisory Council of Volunteer Ascension, President of the Oak Alley Estates HOA, and active in his church, Trinity Baptist. He founded the organization MOSS (Men Of Sixty Something) in 2011, and The Adventures of the MOSS is his first novel.

Page Blank Intentionally

Preface

When we are young, we lack the wisdom and experience necessary to be certain of the decisions we make. In fact, it is in the bad choices that we make that we start to compile the life knowledge we need to make the necessary future corrections.

As we age, those life experiences congeal into the wisdom we will take into our later years. That's not to say that everyone who reaches what is arbitrarily referred to as 'senior citizen' status is wise. The fact is, some of us just never learn. That might be more evident in Washington, DC, than anywhere else.

But some of us do learn. We learn that keeping active, staying in touch with friends, regular attendance and involvement in our churches, surrounding ourselves with a loving family, and volunteering our time to help others keep us healthy both mentally and physically. We can't and won't avoid the inevitable, but we can enrichen our last years and perhaps the waning years of others by continuing to make meaningful contributions to society for as long as we're able.

Part One

Chapter One

"So Tony, what are we going to call this group," asked Uncle Joe.

I hadn't thought of that. "Why do we have to call it anything?" I responded. "We're just some old friends having breakfast."

Uncle Joe then says that we ought to call ourselves something because if we're a group, we might get a discount on breakfast. He's always thinking of some way to save money.

Dustin chimed in with, "How about 'The Old Men's Breakfast'?"

"Well, that's descriptive alright, but I don't like the acronym," I said. "TOMB". The four of us thought for a while; Kevin and I doodled on the paper tablecloth with crayons that some kids must have left in the Sweet'N Low dish.

Kevin suggested, "How about 'Men of Sixty Something'? We're all in our sixties, right?"

"But I'm seventy-one," complained Uncle Joe, who you could tell wasn't crazy about being the oldest guy.

"No," I countered. "You're sixty-eleven. You qualify. And I like the acronym – MOSS. Moss is grey and grows on stately oaks. It's a fitting name for this group."

Someone else suggested that moss is a fungus, but I don't think so. I'll have to Google it.

The way this got started was, one day soon after my 60th birthday, my wife Darlene and I were having breakfast at Frank's Restaurant in Prairieville when I noticed a group of older guys (even older than me) at a corner table chomping on sausage biscuits, slurping coffee, and laughing and gabbing away. They looked like they were having a great time. I decided then and there that I wanted to get together once a week with friends my age. Guess I was feeling nostalgic or something. That's when the idea for the gathering that we later named MOSS was born.

So I called my Uncle Joe, who was my dad's youngest brother and not that much older than me and told him my idea about meeting for breakfast every Friday. He was all for it, being retired and, like a lot of us when we got older, unable to sleep past 5:30 a.m. anyway. Then I called Dustin, whom I've known since I was 6 years old when we were in Sister Marie's first-grade class together. Dustin, his wife Connie, and Darlene and I spend most Friday evenings together. He liked the idea too and said he was pretty sure our friend Kevin would join us because his wife got him out of the house early on Fridays so she could have the neighborhood women over for pilates, whatever that is.

We started meeting on Fridays at Frank's at 8:00 a.m., but that proved to be a mistake for a couple of reasons. One, most of us had already had about a gallon of coffee at home by that time, and two, I had to pick up Uncle Joe, who couldn't drive because of a stroke, and he lives right by Dutchtown High School. The traffic when I went to pick him up was so bad you'd swear that every kid and teacher at the school each drove two cars there. So we moved it to 7:30, but after a couple of months, everyone started showing up at 7:00. I drew the line at 7:00. Yes, I get up at 5:30, even on weekends, but I like to take care of my "regular" business at home if you know what I mean.

Kevin and my Uncle Joe are both retired. Uncle Joe had to quit working when he had a stroke. You'd never know by looking at him that he had a stroke, but he can't see anything in his right field of vision, so he can't drive. He thinks he should still be allowed to drive if he made only left turns, and my aunt Millie and I had to prove to him that he wouldn't even be able to get out of his own subdivision before he'd give up on the idea. Kevin Farmer retired after he sold his grocery store, Farmer's Market, for a gazillion dollars to a regional chain. Of course, he now says that if he had held out for another year, he could have got two gazillions, so he's a little bitter about that.

Dustin, a retired teacher, and I still work part-time, and full retirement doesn't seem like it's in the picture anytime soon for either one of us. I try to drum up work for a local engineering firm, and Dustin teaches some nights at the local community college. But we can't complain – part-time jobs give each of us a lot of latitude when it comes to what we do with our time. Uncle Joe said that I didn't have a job; I had a position. Whatever. I call what I do at Frank's on Friday morning "business development." I don't know exactly whose business I'm developing, but you never know when someone might need a consulting engineer. I always feel like I should be in heavy demand.

Before you know it, other friends were asking if they could join us. The four of us talked about it and decided that anybody who joined us should have some sort of qualifications, so we decided that members of MOSS had to be:

1. Male

2. 60 or older

3. Wise

We took a chance that excluding women wouldn't result in some sort of protest, but our wives were so happy to get rid of us for a couple of hours once a week that none of them objected. We also decided that the "wise" requirement was a self-judgment thing. Otherwise, maybe the four of us wouldn't qualify either. But then we figured that anyone who survived for at least 60 years must have picked up some wisdom along the way, even if it was accidental.

Within a year, we had over 30 guys in the group, including my brother T-Joe. He was named after our Uncle Joe, so to avoid confusion, the family called him Tiny Joe, later shortened to T-Joe. He is only 14 months younger than me and had just turned 60, but we never had more than a dozen or so show up on any given Friday. Mostly it was the same guys every week – the ones who either had nothing else to do or whose wives put them out in the morning with the garbage. Besides, for the ones I already mentioned, there was Terry Parmenter, who used to run a wastewater plant before he retired; Rodney Keets, who retired from a big oil company; Donnie Ourso, woodworker and retired shop teacher whose wife Marlene was in my high school class, Ronald Burgoyne, who owns three or four of those urgent care facilities, Jack Roussel, a retired cane farmer and self-proclaimed local historian, Alden Roussel, attorney and Jack's cousin, Slim Pickens, barber, and Jed Wally, retired Sheriff.

I guess you could say that we were birds of a feather, flocking together. We called our get-togethers "gatherings" because of that old proverb, "a rolling stone gathers no moss." I know it doesn't actually make any sense to call our breakfast meetings "gatherings" for that reason, but that's what we call them. I never claimed it was brilliant or anything.

So now that I had my wish about having breakfast once a week with friends, you would think that I would be satisfied. You would be wrong. Having never learned the art of "leaving well enough alone," I decided that there must be some overriding cosmic purpose for such a group to get together, and it was up to me to figure out what that was. I could not accept that we were there solely for the stuffed French toast with a side of bacon – although I admit that's a pretty good reason for showing up.

I had this idea while reading the newspaper one morning. Yes, Darlene and I still get the newspaper delivered, and I bring it into the bedroom on a tray with a pot of coffee and two pre-heated mugs every morning around 6 a.m. Pre-heated mugs may be the secret to a long marriage. We read the entire paper, including the obituaries. I don't know when that started, but it's practically a ritual now. Some days when there are a lot of obits, I add up the ages of everyone who died to see what the average age is. I throw out the outliers – you know, the ones that died really young in accidents and such – and try to include only those who it seemed like died from natural causes. On some days, the average is alarmingly close to my age. I've been thinking that I should stop reading the obituaries, but the rest of the paper is even more depressing. Also, on the plus side, the obits are the absolute best place to find nicknames.

Anyway, I was reading that there are almost 2,000 think tanks in the United States. These think tanks focus on any number of things, but most of them work on solving one world problem or another – and I guess they never run out of problems to solve because new ones seem to pop up about every other day.

So I figured that MOSS could be the think tank for Ascension Parish. We could look at the problems in the Parish and figure out possible solutions. I was sure that everyone would really like this idea.

"I really don't like that idea," said Uncle Joe when I suggested at the next gathering that MOSS become the think tank for the Parish. I swear he can be so negative.

"Why don't you like the idea?" I asked him.

"Because all that's going to happen is that when things go to hell in a handbasket after they try out our recommendations, we get to be the scrapegoat," he said. I tried to tell him he meant to say "scapegoat," but he said scapegoat doesn't make any sense, and what did I know anyhow? I was just an engineer.

"I kind of like the idea," offered Dustin. A few of the guys sided with Dustin and me on this, but a couple of others thought that Uncle Joe might be right.

I suggested that we put it to a vote, and Uncle Joe said that we ought to have a secret ballot because he thought most everyone would support him if they didn't have to come right out in public and do it. So we borrowed some pages out of our waitress Wendy's order book for the vote. If you thought we should become Ascension Parish's think tank, you voted "yes," and if you thought we'd better not, you voted "no." We asked Wendy to pick up the votes and count them in the other room. She came back in a few minutes and told us "There were eight 'yes' votes and five 'no' votes." That was okay, except there were only twelve of us there that day. We already had a voter fraud crisis.

"Okay, who voted twice?" I asked the group, after recounting the votes to make sure Wendy didn't miscount. I was pretty sure Wendy hadn't miscounted because, although she never got our orders right, she could tell you to the penny what a 20% tip on your bill was, in case you needed to know.

Uncle Joe admitted that he cast a proxy vote for Terry, who couldn't make it that morning. I told him that made no sense because we had no idea we would be voting on anything. In fact, this was the first vote we ever had. He just insisted that Terry told him that if he didn't show up, he should tell everyone that he was sorry he couldn't make it today. Uncle Joe took that as a proxy, and it was no use arguing about it. Since it didn't make a difference in the outcome, we just dropped it. Not exactly Robert's Rules of Order.

Since this think tank thing was my idea, I was expected to take the lead on it and figure out just how it was going to work. What problems would we tackle? How would we go about determining solutions? Who would even care about what we thought? Very good questions. But all Uncle Joe could think about was, would anybody pay us to be their think tank? Nothing but money on the brain.

I figured that the first thing to do was to get the word out about MOSS being a think tank. Even though I'm not a big fan of social media and the like, sometimes you have to get with the program. There are two e-newspapers in Ascension – The Crawfish and The Premium Post. I know the owners of both, so I figured what I'd do was to send them a human-interest story about the MOSS group, telling about how us old friends get together and discuss what's going on in Ascension Parish while having breakfast in a local establishment and therefore supporting the economy. I would also throw in a blurb about how we're a bunch of experienced and wise men who offer their services as a think tank to anyone interested. I sent the story off and got a call from both of them. The conversations were eerily similar.

"Tony, you too cheap to buy an ad? We have to survive, too, you know."

"I know, I know, but look, if you run this story I sent you, and we get any paying customers from it, I'll run an ad for a year." They both bought it. Suckers. Who would pay a bunch of geezers to be a think tank? I figured if we got any bites, we'd do it just for fun anyway.

The story I submitted read like this: "Announcing the formation of the MOSS (Men Of Sixty Something), a group of old friends who are wise and experienced men of sixty years old or older, who meet once a week for breakfast and discuss the issues facing Ascension Parish. They are the Parish's premier think tank, ready to lend their brainpower to the study of any problem, big or small, presented to them. If you have a problem you'd like the MOSS to analyze, or if you think you might qualify to join this august and noteworthy group, contact tony.campachi@gmail.com. Crazies need not apply."

I also sent a photo of twelve of us that I took the day of the questionable vote, with the names of everyone included. This was a little risky because not everyone was sure yet that they wanted to be so publicly identified with MOSS – at least not until we gained some respect and credibility. Also, the four guys on the losing side that day (the ones actually present, no proxies) looked kind of like they were snarling or something. I caught some flak later from Uncle Joe because I didn't get his permission to publish his likeness on the websites, claiming "invasion of privacy." He watches way too much television. He didn't make too big a deal out of it, though, because I could tell that he loved having his picture in the news, even if it was only an e-paper.

Chapter Two

Time went by, as it tends to do, and before you could say, "Wendy, would you pre-heat my coffee mug?" we got a bite from a reader of The Premium Post. Here's the email I received:

"Tony, I am the HOA Secretary for Elms on the Hill subdivision. The President of the HOA, Gerald Cloutier, asked that I reach out to you regarding a problem we're having. Several residents have joined forces and are threatening to sue the HOA because of dog waste that is constantly left on and next to the walking trail around our lake. They think that the HOA is responsible for policing the area and fining the people who don't pick up after their dogs. We do have a schedule of fines that includes this infraction, but we can't catch who's doing it. We're considering raising dues for all dog owners, and the dog owners have banded together and are also threatening to sue the HOA. Our by-laws require that we try to settle these sorts of issues by non-binding arbitration before going to court. Would some of the MOSS group consider being our arbitration panel? We can't pay anything, but my husband will cook a jambalaya for y'all, and I'll make some bread pudding with rum sauce. Please let me know. Thanks," "Marlene Lalonde, Secretary, Elms on the Hill HOA," and she gave me her phone number and email.

This was right up our alley. I got the email on a Wednesday morning, so I called Marlene and told her that I would run it by the MOSS Board on Friday and let her know. We didn't actually have a Board, but I figured if we were going to be in the think tank business, we'd better get professional about it. Come Friday morning, I brought the matter to the gathered group, which was 13 of us, knowing that they'd be really excited about this.

"I'm not really excited about this," said Uncle Joe. "HOAs can get nasty. They can turn on you like a cornered possum. What are they going to pay us?" I figured that's what it would come down to.

"Marlene said her husband would cook us a jambalaya, and she'd make dessert," I told him.

"Hey, I know Marlene Lalonde," said Slim. "Her husband is No-Neck Lalonde. He was the World Jambalaya Champion 10 or 12 years ago. Man, I bet he can make a mean jambalaya!" Slim is a barber who is 5 feet 7 inches tall and weighs about 240 pounds. Slim's given name is Clyde Pickens, and he hated the name Clyde, and his grandpa was a big Slim Pickens fan, so he started calling his grandson "Slim." Of course, Slim wasn't so stout back in those days.

I told the guys that I sort of suggested to Marlene that we had a Board of Directors that would review her request and decide if we wanted to tackle her problem.

Dr. Dart offered, "I think that the four of you who started the MOSS group ought to be the Board of Directors, with Tony as the Chairman. You all have been here the longest." Dr. Dart is not a medical doctor, unfortunately, because we could have used one of those. He has a doctorate in medieval history or something and runs the local community college. My nephew tells me that the kids there started calling him "Dr. Darth Vader," just behind his back, though, because he wears black most of the time.

"I move that Tony, Uncle Joe, Kevin, and Dustin be elected by acclamation as the MOSS Board of Directors, with Tony as the Chair," Dr. Dart continued. Everybody cheered, and Slim spilled his coffee on Terry's lap, so the cheering also included a "Yeow! You idiot!"

Uncle Joe immediately asked if the Board members would get a per diem. I reminded him that we didn't have any membership fees or dues or such, so there was no money with which to pay a per diem. "Well, maybe the members of MOSS – all except the Board, that is – should pay dues," he suggested. "I make a motion that all non-Board members of MOSS pay 10 bucks a month for dues." Needless to say, that motion failed for lack of a second.

"Okay," I said, "thank you all for your confidence in us. Now we need to decide if we're going to take on this HOA thing. This might affect the whole group, so it ought to not be just the Board deciding. Anybody got any thoughts about it?"

"I have some experience with using an arbitration panel," offered Ronald. "My urgent care places get threatened with lawsuits every week. I wouldn't mind being on the panel if we decide to do this."

Uncle Joe, who was still sulking about the per diem thing, said that we should leave him out of it. Terry told us that his sister Patty lived in Elms on the Hill and that she had a 90-pound Goldendoodle who could compete with a cow in the poop department, and he wasn't sure if his sister picked up the stuff, so he begged off. Terry used to run a wastewater plant, so he knows something about poop.

Jack volunteered for the panel, as long as we were okay with the fact that he thought that anyone who lived in a subdivision in the first place was an idiot, present company excepted, of course. Jack lives on a 10-acre plot of land on the river road and cuts his grass himself with a John Deere. His youngest son, Harold, lives in my subdivision, and Jack doesn't even like to visit him.

Slim asked if you had to be on the panel to get No-Neck's jambalaya, and I said "yes," so he also volunteered. I put my hat in since it was my idea, and we cut the panel off at four. We were all set. I called Marlene Lalonde right after we finished breakfast and told her we were good to go.

Chapter Three

Elms on the Hill doesn't have a community clubhouse or anything, so I'm told that the HOA usually meets at someone's home and, by default, that someone is usually the President. But when I called Marlene to tell her that we were ready to get started, she said that the Board of the HOA suggested meeting at a local church. The HOA treasurer was a member of the church and said that he could talk the pastor into letting them use their sanctuary for the meeting.

"Marlene, that's a great idea," I told her. "That should keep the fighting down to a minimum. Who would want to desecrate a church sanctuary?"

"Ha! You don't know these folks. We got some real troublemakers in this subdivision," she said. She sure didn't talk like that when she first asked the MOSS group to get involved. I was starting to get a little anxious. She asked me how many of us would be on the panel.

"There will be four of us, including me," I told her. "When do you want to have the meeting?"

"Our by-laws require that we give everyone in the subdivision a 7-day notice for a special meeting, so the earliest we can meet is next Friday night. Will that work for y'all?" she asked.

I told her that we could since the LSU Baseball team was playing Arkansas away, and as long as we could check on the score now and then, we could make it next Friday. I then told her that the guys were going to ask me when No-Neck was doing the jambalaya.

"He said he'd cook on Saturday afternoon, assuming the meeting would be over by then," she laughed. Now I was starting to worry. "He'll make enough for thirty, so bring your wives if you like. I'll make plenty of my bread pudding. We'll set up tables under the carport at my house." The guys would be happy about that – not the part about "bring your wives" but that they could all come.

So we agreed to meet on the following Friday at 7:00 p.m. at the "Fountain Community Church" in Prairieville. I had until then to become an expert in arbitration. Naturally, the first thing I did was call an attorney friend, Alden Roussel, who was a member of MOSS but didn't make too many gatherings. Alden was retired and traveled in his RV with his wife a good bit but usually answered his cell phone. I caught him stopped at a gas station in Santa Fe and filled him in on what was going on.

"Are you out of your mind? Whatever possessed you to think that it would be a good idea to get involved in an HOA dispute?" was his immediate response. "I've seen fistfights in court over HOA lawsuits. Something happens to people who live in subdivisions where the houses are too close together. They go nuts." Alden lived on 4 acres on the river road near Jack and paid someone to take care of his yard. Alden didn't "cut his grass" like the rest of us. He had someone "mow his lawn."

"We can't back out now," I said. "We're committed."

"Yeah, you ought to be committed, alright," he said. "Just make sure that both parties to the arbitration sign an agreement that holds you and the MOSS group harmless of any repercussions as a result of your decision. Otherwise, you'll need an attorney yourself because it's guaranteed that one of the two parties will not like the outcome." Man, Alden is another one who can be so negative. This was just a little argument over some dog poop. How bad could it get?

After the conversation with Alden, I decided to look up "arbitration" and figure out the ground rules. Here's the definition from the Legal Dictionary: "Arbitration – the submission of a dispute to an unbiased third person designated by the parties to the controversy, who agree in advance to comply with the award – a decision to be issued after a hearing at which both parties have an opportunity to be heard."

That sounded easy enough. I did a little more research and decided we needed to line up a few other things in order to be really professional about this:

1. Someone to take notes

2. A gavel

3. A big guy moonlighting from the Sheriff's department to keep the peace

Slim's wife Barbara used to be a secretary for the school board, and she volunteered to take notes, I think mainly because she had heard a lot of gossip about the whole dog poop controversy and thought it would be fun to be there.

I already had a gavel for being Past President of the Rotary Club, but I had to take it off of the plaque it was glued onto. I could just glue it back on later unless we got more of these arbitration gigs.

Marlene said that the HOA would spring for some security at the event if I knew anyone who would work cheap, so I called T.J. Morales, a deputy with the Sheriff's department. He played football at St. Amant High a few years back, and they called him "Wide Load" Morales because, as an offensive lineman, he was so big that he could block two defensive tackles at a time. Also because he took up two folding chairs to sit down. If it hadn't been for bum knees, he would have played college ball for sure.

Sheriff Rob Pepper, whose son played with T.J. at St. Amant, hired him right out of high school, but he couldn't put him in a patrol car without making major modifications to the seats, so he had T.J. working the jailhouse in Donaldsonville. I'm told that T.J., who was actually very soft-spoken and kind-hearted, was nevertheless an intimidating presence at the jail.

T.J. said that he would do it for $40 an hour and a seat at the jambalaya dinner – actually, two seats. I would have to tell No-Neck that he would need to add a few pounds of rice and sausage.

We were ready for the big event.

Chapter Four

At exactly 7:00 p.m. on the following Friday, in the sanctuary of Fountain Community Church, Gerald Cloutier called the meeting to order.

"Now we're all friends and neighbors here," began Gerald, "and we're in the house of God, so let's all sit back and relax, and we'll get this arbitration hearing started. You all agreed to participate in this thing and to abide by the decision of this panel. This here is Tony Campachi, and he'll introduce the members of the arbitration panel, and give you their credentials, and tell you how this hearing is going to proceed."

Credentials? I thought to myself. I was taken by surprise by this and was going to have to come up with something quick. I didn't know Gerald was going to ask for credentials, and I just hated to lie in the house of God.

The church had three sections of pews separated by two aisles –

one section on the left, one on the right, and a section in the center. In the center section of pews were a few of the MOSS members who decided that this might be entertaining – Kevin, Terry, and my brother T-Joe. All of the dog owners were on the left, and all of the non-dog owners were on the right. It was pretty easy to tell who the dog owners were because they all had leashes around their necks and hand-drawn signs saying stuff like "Dogs are people too," "Dog lovers unite," and "Poop is a natural fertilizer." Some had t-shirts with a picture of their dog on the front.

Most of the non-dog owners wore rubber boots and held signs with blown-up photos of an actual pile of dog poop with a red circle and a line through it, with the caption "Pick it up or hold it in." The two sides were glaring at each other. This could get ugly.

The table for the four of us on the arbitration panel was in the front, facing the mostly empty pews in the middle. In front of the table and facing it was a microphone on a stand. Barbara Pickens sat at a separate card table next to us with her notepad and some sharpened No. 2 pencils lined up on the table and a big grin on her face. She also had a tape recorder the size of a boom box on the table so that she wouldn't miss anything.

Standing conspicuously to one side of our table was T. J. Morales, trying somewhat unsuccessfully to cross his arms over his chest. He settled for resting them on his stomach. Pretty much everyone present knew T.J. because a lot of them had sons that played for Dutchtown High, a big St. Amant rival. They all had nightmares of Wide Load Morales falling on top of their kids.

The HOA Board members were milling around behind us, and after Gerald gave his opening remarks and put me on the spot, he and Marlene, and the other Board members sat in the middle pews so as not to appear to side with one group or the other.

It was time to get started. I took a deep breath and almost swallowed the cough drop that Darlene said I should suck on so I wouldn't sound as raspy as I usually do. I started choking, so T.J., who was standing close by, popped me on the back so hard I saw stars and had tears in my eyes. Not a great start, but it did get the crowd laughing a bit.

After catching my breath, I said, "Friends and neighbors and fellow Ascensionites, I'm Tony Campachi, Civil Engineer by training and trade, and I've served several times in court as an expert witness. I've also been involved in numerous construction contracts that relied upon arbitration to resolve disputes."

I didn't bother to explain that my expert witness testimony was almost always about some construction practice or another and that not a single construction contract I was ever involved in that required arbitration to resolve disputes ever actually resulted in arbitration. In other words, I had squat for experience.

"With me on the arbitration panel tonight," I continued, "are Ronald Burgoyne, Jack Roussell, and Slim Pickens." Each of them gave a weak little wave to no one in particular, not wanting to make eye contact with anyone.

"These men are all professionals and have lived and worked in this community for many years. We all fully understand the issues facing your neighborhood and are prepared to listen to both sides with open minds." Boy, that sounded pretty good, if I say so myself.

"Also helping out tonight is Barbara Pickens, who will be taking notes and recording the hearing," (the murmuring started at this point) "and Deputy T.J. Morales, who will maintain order if necessary, and I'm confident T.J. won't have a thing to do tonight." I wasn't confident of this at all, but I thought it would get a laugh. There was no laughing this time, and I could hear someone say "Wide Load" and certain disparaging remarks being loudly whispered throughout the church. T.J. stood there like a granite statue with a slight smirk on his face. I wondered if his hand hurt as much as my back did.

I continued. "This is how we're going to proceed tonight. You were all previously advised by Mr. Cloutier as to what to expect. So I need a representative from each side of the dispute to leave your signs and leashes and such at your seat and come up, and we'll have a coin toss to decide which side will make their presentation first. The winner of the coin toss can elect for their side to present first or elect to wait and let the other side go first. Just like a football game – the winner of the coin toss will decide whether to kick off or receive." I thought that was a really clever thing to say and would relax everybody, but apparently, it just reminded some of the parents of the damage that Wide Load Morales did to their kids, and the murmuring started again.

Two ladies walked to the front, and I asked them to give their names to Barbara for the record.

"I'm Cora Fontenot Givens, lover of animals, and I represent the dog owners," said the first woman, to wild applause from the left side of the church and a few boos from the right.

The second woman stepped up to Barbara's table and said, "I'm Clara Fontenot McManus, and I speak for the people with dog candy on their shoes." There were audible gasps from the dog owners and the Board members. The right side of the church stood up as one and pumped their fists in the air and yelled, "You tell 'em, Clara!"

I should point out that the audible gasps were because Clara didn't really say dog candy. I decided to keep the record clean, so I substituted "candy" for anything said that shouldn't have been said in church. Just use your imagination.

I could see out of the corner of my eye that Barbara was frantically trying to get my attention. So while T.J. walked around in a threatening manner, trying to calm everyone down, I went over to see what Barbara wanted. "Those two women are sisters!" she said. "I was looking at the Elms on the Hill Facebook page last night, and those two women are not just sisters; they're identical twin sisters!"

"They don't even look that much alike," I said. "One's blond, and one's a redhead, for one thing." Barbara looked at me the way that Darlene often does – like I just fell off of the turnip truck and didn't know the way to town.

"They are probably both brunettes, Tony," she told me like I was 12 years old.

"Oh," I said. So not only was this an argument between two groups of people in the same HOA, but it was also a family squabble. Marlene sure didn't mention that detail.

I pulled out a coin that I had brought, especially for this occasion. I had to dig it out of my golf bag because I usually use it as a ball marker. It was a Rotary coin, with the Rotary wheel and the Rotary motto "Service Above Self" on one side and the 4-Way Test on the other side. The 4-Way Test is four questions that we Rotarians ask ourselves about everything we think, say, or do:

1. Is it the Truth?

2. Is it Fair to all concerned?

3. Will it build Goodwill and Better   Friendships?

4. Will it be Beneficial to all concerned?

I showed the coin to Cora and Clara and read the Rotary motto and the 4-Way Test to everyone in the audience. I remember thinking at the time what a brilliant psychological ploy this was and that maybe just reading the motto and the 4-Way Test would cause everyone there to say, "Hey, why can't we just all get along?" No such luck.

"Okay, ladies," I started, "the Rotary wheel will be heads, and the 4-Way Test will be tails."

Cora said, "Wait a minute, I think the 4-Way thing ought to be heads."

Clara countered with, "You're out of your mind, Cora, as usual. Clearly, the wheel thing is heads, just like Mr. Campachi says."

Cora came back with, "Clara, you don't know a wheel from candy!"

Then Clara spit out, "I know that the wheel on that coin is heads because it looks a lot like your big fat fake redhead!"

"Oh yeah?" yelled Cora. "May I remind you that we used to be identical twins until you decided to get fat and that my red hair looks a whole lot better than those black roots under that blond rat's nest you call a hairdo!"

I motioned to Wide Load to get between the two because they had each taken a step toward the other during the exchange of compliments.

I put the Rotary coin away and pulled out a quarter. "Okay, let's try this again. Here's a quarter. Heads will be heads, and tails will be tails. Clara, call the coin in the air."

"Wait a minute!" cried Cora once more. "Why does she get to call the coin toss?"

"Oh, for crying out loud, Cora, you've been a crybaby your whole life. You can go ahead and call the coin toss, you loser!" sneered Clara through clenched teeth.

Cora called "heads," so I flipped the quarter up, a little too high as it turned out, and it pinged off a rotating ceiling fan that was hanging much too low for my taste and hit Clara, who was tracking the thing closely, squarely in her left eye.

"Yi!" Clara cried out, and Cora started laughing, which didn't help matters. Clara started chasing Cora around the table while holding her hand over her injured eye, both going too fast for Wide Load to catch up with them. Ronald Burgoyne jumped to the rescue and got Clara calmed down enough to stop yelling for her husband Monroe to "sue the candy out of everyone" so he could take a look at her eye. Monroe McManus was one of the Parish's Assistant District Attorneys until he ran for judge and lost, and now has a little law practice on the side exclusively for personal injury cases, all of which he settles out of court.

Monroe, wearing waders that he had to hold up with one hand and a t-shirt proclaiming "This Place Has Gone To The Dogs!" finally made his way to Clara as Ronald was examining her eye.

"What do you think, Ronald?" asked Monroe. Ronald and Monroe knew each other primarily because Ronald's urgent care facilities saw a lot of ambulances that Monroe was usually chasing.

Ronald said that Clara's eye was a little red and she should put some ice on it, but it looked as though she could see okay based on how she was giving Cora the evil eye with it. That satisfied Monroe, and he thanked Ronald and waddled back to his seat. Because Ronald owned several urgent care facilities, no one questioned his ability to diagnose Clara in spite of the fact that he had no medical training whatsoever and didn't know a suture from a seizure.

After bouncing off of Clara's eye, Slim spotted the quarter rolling under the table. I thought that we should flip it again, but that idea was met with protests all around, so I crawled under the table, found the quarter, and announced that "heads" had won. By that time, I had forgotten whether Cora had called "heads" or "tails," so I conferred with Marlene. She played back the episode on her recorder and confirmed that Cora had, in fact, called out "heads" before the eyeball fiasco, so Cora was called on to either present her side's case or to defer. Cora elected to go first.

"I represent the interests of the dog owners of our subdivision," she began, reading from prepared notes. "More than half of our 220 homeowners have dogs. Our dog is a member of our family."

Someone from stage right whispered, "I can see the resemblance." This was met with guffaws from the crowd on the right, and even Slim snickered, so I banged the gavel and called for quiet, and told Cora to please continue.

"As good dog owners, we exercise our pets regularly—and as good residents of Elms on the Hill, we pick up after our dogs." This statement was met with hisses of derision from the non-dog owners, some waving their big photos of dog poop.

"Okay, quiet down now, and let's let Mrs. Givens finish her presentation," I asked while lightly banging the gavel again. I hoped I didn't have to bang it very much more—the head was already loose.

Cora took a second to find her place in her notes and continued. "I have personally interviewed every one of our dog owners, and to a person they each have signed a statement, witnessed by me and by Muriel Spitzvaden, who accompanied me, swearing that they always carry poop bags on their walks, and always, always pick up their dog's droppings, and properly dispose of them in their own garbage cans. I am hereby offering a copy of these signed statements to the arbitration panel for their inspection." She did just that, presenting us with a pretty impressive stack of legal-looking signed and witnessed papers.

Monroe McManus, ever the attorney, asked to see these "so-called affidavits." I tried, but it didn't do any good to point out to him that no one had called the things "affidavits," but I offered to read the statement that all of the dog owners had signed. Here's how it read:

"To Whom It May Concern, we, the undersigned, acknowledge that we live in Elms on the Hill Subdivision and own one or more dogs that reside with us. We further acknowledge that we, on occasion, exercise our dog(s) on or near the walking paths within the subdivision. We also acknowledge that our dog(s) will, on occasion and as nature intended, relieve him/herself of number 1 and number 2 (see footnote) while exercising. We hereby swear in front of witnesses that we always carry with us on these exercise walks plastic, impervious bags with which to pick up our dog's number 2 (see footnote). We also swear that we dispose of these bags in a proper and environmentally safe manner."

It was signed by each of the dog owners of the subdivision. The footnote said, "Note: number 1 is urine, and number 2 is feces." Personally, I didn't think that explanation was necessary, but I'm no lawyer.

"Mrs. Givens, are you done with your statement?" I asked.

"No, I have one thing more to say," she offered, going back to her notes. "It is our belief that the complaints lodged by our non-dog-owning neighbors are due to droppings left in the dead of night by some interloper to Elms on the Hill and not by the pets of our resident dog owners. We hereby petition the HOA to set up a patrol or cameras or some other device to catch this trespassing squatter while the trail is hot." She then sat down to cheers and applause from the left side of the church.

"See what she did?" Ronald whispered to us. "She went on the offensive. The best defense is a good offense."

"Yeah," Jack whispered back, "that was pretty slick. I think she's made a good case. I'm voting for her."

"We haven't heard the other side yet, Jack," I told him. "After we hear the other side, we're going to huddle together, discuss it, and then decide." I think that Jack might have been influenced by Cora's red hair. Jack married a redhead who passed away after 12 years, and a few years later, he married another redhead. He clearly liked his redheads. I was beginning to wonder if Jack could be unbiased about this.

The place quieted down a bit, and I called Mrs. McManus to the front. She stepped up to the microphone and began with, "Well, that was just something, Cora. I guess you expect that just because you typed up a fancy legal-sounding statement and got everybody to sign it, we're supposed to believe that you're all not just a bunch of lying … (and here we could see that she was struggling to find the right word) … liars."

"Well, we don't buy it," she continued. "You would have these good, smart people (pointing to the panel) believe that someone from a neighboring subdivision drove over in the dead of night to let their dog drop bombs on our walking trail. Well, that's just laughable. Ha!" she said loudly to show just how laughable it was. That got a few "Ha!"s from the right side too.

"But just to show you that we're reasonable people and that our hearts are in the right place, we don't think that every dog owner in Elms on the Hill is not cleaning up after their dog. We've done our own research, see, and we believe that all the poop bombs (this was the first time this term was used) are possibly from one or maybe two very well-fed and productive dogs. All we're saying is, 'You know who you are!'"

"Mrs. McManus, can you tell us how you know all of the poop bombs (the term was a catchy one, apparently) were from one or two dogs?" asked Slim. Slim was out of order, as he didn't first get recognized by the Chair – me – but it was a good question, so I let it slide. In fact, in order to reestablish my authority, I followed up with, "Yes, Mrs. McManus, explain to the panel why you believe the poop bombs (it was pretty catchy) were produced from one or maybe two animals?"

"Easy," she said. "We took photos of every pile we could find, and they were distinctive in size, shape, and color. Here, take a look at these – we offer these photos as our Exhibit 1." She must have been coached by Monroe.

She handed me a dozen glossy, 8 x 10 close-up color photos of dog poop. Each had a caption explaining where it was found along the walking trail and the time and date it was discovered. There was also the letter S, W, or C next to each caption. I passed the photos around the table and noticed that both Slim's wife, Barbara, and Wide Load Morales were standing nearby, looking over their shoulders at the new evidence.

I had to ask and was sorry I did. "Mrs. McManus, what do the letters S, W, and C stand for?"

Clara responded, "The letters stand for Steaming, Warm, and Cold. We figured we could better pinpoint that actual time of delivery if we knew the temperature of the package when found." I didn't want to ask how they determined the temperature. Of course, "Steaming" sort of spoke for itself. "We also took samples of each pile and put them in separate Tupperware containers to preserve the evidence," she added. Remind me never to go to a pot-luck at Elms on the Hill.

I asked Clara if she had anything more to say. She concluded with, "So we think we're only looking for one or two culprits, not half of the subdivision. We just want y'all to turn in the guilty party so they can be appropriately fined and reprimanded. Somebody in here must know who it is."

The dog owners on the left were looking at each other and shaking their heads. It sure didn't look like they were hiding anybody. I figured if somebody knew who it was, they would speak up and get this whole thing over with. Nobody spoke up.

I banged the gavel one last time – it was the last time because the head flew off of it and hit Wide Load in the leg, and he didn't even flinch – and called the meeting back to order. Wide load tried to bend over and pick up the gavel head, but that wasn't going to happen, so he nudged it under the table with his size 14s. "The panel will now review the information provided, discuss the statements made, and render its decision shortly." We went into a small office adjacent to the sanctuary, dragged in a couple of chairs with us, closed the door, and began to deliberate.

Of course, Jack had already decided for the red-headed Cora, but the rest of us were at a loss. "Anybody got any ideas?" I asked.

"I got something to say," offered Slim. "Anybody who takes close-up color photos of dog poop, and on top of that, saves specimens in Tupperware, is one sick individual." We all pretty much agreed with that.

Ronald, who had been pretty quiet since tending to Clara's eye, said, "You know what? I think we have a real opportunity here. Clara's group has actual samples of the dog poop. We can take the samples that Clara's group collected, have the DNA checked, and then get the DNA from all of the dogs in the subdivision and figure out who the guilty parties are!"

"But Ronald," I said, somewhat skeptically, which is my nature, "how much would that cost, and how long would it take to do?" Those were good questions, I figured.

"Those are good questions," responded Ronald. "I'm not really sure who would do a DNA test on dog poop. And it would probably cost a lot and take weeks to do."

"Maybe we don't have to actually do the tests," suggested Jack. "What if they just think we're going to get the stuff tested? Maybe we can flush out the guilty party."

Jack told us his idea, and we found out for the first time just how conniving Jack could be. But we liked the plan, so we spent a few more minutes working out the details and decided we'd better inform Gerald Cloutier about our scheme. I stuck my head out of the door and motioned for Gerald to join us.

"Gerald," I started, "we have this idea we'd like to run by you before we go with it to make sure you buy into the plan." Then we proceeded to fill him in on the details.

"I don't think we have anything to lose by giving it a try," was Gerald's response. "Let's go for it."

So I called the meeting back to order. Not having a working gavel, I rapped my knuckles on the microphone. "Ladies and gentlemen, having heard from both sides tonight, we've come to the following conclusion: the problem of the dog poop appears to be caused by only one or two dog owners. It doesn't seem fair to fine or to raise the dues for all the dog owners because of the failure of one or two of them."

This was met by raucous yells and applause by the left side of the church, with high-fives all around.

"Here's what we're going to do," I continued. "Since we have samples of dog poop that have been meticulously collected, labeled, and preserved, and we're satisfied that the chain of evidence is intact, we're going to have DNA tests run on each sample." I had just watched a re-run of Law and Order the night before and picked up that "chain of evidence" jargon. I could tell people were impressed.

"Then," I went on, "we're going to require every dog owner to bring their dog to a local vet, have a blood sample drawn that we can submit for DNA testing, and compare the results. Each owner will have to pay the up-front cost, but the HOA Board has agreed to require the guilty party to cover all costs incurred, even if they have to put a lien on the property."

There was some serious murmuring going on after that statement.

"How much will this DNA testing stuff cost?" someone yelled out. "And how long will all of this take?" You'd swear that someone must have been channeling my brain waves. Or it could be there was another engineer in the group.

Ronald answered that, with the vet's bill and the lab costs, he figured it might come to about $200 to $250 per dog.

Someone over in the dog owners group did some quick math and figured that if the guilty party was identified, it would set them back from $25,000 to $30,000. That caused some real squirming around over there. No one wanted to shell out $200 for the test, much less $25,000 or more in penalties.

Cora finally spoke up. "So what happens if the guilty party confesses before all of this DNA nonsense starts up?"

"I suggest that we ask the HOA Board what might happen if that turns out to be the case," I offered.

Gerald Cloutier and the other members of the HOA Board quickly huddled together in the middle of the room, and after a few minutes, Gerald strode to the microphone. "Ladies and gentlemen, the Board has agreed that should the guilty party or parties come forward within the next three days – by this time Monday at the latest – a fine of $250 would be imposed, which would be donated to Fountain Community Church for the hospitality we've been shown. Also, the fine will be doubled for each future similar infraction of the by-laws."

Clara loudly suggested that the perpetrator also pay Meriam Boudreaux for the Tupperware she contributed, but Gerald ruled that she would just have to write that off as a loss.

Gerald continued, saying, "The Board also recommends that the guilty party may admit their guilt and pay the fine through Mr. Campachi in such a way that no one who lives in Elms on the Hill will know who it is. But if this admission of guilt and payment of the fine does not happen by Monday before (looking at his watch) 9:15 p.m., then the Board will have no alternative but to pursue the DNA testing."

Chapter Five

There just wasn't anything else to say. People started quietly filing out with their signs and leashes and boots and such. Gerald and the HOA Board gathered around our table and expressed their gratitude. They felt that the whole arbitration thing was a success and would resolve the issue in short order. At least they hoped it did because they had no intention of going the DNA route.

I didn't feel like it could be considered a success until someone confessed, and the mystery was solved. And it didn't take long.

The next evening, late on a beautiful cool March day, 18 of us showed up to feast on No-Neck's jambalaya and Marlene's bread pudding. Only a few wives, including Darlene, came. Some of the guys told their wives that the invitation was for the members of MOSS only – a fabrication that would soon catch up with them and cost them dearly. Pictures of us sitting on folding chairs pulled up to a couple of pieces of plywood on sawhorses, chowing down under the Lalonde's carport, were on Facebook before we even digested the first bite. Having previously had an embarrassing experience with a folding chair, Wide-Load brought his own home-made stool with 4 x 4's for legs and 2 x 6's for the seat, and the thing still creaked when he sat down.

We all brought diet cokes and beer and such, and No-Neck was good enough to heat up a couple of big cans of Blue Runner white beans to go with the jambalaya, along with several loaves of Leidenheimer French bread and tubs of butter. He had cooked the jambalaya in one of his medium-sized cast-iron pots over a propane burner that he said he also used for boiling crawfish. Uncle Joe told No-Neck that he was surprised that the jambalaya wasn't cooked over wood as they do in the annual Gonzales jambalaya festival. No-Neck told him they had to use wood in the contest because it was in the rules – but it was a pain in the butt, and he sure wasn't going to cook on wood if he didn't have to. Naturally, Uncle Joe had to grumble that it wasn't authentic jambalaya if you used propane. Didn't stop him from eating, though.

We were finishing up our second and third helpings of jambalaya and about to start in on Marlene's bread pudding when Terry Parmenter's sister, Patty, walked into the carport. Patty, a petite and pretty brunette, was married to Manny Morvant, a short, cigar-smoking hustler who owned a small car dealership in south Baton Rouge. Patty had been at the meeting the night before. I remember her because she wore a bright pink shirt with a picture of her dog Titus on the front – a smiling Goldendoodle. I didn't think that dogs could actually smile, but I swear this dog was smiling.

Patty and Marlene apparently remained friends through what we were now calling "The Dog Candy Caper" because she walked up to her, and they hugged each other. I could see Patty asking Marlene something and pointing towards me, then Marlene came and whispered into my ear that Patty wanted to talk to me in private. Darlene, who doesn't miss a trick, heard what Marlene said. I excused myself, and Darlene gave me "the look," which I interpreted as "don't do anything stupid."

Marlene led Patty and me into the kitchen, and we sat at a small table set next to a bay window. Patty told Marlene that it would be okay with her if she listened to what she had to say, but Marlene said no, she had to go serve the rum sauce before it got cold. She grabbed the pot from the stovetop and headed for the carport door.

"Mr. Campachi," Patty began.

"Just call me Tony," I suggested.

"Well, I'm Patty Morvant—call me Patty—and I want to make sure I understand what happened last night at the meeting," she said.

I should probably mention that Patty Morvant is something of a looker, if you know what I mean. I met her husband Manny once when I did a make-up meeting at the Baton Rouge Rotary Club and happened to sit next to him. Patty was with him at the meeting but was sitting together with some of the other wives. They were there because Dee Dee Breaux, the long-time coach of the LSU Women's Gymnastics Team, was the guest speaker, and Patty's step-daughter – Manny's daughter from a previous marriage – was on the team. I think that Patty and her step-daughter got along so well because they were close to the same age. Manny pointed Patty out to me and said, "that's my trophy wife over there – the one with the cleavage." So that's why I got "the look" from Darlene.

"Well," I started, "the deal is this. If somebody comes out before Monday night and confesses to being the dog owner who's not been picking up after their pet, they'll have to pay a modest fine and be required to do a better job at poop patrol with their dog. Then the whole matter will be forgotten. Why are you asking, Patty – do you know who might be doing this?"

"Mr. Campachi – I mean, Tony – that's why I'm here. It's my husband, Manny," she confessed. "When he gets home at night, sometimes pretty late, he takes Titus – that's our Goldendoodle – out for a walk while he smokes his vile cigar. I won't let him smoke in the house. I make sure he takes poop bags with him every time. He wasn't at the meeting last night, but when I told him what happened and that there might be DNA tests and stuff that someone was going to have to pay for, he told me what he was doing.

"He would walk to the back where the trail goes around the lake," Patty continued, "and he would sit on a bench in the dark and let Titus run around while he smoked his cigar! I was shocked! There I was last night, acting like a fool, like an innocent bystander, and it was my own husband causing the problem. I told him that I wished the mosquitos had eaten him alive for doing that. He said that the cigar smoke keeps the mosquitos away."

"Patty," I said, "I'm glad you came forward. It will save everybody a lot of trouble. And no one but me has to know who it was – but I guess Marlene might already suspect."

"That's all right if Aunt Marlene knows. She's not really my aunt; she's my Godmother," Patty explained. "Actually, she's my mother's best friend. They went to high school together. And she knows that Manny can be… difficult."

"So is Manny going to pay the fine and promise to quit letting Brutus…."

"Titus," she corrected.

"…I mean, quit letting Titus off-leash to drop bombs all over the walking trail?" I asked.

"Yes, he sent me over here with $250 in cash," Patty said. "He was too embarrassed to come over himself, and besides, Aunt Marlene doesn't trust Manny ever since he sold her that Olds Omega. I think that she feels sorry for me, though."

Patty handed over a plain letter-sized envelope with a "Man, You'll Love Manny!" used car sale ad inside, folded over five fifty-dollar bills. I offered to write her a receipt on the back of the flyer, but she said she didn't need it unless it was tax-deductible. Manny would want a receipt then, for sure. I told her that I didn't think it was. Patty asked me if I was going to tell anybody about this, and I assured her that the secret was safe with me and that part of the deal was that the guilty party could remain anonymous as long as the fine was paid and the practice of allowing free-range dogs in the subdivision was nipped in the bud. I would just hand over the money to Gerald Cloutier the next day and let him know that the Dog Candy Caper was a thing of the past.

Patty thanked me and apologized again on behalf of her husband, then went out and told Marlene she was headed home to feed her two boys – Manny and Titus. Marlene gave her Tupperware containers of jambalaya and white beans to take home. I hoped that she didn't get them from Meriam Boudreaux.

I went out to the carport just in time to see T. J. "Wide Load" Morales finishing off the last of the bread pudding right out of the aluminum pan Marlene cooked it in. All of the guys were standing up and milling around, trying unsuccessfully to hold their stomachs in while Marlene introduced her Godchild Patty to the group, telling them that she had invited Patty over to get some jambalaya. I went and sat down next to Darlene again, hoping that she had saved me a bite of bread pudding.

When I told Patty that her secret was safe with me, I wasn't thinking about just how persuasive Darlene could be when she wanted to pry something out of me, especially after I spent what she called "way too much time" in the house with that "Patty Morvant person." I told Darlene that I'd tell her about it later and that I couldn't say anything right now. I got "the look" again. And no bread pudding.

Sunday morning after our church service, I dropped by Gerald Cloutier's home in Elms on the Hill (Marlene had given me his address) and gave him the cash. I had taken out the flyer, though. Neither Gerald nor anyone else was supposed to know who had confessed and paid the fine. I suspected that the rumor mill was grinding away, but no one got anything out of me except for Darlene, of course.

Part Two

Chapter One

Word quickly spread of our success in resolving the HOA issue at Elms on the Hill, and I started getting emails and notes from all sorts of folks, including two other HOAs. In the week following our arbitration hearing at Fountain Community Church, I got the following comments:

"You guys are not a Think Tank, you're a Stink Tank!" – *anonymous.*

"There's nothing in our subdivision restrictions that specifically says residents can't put up solar panels, but the Architectural Control Committee (ACC) is denying all such requests, and some homeowners are threatening to take action. We may need to go to arbitration. Please call me." – *Maynard Krebs, President, Oak Harbor Estates.*

"You grew up in Donaldsonville, so don't act like you know anything." – *anonymous.*

"It floods here when it rains a lot. Can y'all find out if there's a connection?" – *name withheld by request.*

"I think the Jambalaya Queen contest is rigged because I lost 3 times. Can your tank think about that?" – *former contestant who asked not to use her name.*

"Y'all are good at the dog stuff. Can you find my dog? She ran away two years ago. Her name is Bunny, but she answers to Foo Foo." – *former dog owner in Gonzales.*

"Me and some friends own cemetery plots in the Garden of Memories on Highway 74, and we don't think the caretakers are doing a good job, so we want to form a Plot Owners Association – a POA. Can y'all help?" – *Nolan "Nobby" Narcisse, Chairman of the proposed Plot Owners Association of the Garden of Memories.*

"Can you all think of a better way than voting to get people elected? I quit voting 20 years ago because the Parish Council was doing such a bad job – and it hasn't got any better. Someone ought to do something." – *former Ascension Parish voter.*

"Does your think tank believe that if someone went to jail for 5

years for robbery, that when they get out, they have to say that in a job interview? It wasn't armed robbery because the gun wasn't loaded. A friend wants to know." – a friend of a felon.

I brought these comments and requests to the next Friday's breakfast gathering and shared them with the guys. I was pretty excited about this.

"I'm not too excited about this," responded Uncle Joe. "I think y'all lucked out with the dog poop thing. I mean, what if no one had confessed? You'd be up candy creek without a paddle."

Dustin Sonnier contributed, "I don't think we can do the Garden of Memories thing. Too many of us have plots there." Darlene and I had one plot in Garden of Memories for the two of us because she wants to be cremated. She can't stand the thought of roaches crawling over her in the casket. I didn't bother telling her that she wouldn't notice if they did – it would just be a waste of breath.

"I agree," I said. "I don't think we can touch that one. But I am interested in joining the POA if they ever get that going. I'll call that guy Nobby about it."

"I don't think that any of the MOSS live in Oak Harbor. Maybe we could do that one about the solar panels," offered Jack Roussel.

Wendy, who was taking our orders at the time, mentioned that her mom and stepfather lived in Oak Harbor, and they believed that solar panels caused cancer, so they were really against allowing them.

"I heard about the cancer thing and solar panels," chimed in Uncle Joe.

"I've never heard of such a thing. Where did you hear that?" I asked him.

"From Wendy just now. Didn't you hear her? You better start paying attention. You missin' everything," he responded.

"Okay, so is anyone opposed to taking on the Oak Harbor thing about the solar panels?" I asked. No one had any objections, so I offered to call the HOA President, Maynard Krebs, to tell him we were interested.

"Wait a minute, wait a minute," exclaimed Dustin, laughing. "Is his name really Maynard Krebs? Like Maynard G. Krebs? So who's the Vice-President, Dobie Gillis?"

I responded, "I guess that's his real name. Maybe his parents really liked the show. They'd have to be at least our age to have remembered it. So Maynard must be the same age as our kids."

"Poor guy," offered Kevin. "Imagine having to go through life telling people your name is Maynard G. Krebs."

"Well, like I said before," I told him. "Unless you're at least our age, you probably wouldn't even know who Maynard G. Krebs was. And we don't know if his middle initial is 'G' either."

After breakfast, I called the number Maynard had provided in his email to me. A woman answered the phone. "Krebs and Cangelosi Disposal Services, to whom may I address your call?"

I told her that I was calling for Maynard Krebs. She asked, "May I tell Mr. Krebs who's calling?" so I told her my name. Then she asked, "May I tell Mr. Krebs what your call is regarding?" By this time, I'm thinking, "Holy cow, what is this, the CIA or something?" I gave her a brief description of Maynard's email to me and assured her that Mr. Krebs would want to speak to me. She put me on hold, and I listened to Smooth Jazz, interrupted every 20 seconds with a commercial for Krebs and Cangelosi Disposal Services, "No job is too small, too large, or too disgusting." Hmmm….

"This here is Maynard Krebs. What can I do you for?" suddenly came booming over the phone, causing me to forget for a second what the heck I was calling for.

"Mr. Krebs, this is Tony Campachi. You emailed me regarding an issue you're dealing with in the Oak Harbor Estates neighborhood – something about solar panels?" I answered.

"Oh hell yes," he said. "We have to nip this matter in the butt. I sure hope you can help us with this," he bellowed.

I almost said, "You mean 'nip it in the bud,' don't you?" but Darlene is always warning me about correcting other people.

"Well, I'm sure we can be of help to you in this matter," I quickly replied. "I'd like to meet with you and get a little more information before we commit to anything, though."

"Hell yes, why don't you come on over to my office Monday morning around 10:00, and we'll hash it out," he yelled. I swear it sounded like he was talking through a megaphone. "I'll get the HOA ACC Chairman, Nobby Narcisse, to join us."

Nobby Narcisse, I pondered to myself. Small world. I'll have to ask him about the Plot Owner's Association idea at the Garden of Memories. "Sure," I told Maynard Krebs. "I'll be there." He told me where his office was, just behind the new WalMart on Airline. I called Jack Roussel later in the day, and he agreed to accompany me to Krebs and Cangelosi Disposal Services on Monday.

Chapter Two

Jack and I met in the Walmart parking lot at about 9:50 a.m. My truck was in the shop for an oil change, so I was in Darlene's Cadillac. I parked it and got into Jack's truck. We found Krebs and Cangelosi Disposal pretty easily behind the Walmart, as Maynard Krebs had described. He hadn't mentioned that it was in a double-wide trailer in a massive yard surrounded by a 10-foot chain-link fence topped with barbed wire. It looked like a prison compound. There was a guard shack at the entrance manned by two uniformed, armed people. The first one to approach the truck as Jack braked to a stop was a skinny short Black woman with purple hair tied in a ponytail sticking out of a brown billed uniform hat. Behind her in the doorway of the shack was a hulk of a White man I judged to be about six-foot-five inches and much-tattooed, looking every bit like a disgruntled ex-prisoner seeking revenge for something. His brown uniform was bulging at the seams, and his hat was just perched on the top of his bald head, which was clearly too large to accommodate it. He was leaning against the door jamb, and I swear the shack was listing to starboard.

"What ya'll want?" asked the young woman whose name badge read "Yolanda".

"We have an appointment with Mr. Krebs and Mr. Narcisse," I informed her.

She had us write our names on a tablet on a clipboard and note the time we arrived. She made note of Jack's license plate number and checked out the inside of the truck as well as the truck bed as though we were entering a high-security military base. Then she pointed us in the direction of the double-wide with a huge sign on the side of it designating it as the "Office". There were 7 or 8 vehicles parked in the front and on the sides of the trailer – all pickup trucks, most with huge tires and all with gun racks and trailer hitches. Man, was I glad we weren't in Darlene's Cadillac. I would have felt like a wuss.

There were steps and small landings leading to the two doors on one side of the office. One was clearly marked "OFFICE" in large letters on the side of the door. The other was labeled "PRIVATE – DO NOT ENTER." There was another uniformed and armed guard sitting in a chair on the landing next to that door. The only open parking spot was just between the two doors. The guard gave us the evil eye behind his reflective sunglasses – okay, we couldn't really see his eyes, but I felt the presence of evil when he glared at us. We opted for the OFFICE door.

We walked into a surprisingly large reception area and were immediately greeted by none other than Clara McManus, a protagonist in the Elms on the Hill dog candy incident. She had on more makeup than I'd ever seen Darlene wear in a year, was smartly dressed in a low-cut white frilly blouse, 4 or 5-inch black high heels, and a tight black skirt that showed off her knees and a good bit of her thighs. Her blond hair was teased up into a hairdo that almost touched the low trailer ceiling.

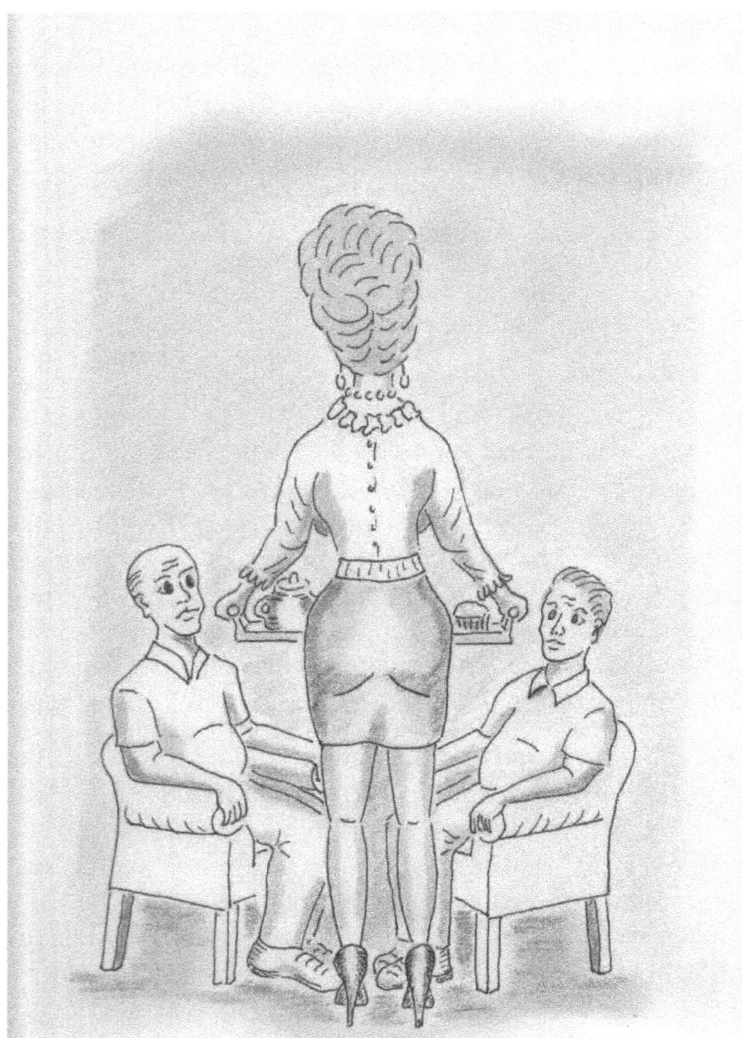

"Hello, Mr. Campachi, remember me? It's Clara McManus. It's so nice to see you again!" she exclaimed enthusiastically, grasping my right hand with both of hers, then sliding her left hand up my arm to the elbow and cradling my right hand between her substantial breasts. "I told Maynard all about how you all solved our dog candy problem over at Elms on the Hill, so that's why he contacted you. I'm just positive that you can help him with his problem. You all were so good!"

I was speechless. Jack kept going, "Ahma ahma ahma…." I finally managed to stammer out, "Clara, of course I remember you! Please call me Tony, and this here is Jack Roussel. Say, how's your eye?" I immediately regretted asking that, thinking that she might be sensitive about the coin flip thing. I also felt it was sort of my fault that she got hit in the eye.

"Oh, you don't worry about that!" she replied. "A little makeup took care of that, and it's mostly healed by now. I really don't blame you at all." It sounded like she really blamed me. "Maynard – I mean, Mr. Krebs – is in a meeting, but I think they're almost done. Y'all sit down. Let me get you both some coffee. We have a brand-new Keurig. I just love them little K-cups, don't you?" She bustled off through a door into what I guessed was her office, and we took a seat on a couple of very nice leather-covered low-back chairs that looked like they were embarrassed to be in a double-wide. There were six other such chairs in the room, with a small table between each pair.

Clara's door opened, and she reappeared carrying a silver tray with mugs of coffee, a creamer, a sugar bowl, and muffins. She set the tray down on the table between Jack and me. "I made these gingerbread muffins this morning, so y'all don't be shy now! Dig in!"

The door to Clara's office was still open, and it must have led to Maynard's office because all of a sudden, through her door, we could hear a yell and a loud thud like someone dropped a hundred-pound sack of potatoes. I swear I felt the trailer shake. Clara smiled and said, "I think they're wrapping up their meeting now. Y'all enjoy your coffee and muffins, and I'll come and get you in just a minute." She strutted back into her office, heels clicking noisily on the tile floor, and closed the door behind her.

Jack and I exchanged a look, and he gurgled out what I was thinking – "What the heck are we doing here? Should we leave?" But how would we explain that to Clara? She seemed genuinely happy that we came, and we would have looked like a couple of wusses if we had just up and left because we heard what might have been a dead body fall to the floor. I was starting to regret I hadn't called Wide Load Morales to come with me instead of Jack. We silently decided that discretion was called for and reached for the coffee and muffins and acted like nothing at all was out of the ordinary. Plus, I hadn't had any breakfast because Darlene had a Zumba class and refused to eat before going because the one time she did, she threw up on her new leotards. And the muffins smelled great.

Just as we were finishing our second muffin and I was wiping the crumbs from my stomach shelf, Clara opened the door and, smiling, asked us to follow her. We timidly walked behind her, and I couldn't help but think of that Three Stooges scene when a shapely woman beckoned them to "walk this way, boys," and they sashayed behind her, mimicking her swaying hips. We went through Clara's office and into Maynard Krebs's. He sat behind a massive wooden desk that must have been custom-built in the room because there was no way that thing got through the trailer door.

"Well, hello boys, how the heck are ya!" Maynard enthusiastically greeted us. "Have a seat. Clara, did you offer these gentlemen coffee and all?" he asked her.

"I sure did, Mayn...uh...Mr. Krebs," she said. "And my gingerbread muffins too!"

"Well, isn't that nice! Thank you, Clara, you can go on back to your office now. I'm sure you have stuff to do, right?"

"Oh yes, sir, I sure do. Y'all call me if you need anything," she said over her shoulder as she left the room and closed the door.

Maynard Krebs was an imposing man, about six-one or two, I'd guess about 240 pounds, with bushy black eyebrows, a long face, and thinning black hair with streaks of gray, combed straight back. He reminded me of a young Abe Vigoda. Not Abe Vigoda from Barney Miller, but Abe Vigoda from The Godfather, which didn't make me any more comfortable.

"I sure appreciate y'all coming over this morning," Maynard boomed out. "Clara speaks very highly of the job y'all did for them HOA folks at Elms on the Hill. I sure hope y'all can do the same for us. We're about ready to give up being able to solve our problem peacefully, if you know what I mean."

I did not know what he meant, but I grunted and nodded in understanding. I was just wondering where the folks who had been meeting in here had disappeared to when a hidden door in the paneled wall to the left of Maynard's desk opened, and in walked a man that looked familiar, but I couldn't recall how I knew him. He was about five-foot-seven, balding, maybe 60 or so years old, with wide shoulders and large biceps and forearms. He worked out for sure.

"Jelly! Glad you could join us," Maynard yelled. "Jelly, this here is Tony Campachi – I hope I got that right – and Jack Roussel. Fellas, this here is my partner, Jelly Cangelosi."

We stood up and shook hands with Mr. Cangelosi, who had a bone-crushing grip that made me wish I'd spent more time at Anytime Fitness. That was when I recognized him as one of our Parish Councilmen. I'd been to a Council meeting with my Rotary Club a couple of months back to thank the Council and Parish President for supporting one of our projects. I remember him because when we took a group photo, he had to stand in front with the other shorter folks. I also remembered that his real name was John.

Maynard pulled Jelly aside and whispered something to him. Because Maynard's whisper is pretty much the same in volume as my normal voice, I heard him ask, "Did you take care of our little problem?" And Jelly responded, "Oh yeah, he'll be okay; I got Yolanda to bring him to an urgent care. His leg was hurting too bad to drive."

Maynard then turned back to us. "I'm sorry Mr. Narcisse won't be joining us for this meeting. He had a little accident in here earlier. Tripped on a rug."

I didn't see a rug, but I didn't say anything. I guess they got rid of it. Maybe rolled up Nobby Narcisse in it for tidy disposal. My imagination was working overtime. As Maynard sat back down behind his desk, my eyes followed him and settled on a brass nameplate right in front of me – holy crap, "Maynard G. Krebs, President." His parents either had a strange sense of humor or were just plain cruel.

"Look here, Tony – can I call you Tony?" Maynard asked, then continued before I could answer. "We need y'all to jump on this solar panel thing and get it figured out as soon as possible. The main thing – the main problem is – Nobby and his Architectural Control Committee are dead set against allowing solar panels in the subdivision, but he and I are not seeing eye to eye on this thing. I've looked, and I can't find nothing in the subdivision restrictions that says we can't have solar panels. Plus, they're good for the environment and all. You know, all of that green stuff."

He then yelled, "Clara, come here for a second." She popped her head in. "Clara, get these gentlemen a couple of copies of the Oak Harbor Estates subdivision restrictions, would you?"

"Yes, sir," she replied. "I already made some extra copies. How many would you like, Mr. Campachi?"

"Well, really, one copy ought to be….well, maybe two copies would be best if you don't mind," I answered.

Maynard continued, "Now y'all study this thing and call me direct and tell me what you think. How much do y'all charge for doing this?"

Wow, I hadn't thought about someone willing to pay us for our services. I was about to say, "Just some jambalaya and bread pudding is what we usually charge," but what I said was, "We don't really have fees – we sort of negotiate depending upon the complexity of the problem." I thought that sounded very professional.

"Well, look here," Maynard said. "We can pay $200 an hour for your time. You just send me your bill when you're done. I figure it'll take you 3 or 4 hours to study these restrictions, and then whatever time it takes for you and your Board or whatever, to come to our next HOA meeting and settle the thing."

I asked him, "When is your next HOA meeting?" I wanted to make sure we had time to study the subdivision restrictions and form an opinion.

"Hell, I'll just call a special meeting anytime we need to," he bragged. "You just call me when you're ready. Now if you don't mind, I got other things to take care of today, so Clara will show y'all out. You call me now!"

Clara came in and handed us each of copy of the subdivision restrictions for Oak Harbor Estates – about one inch thick – and this time she literally said, "Y'all walk this way."

She led us out through her office and into the reception area toward the entrance door and then whispered to me, "Mr. Campachi, Mr. Krebs really, really needs to get these solar panels approved for his subdivision. He's taking it real personal."

"I know he said he disagreed with Nobby Narcisse about it. How do the other residents feel?" I asked.

"I don't know for sure," she replied. "I just know he – Maynard – Mr. Krebs – he really wants to see them approved."

Chapter Three

I emailed the MOSS group on Monday afternoon and asked them to come to our gathering on Friday if they could. I really wanted as many as possible to chime in on this one. In the meantime, Jack and I would study the subdivision regulations so that we could discuss the matter as intelligently as possible when we met with the rest of the guys.

Most of the regulars showed up on Friday. Besides me, there was Uncle Joe, who was picked up by Jack Roussel, Dustin Sonnier, Rodney Keets, Kevin Farmer, Slim Pickens, Terry Parmenter, Dr. Dart, Ronald Burgoyne, Alden Roussel (Jack's cousin), and my brother T-Joe. I was glad Alden came in case we needed some free legal advice.

Frank's puts together several tables in a large square for us every Friday, with three or four of us on each side. After Wendy brought coffee and took our orders (everybody ordered what they always order, so I don't know why she bothered), we got down to business.

"I call this meeting to order," I said as I tapped my butter knife on my glass. Since this was the first time I ever said that, it took everybody by surprise. A couple of the guys looked around like they might be in the wrong place.

"Here's the situation," I began. "Y'all remember we agreed last week that we'd look at that solar panel thing at Oak Harbor Estates? Well, Jack and I went and met with Maynard Krebs, whose middle initial is 'G,' by the way (guffaws from Dustin), and he explained the situation to us. He also gave us each a copy of their subdivision restrictions, and Jack and I have been going over them for the past couple of days."

Jack chimed in excitedly, "And guess who is Maynard G. Krebs's personal assistant? None other than Clara McManus! Man, you should see how she dresses to work in a double-wide trailer for a garbage company!" When we met with Clara, all he could say was, "Ahma ahma ahma."

I called the meeting back to order, and about that time, Wendy started bringing in our food, so I waited a minute until everyone was served and got more coffee, and half of us went to the restroom and back, and then I started again. "So what Mr. Krebs wants us to do is to give him our opinion on whether or not the subdivision restrictions prohibit the homeowners from putting solar panels on the roofs of their homes. We're supposed to call him and tell him when we're ready to present our findings at an HOA meeting."

"I guess we're not getting paid for this one either," grumbled my Uncle Joe through a mouthful of grits.

Jack said, "Maynard wants to pay us $200 an hour for our time— can you believe it?"

"Now we're talkin'," said Uncle Joe, spitting grits all over the table.

I told everyone that I didn't think we should charge anybody for what we do, and I thought Uncle Joe was going to have another stroke right at the table. After he said some pretty unkind things about how I was raised and what in hell did they teach me at LSU, Alden had a few things to say in my defense, sort of.

"If you're going to take a fee for this consulting you're doing, you'll have to incorporate with the state first, set up an account with a bank, have an annual audit, and there are all sorts of other implications. And if you think you're going to get free legal advice from me, think again!" cautioned Alden. "I warned you not to get involved with HOAs. They're the worst." There went my idea of getting free legal advice.

Uncle Joe wasn't finished. "Look here, if he pays us in cash, who's gonna know?"

"Look, I don't want to be tied up with something illegal," I said. "The firm I work for does some work for the Parish. They could get fired if I did something sketchy like that."

"Ha! If that were the case, everyone working for the Parish would be fired!" chortled Uncle Joe, which was followed by laughter and general agreement from the rest of the guys. I thought that was a little unfair. I mean, it couldn't be "everyone."

"Like I said earlier," I said loudly, trying to get this meeting back on track, "Jack and I spent some time looking over the Oak Harbor

Estates subdivision restrictions, and here's what we found that we think might be germane to this case."

"Who's Gemaine?" asked Uncle Joe, who, after finding out we wouldn't be getting paid, had lost interest and wasn't paying attention. "You talkin' about Gemaine LeBlanc, who runs The Chicken Shack? What does she have to do with this?"

"No, I'm not talking about Gemaine LeBlanc," I said in exasperation. "I just meant that we found something in the subdivision restrictions that might help us figure out if solar panels can be prohibited."

"Well, why didn't you just say so," replied Uncle Joe. "I don't see why you want to bring Gemaine into this."

I was close to losing it by this point. My brother T-Joe tried to help by distracting Uncle Joe with some bacon he had left. I could hear them talking about how good the chicken was at the Chicken Shack.

After the dust settled, I read to the group the parts of the restrictions that Jack and I thought might apply:

"No noxious or offensive activity shall be conducted on any lot, nor shall anything be done thereon which may become an annoyance or nuisance to one's neighbor or the neighborhood. This shall be at the sole discretion of the Architectural Control Committee (ACC). "

Another section read, *"No outside lines, outside television antennas, satellite dishes, above ground improvements including without limitation, basketball goals, swing sets, children play houses, or hanging devices shall be allowed without the prior written consent of the Architectural Control Committee. "*

The last thing we found said, *"The Architectural Control Committee must approve exterior paint and trim or alterations thereof with regard to any building or improvements. The Architectural Control Committee reserves the right to approve decorations and lighting of any building or improvements... "*

"That's typical of subdivision restrictions," offered Alden. "The ACC has the ultimate say-so unless they're overruled by the Board of Directors, which rarely happens because then the Board might open themselves up to a lawsuit. They would have to explain why they didn't follow the recommendations of the ACC. That's assuming the ACC didn't grossly misinterpret the restrictions." I was shocked that Alden offered this legal-sounding opinion without being asked.

"There's nothing mentioned in there about solar panels," offered Jack.

"There's also nothing specifically said about keeping a spaceship on your roof," countered Alden. "That's why they use the term "at the sole discretion of the Architectural Control Committee."

By this time, most of the group had other things to do, and besides, Wendy quit bringing free coffee refills after about half a dozen trips, so the meeting broke up. I asked Dustin, Kevin, and Uncle Joe (the MOSS Board members) to stick around for a few more minutes to see if we could agree upon what to tell Maynard Krebs.

"It sounds to me like the ACC has a lot of say in this," Dustin offered. "If they tell the Board 'No solar panels are allowed,' the Board will either have to agree or disagree with them. It's up to the Board if they want to take a chance and go against the recommendations of the ACC. At least that's what Alden was saying."

Kevin suggested that maybe if most of the homeowners wanted solar panels, they could maybe revise the restrictions to allow them.

"We should have asked Alden if that was possible," I replied. Then, to appease Uncle Joe, I asked him for his opinion.

"I heard them solar panels cause cancer, so I don't think they ought to let people put them up," was his reply.

"According to Maynard Krebs, the ACC is saying 'no solar panels.' Do we agree that we need to tell Maynard that the ACC has the authority to make that call?" I asked.

Everyone agreed that this was the case, and we should tell Maynard Krebs what we thought. After one more trip to the restroom, we paid our bills and headed out. I brought Uncle Joe to his house, listening to him complain the entire 20-minute trip about not accepting pay from Maynard Krebs. I was mentally exhausted, so I decided to wait until Monday to give Maynard a call.

Chapter Four

Darlene and I were headed to Cracker Barrel the following day for a late breakfast when I got a call on my cell phone from a number I didn't recognize. I usually don't answer if I don't recognize the number because I don't need my automobile extended warranty renewed. I decided to answer this time because MOSS has become somewhat famous and, who knows, it might be Channel Nine News asking to do an interview.

I answered, "Hello, this is Tony Campachi." Darlene thinks I shouldn't give my name like that because the next time they call me to renew my automobile extended warranty, they'll act as if they know me.

"Mr. Campachi, this is Nobby Narcisse with Oak Harbor Estates. Do you have a minute to talk?" he asked.

"Well, hello, Mr. Narcisse. You can call me Tony. What can I do for you?" I responded.

"Please call me Nobby," he said. "I hear that Maynard Krebs asked your MOSS group to weigh in on our disagreement regarding solar panels. I wondered if you've decided on what you're going to recommend."

I had Nobby on speaker in my truck, and Darlene was giving me the index finger on the lips, which could mean "Be quiet," or "Don't say anything," or "Do I need to touch up my lipstick?" I can never tell.

I said, "Nobby, the MOSS group has arrived at a recommendation, but I'm not at liberty to say anything until I meet and discuss it with Mr. Krebs."

"Oh sure, I understand that," Nobby answered. "So, when might you meet with Mr. Krebs?"

"I plan on calling him on Monday and setting up a meeting then. He might want you in the meeting," I suggested. "Oh, by the way, how's your leg? I heard you had an accident."

"Uh, yes, I...uh, hey, what did you hear?" Nobby asked.

"Maynard said that you tripped on a rug in his office," I answered.

The invisible mystery rug.

"Yes, that's right. Really clumsy of me. I don't know how that happened," Nobby offered. "Tore some ligaments in my knee. I don't know yet if I'll have to have surgery."

Hmmm, I thought to myself. I was about to ask more questions, but we were in the Cracker Barrel parking lot, and Darlene was already heading to the door.

"Hey, I sure hope you get better soon," I offered. "Thanks for calling. Sorry, I couldn't really tell you anything. I'm sure Mr. Krebs will let you know when we're going to meet to discuss this."

We said our goodbyes and hung up. Cracker Barrel was pretty crowded at 10:00 a.m. on Saturday, and I caught up with Darlene waiting in line. "What kind of name is 'Nobby'?" she asked. "Is he missing a hand or a leg or something? That's a very mean thing to call someone who has a handicap."

I thought to myself that he might have come close to losing a leg, but I didn't say anything about it. "Who knows," I finally said. "A lot of folks around here have nicknames. Nobby's real name is Nolan, and I've never met him in person, so I don't know why that's his nickname. I'll ask him if I get the chance. I mean, if it's not obvious."

We got a table near the front window, and for fun, we started going through all of the nicknames of people we knew. There was Boo-Boo, Tetaunt, Big Lou, T-Boy, MoJo, LaLa, CooTan, GaGa and Little GaGa, Peanut, Chalou, Bean, Shorty, Longjohn, No Neck, Wide Load, PutPut, TiJohn, Stots, and Nobby of course, and a number of others. Darlene, who's been married to me since the Stone Age and should already know this, asked if I ever had a nickname growing up besides Tony, my birth certificate name being Anthony.

I thought for a minute. "I guess you could say I had two nicknames. One of them was 'Man.' Paul, the barber who had a barbershop with his father on Mississippi Street in Donaldsonville, called me 'Man' because he could never remember anybody's name. He probably called everybody 'Man.' The other was 'Bubba.' That's what my brother T-Joe called me because he couldn't say 'brother' when he was little. Heck, he called me Bubba until we were both in high school. I'm really glad that didn't catch on with anybody else!"

After that, we made up nicknames for people we saw at Cracker Barrel while we ate. My favorites were 'Grit-face' and "Egg-lip."

Chapter Five

First thing Monday morning, I called Maynard's office. Once again, the Inquisitor answered. "Krebs and Cangelosi Disposal Services, to whom may I address your call?" I told her that I was calling for Maynard Krebs. She asked, "May I tell Mr. Krebs who's calling?" so I told her my name. Then she asked, "May I tell Mr. Krebs what your call is regarding?" I told her that he'd know why I was calling and that he was expecting my call. I guess he must have some kind of answering service because I didn't see a receptionist-type person at the trailer.

It turns out that Maynard wasn't in, and I was routed to Clara. "Mr. Campachi!" she answered excitedly. "Mr. Krebs had to step out, but he told me to expect your call. He's anxious to hear what you have to say. Can you meet with him this afternoon?"

We decided on 3:00 p.m. at his office. I thought briefly about asking Wide Load Morales to join me but decided I should have another Board member, so I called both Dustin and Kevin. No way was I bringing my Uncle and all Jack contributed last time was "ahma ahma ahma" and help with eating muffins. Dustin was tied up, but Kevin could make it.

Kevin met me at 2:50 p.m. at the Walmart parking lot right near Maynard's office, parked his suburban, and got into my truck. A couple of minutes later, we were cordially greeted by Yolanda and The Hulk. "What y'all want?" asked Yolanda sweetly. I told her our business, signed the form on the clipboard, endured a careful visual inspection of my truck and our bodies, and was then allowed to proceed inside the security fence. The Hulk looked as though he might have wanted to do a body cavity search.

Yolanda must have let Clara know that we were there because she was waiting for us just inside the door. "Mr. Campachi, so good to see you again! Oh, and this isn't Mr. Jack –"

"No, this is Kevin Farmer, one of MOSS's Board members," I replied. "Jack really wanted to come, but his wife had other ideas for him this afternoon. Kevin, you remember Clara McManus from that Elms on the Hill thing we worked out."

"Yes, of course, I do; hello, Ms. McManus," replied Kevin politely. Dealing with customers in that grocery store he owned for so many years gave him a lot of experience in being nice, even if it was faked.

Clara smiled and told us that Mr. Krebs would be with us in just a minute. "Can I get y'all some coffee – I just made a fresh pot of decaf – I just can't drink regular coffee in the afternoon; I'd never get to sleep tonight. Or maybe you'd like a Coke or a Dr. Pepper?"

We politely declined, and just then, Maynard Krebs stuck his head into Clara's office, smiled, and yelled, "I'm sorry to keep you all waiting. Please come on in."

Clara shut the door behind us, and I said, "Maynard, I'd like you to meet Kevin Farmer, one of our MOSS Board members. Kevin, this is Maynard Krebs."

As they shook hands, Maynard tilted his head to the right a little, got a quizzical look on his face, and asked, "Didn't you own Farmer's Market Grocery Store before it was bought out by that Metairie chain?"

"Why yes, I did," Kevin replied. "Is that where you shop?"

"No, that's where I tried to get your business for disposal services, but you decided to go with River Road Trash," Maynard replied with just a little bitterness in his voice.

"I'm sorry, I don't recall meeting you before – I'm sure it was just a matter of River Road being the cheaper alternative," said Kevin cautiously.

"I didn't meet with you; Jelly Cangelosi met with you," Maynard grunted. "You know, cheaper is not always better. Sometimes you end up paying more in the long run. The new owners understood that right away and hired us to do their pickups."

I could see that Kevin didn't know what to say to that, so I jumped in and told Maynard that we had studied the subdivision restrictions and had some comments, so we all sat down, and I began.

"Maynard, we studied the restrictions extensively and found several clauses that we believe apply to this situation," I started.

"Although solar panels are not specifically mentioned, the way it's written, it seems that the ACC has a lot of latitude regarding what is allowed and not allowed."

"So what's the bottom line here, Tony?" Maynard asked.

I summed it up. "The ACC has the authority to recommend to the Board that solar panels would be detrimental to the aesthetics and, therefore, the property values of the homes in Oak Harbor Estates. The Board can overrule the ACC, but you might be setting yourself up for a lawsuit. Let me ask you something – has the Architectural Control Committee come out and formally – I mean in writing to the Board – said that solar panels are not allowed?"

"No, nothing in writing yet," Maynard said dejectedly. "I just asked Nobby about it on behalf of a few folks in the subdivision who are thinking about putting them up."

I thought for a minute and said, "What about having the residents vote on whether solar panels ought to be allowed? If most of the homeowners are okay with solar panels, maybe you can vote to change the restrictions."

Maynard grunted and answered, "My daddy always told me, 'Don't underestimate the stupidity of the average voter.' I don't want to trust this in the hands of the residents. Some of them are idiots."

I felt like we were at an impasse. I was about to say that I didn't think there was anything more the MOSS group could do when Maynard piped up. "What if Nobby and his committee changed their minds about solar panels?"

"It's like I said, the ACC has a lot of latitude about these things," I offered. "If they approve the use of solar panels, they might still want to restrict the panels to the backs of houses where they're not so visible from the street, maybe put a limit on the number of panels that can be installed – stuff like that."

"You know what? That's a good idea!" replied Maynard with some excitement. "Maybe I can convince Nobby that solar panels would be okay if they were a little less, uh, uh, what's the word…?"

"Conspicuous?" Kevin offered. He hadn't said anything after Maynard's "cheaper is not always better" comment.

"Yeah, that's it – less conspicuous. I'm going to meet with Nobby and see if I can talk some sense into him," Maynard said, and the look on his face when he said it made me think about Nobby maybe soon having two bad legs.

"Tony, y'all have been a big help with this," Maynard said as he stood up and held out his hand. "I don't know if we'll need you anymore, but if we do, I'll get Clara to give you a call. You just send me your bill now, you hear?"

We shook hands, and I didn't bother to tell him that we figured it was too much trouble to charge for our work as a think tank and that we just decided we'd do this as a community service.

Chapter Six

The next Friday was unseasonably cold and rainy for late April, so we had a pretty big group show up at Frank's for our gathering because there wasn't anything else to do. Even our retired sheriff, Jed Wally, came, and he almost never made it to breakfast. Guess his golf game got rained out.

"Golf game got rained out today, boys," Jed let us know, "so I thought I'd give y'all a treat and show up this morning."

"You buying breakfast for everybody this morning, Jed?" asked Alden. Alden Roussel and Jed Wally were old hunting buddies and rode horses together every year in the Veteran's Day Parade.

"Now you know that is just not very likely," answered Jed with authority. "Me paying for your breakfast is about as likely as your Uncle Joe here paying." Uncle Joe's reputation for being frugal, to put it politely, was well known. Jed, on the other hand, was a very generous sort. It wouldn't surprise me at all if he picked up the tab for the whole table – but we wouldn't let him do that anyway. People were always trying to buy him meals when he was Sheriff, but he always declined. Jed didn't mind if you bought a meal for his deputies, though. I know I paid for a meal or two back in the day. Jed had been a really good sheriff, and he and his deputies were well-appreciated by the Ascension citizenry. Our current sheriff Rob Pepper came up through the ranks under Jed and learned a lot from him about how to deal with people, especially dangerous ones.

After we had eaten and drunk umpteen cups of coffee, Kevin said that I ought to tell everyone about how our meeting with Maynard went. Jed and a couple of other guys hadn't heard about the "public service" we took on for Oak Harbor Estates, so I gave them a quick summary of how we got involved in the solar panel controversy.

"What I couldn't figure out," I said as I was winding up the report, "is why Maynard seemed so interested in allowing solar panels on the houses there. I heard that those are really upscale homes, probably none under half a million. And Maynard didn't strike me as being all that environmentally friendly."

"Ha! I can tell you why he's pushing for solar panels," offered Jed.

"His wife's crooked brother sells them!"

Several of us, in one voice, said, "You've got to be kidding."

"Who are you talking about, Jed?" asked Kevin.

"Maynard's wife's maiden name is Nadine Voisin," Jed explained. "Her brother, Vincent 'Vinny' Voisin, has several times been a brief guest of ours in the Donaldsonville lockup. His brother-in-law Maynard has paid fines, bail, attorney's fees, whatever, to keep him on the street."

"So Maynard's wife gets him to bail out her brother?" I asked.

"Maybe," answered Jed. "I think it's more likely that Maynard is a silent partner in the solar panel business because I don't see how Vinny Voisin could come up with the capital to start a company like that on his own."

"How do you know all this stuff, Jed?" I asked him.

"I have a few well-off supporters that live in Oak Harbor Estates, and I meet with them from time to time," he told us. "They let me know what's going on, you know, stuff that I might like to know about."

Uncle Joe started telling Jed about how solar panels are proven to cause cancer, and the conversation about Vinny and Maynard got sidetracked.

Chapter Seven

Jed's revelation was, to say the least, eye-opening. Growing up in the town of Donaldsonville hadn't prepared me for situations like this. It's true that Darlene and I had lived in Miami for a few years, and we saw some goings-on there that make me blush just to think about them, but overall I'm still what you might call incurably optimistic and naïve. I usually think the best of people, although I admit that, in a weak moment, I thought Maynard or one of his employees might have broken Nobby's leg.

As I was walking out of Frank's, I was telling myself that at least our involvement in the whole solar panel fiasco was at an end when my phone rang and I saw that it was Nobby Narcisse. I thought about letting it go to voicemail, but I'm so programmed to answer the stupid thing that I clicked on it and said "Hello, Nobby."

"Hello, Mr. Campachi, this is Nobby Narcisse," as though I hadn't greeted him by name already. "Did I catch you at a bad time?"

I thought about replying "Yes, I'm in the middle of my hernia surgery" or "I think I'm having a heart attack and I need to hang up and dial 911," but instead I said "Oh no, Nobby, it's not a bad time. What can I do for you?" There's that optimism and naiveté working against me again. I am also cursed with a condition that causes me to say "yes" and raise my right hand a lot. Darlene calls it "volunteeritis."

Nobby started, "I got a phone call from Maynard earlier this week – in fact, a few calls – but I didn't answer them. I just let his calls go to voice mail." I might have to consider Nobby as a role model. "He wants to meet with me to discuss the ACC's position on solar panels again, but I've been avoiding him. I was hoping that, since you already met with Maynard, maybe you can share with me and my committee what your recommendations were."

"Hmmm, let me think for a minute." I had to buy some time. "Can you meet me for coffee at PJ's on Hwy 73?"

"What, you mean right now?" Nobby asked. "Absolutely, I'm not far from there. I can be there in five minutes."

I told him that it would take me closer to 15 but that I was on my way.

A short time later, I walked into PJ's, and there was Nobby waiting at the register. I had never met Nobby, but he was the only guy in the place and the only person on crutches. We shook hands, and he asked what I'd like. I only drink black coffee, sometimes decaf, but never flavored. The only thing I ever put in coffee is a little cinnamon. Of course I do have café au lait with beignets, but that's required.

After Nobby ordered and paid, we sat down at one of the few empty tables. The rest were occupied by young moms who had dropped off their kids to daycare or school and were enjoying a few minutes of calm and caffeine. We talked a little about the unusually cool, wet weather, and the barista called out, "Nolan," but I quickly got up and got our coffees.

"Tony – can I call you Tony?" Nobby began, and I said that, of course, he could. "Can you tell me what you advised Maynard about the solar panels? It's really important that I understand where this matter is headed."

I decided that I wasn't under any obligation such as "attorney-client privilege," "the seal of the confessional," or even "what happens in Vegas stays in Vegas." I said, "We told Maynard that, according to the subdivision restrictions, the ACC had a lot of latitude in interpreting the intent of the language. The Board could always go against the recommendations of the ACC, but that would be somewhat risky. Our advice was to put the matter to a vote of the entire subdivision. If the majority wanted solar panels, the restrictions could be amended or revised to allow them."

"Well, I can tell you in no uncertain terms that solar panels would get voted down," replied Nobby.

That was surprising. I said, "Maynard made it sound like a lot of residents really wanted solar panels. Of course, he also said that he didn't trust the residents to vote in favor, though."

Nobby grunted, leaned over the table, and confided, "There are exactly thirteen homeowners, all on the same street, who would definitely be in favor, and maybe a few more on the fence, but overall, the vast majority of the 175 homeowners would vote it down."

"Thirteen?" I responded. "But how do you know…"

Nobby cut me off with "Because thirteen homeowners were conned into giving Maynard's brother-in-law considerable down payments to put up solar panels. According to the ones who contacted me about getting written approvals so they could get started, this guy Vinny-something told them that the ACC and the Board of Directors had already verbally approved the installation."

"Vinny Voisin is the guy's name," I informed him. "He's had some run-ins with the law, but I'm told that his business is legitimate. What are you going to do?"

"I don't know; I just don't know. Maynard, he can be very forceful in order to get his way," said Nobby as he shifted his right leg and grimaced a bit.

"Say, can you drive with your leg in a brace like that?" I asked.

"Sure," he answered. "I stretch out my right leg on the seat and use my left to brake and accelerate. I'm just glad that I don't drive a standard anymore."

I was picturing him with two leg braces or maybe casts and possibly a wheelchair. I was really starting to feel sorry for him, but I didn't think that there was anything that MOSS could do to help. I wondered if I had been thinking out loud when Nobby said, "I think that there might be something that your MOSS group could do to help me out of this situation." Weird.

"I don't see how we can help at this point," I said somewhat weakly.

"What if I meet with Maynard and suggest that we call a homeowner's meeting and let the MOSS group arbitration panel decide the thing? That would at least get it off of my committee's back," Nobby pleaded.

And right onto mine was all I could think. "Well, alright, I guess. If you and Maynard agree to this, give me a call, and we'll work out something."

We left PJ's at the same time, Nobby with his crutches and me with my indigestion.

Dustin, Connie, Darlene and I have cocktails at our home or theirs on most Friday nights. This time it was at ours. We usually have cheese and crackers or smoked boudin or hog's head cheese or a frozen pizza or something else that's simple and doesn't require a lot of preparation or cleanup afterwards. This allows us to lean back and enjoy my Bombay Sapphire gin martini with blue cheese olives, Dustin's scotch, and Connie and Darlene's cosmos while we watch a British Crime drama on Britbox. We have to start watching the show before we drink too much because if I've had two martinis, I have trouble following the complicated plots and reading the subtitles, and I hate to have to ask Darlene what's going on.

The one thing that we have passed on to our two daughters, besides for blue eyes and bunions, is the tradition of cocktail night. They will invariably call us or at least text us a picture of what drink and snack they're having every Friday night. So when my cell phone rang just when the pathologist was beginning the autopsy of a particularly gruesome corpse, I assumed it was one of the girls, paused the autopsy in mid-cut, and answered, "Hey!"

It was Nobby Narcisse. "Hey, Tony! Glad I caught you. Just wanted to tell you that Maynard agreed to the arbitration. We have to give the homeowners a two-week notice of the HOA meeting, though, and that won't go out until Monday, so about two weeks or so from this coming Monday, we'll have the meeting – that's assuming that your MOSS group can make it. I'll call you to coordinate."

I think that I might have nodded and grunted something back to him, but in any case, he hung up, and I began thinking about a possible third martini.

Chapter Eight

For much of my career, I was blessed with jobs that included a company vehicle. When my last stint with a regional engineering firm ended a few years back and I lost that wonderful freebee, Darlene and I went out in search of a gently used pickup truck. We looked at Toyotas and discovered that the used Toyotas were just about the same price as the new ones. We went next to the Ford dealer and were walking around the lot when we were obviously spotted by one of those salespeople who work on commission because I could see him scurrying out to intercept me before we could escape.

But it turned out to be a friend of ours, the former principal of the Ascension Alternative School, Perry Elton.

"Perry, I didn't know you worked here!" I said in greeting.

He responded "This is my part-time retirement gig. I only work a couple of days a week. I'll probably quit when I've sold a car or truck to all of my friends. What are y'all looking for?"

I told him that I wanted a pickup that had been previously owned by an older gentleman who passed away before he could drive it anywhere, and his family didn't want it because it was too painful a reminder to them.

"I have just the thing," Perry told me. He led me to a shiny black Ford F-150 XLT full crew cab with running boards and a sprayed-in pickup bed. I was in love. "It was leased for a year, then turned in for a new model. It's only a year old with under 27,000 miles."

I wanted it but didn't want to sound desperate. I was waiting for Perry to say he'd toss in a free undercoating.

"This thing is a babe magnet," Perry whispered to me with a grin while Darlene was checking out the passenger seat. He knew he had me but that I couldn't use that as a selling point to Darlene.

After a bit of haggling and a ridiculous amount of paperwork, we bought the truck and I drove it off the lot, feeling like I had been issued a new man card.

It turned out that the truck was, in fact, a babe magnet. Every babe who had stuff to be moved, including my daughters in Kentucky and Texas, began to look at me with yearning in their eyes. I had never been so popular. I thought briefly about running for office.

I spent most of the week following Nobby's Friday night call hauling things to and fro for Volunteer Ascension and for my Rotary Club. When Thursday came around, I sent out an email to the MOSS group to announce an important gathering for Friday morning.

I picked up Uncle Joe the next morning on the way to Frank's. He always greeted me by saying, "If it isn't my favorite nephew." Of course, he knew that he was my favorite uncle because I spent more time with him than I did with my own brothers. We talked about how nice it was to see Jed Wally last Friday because he doesn't come to the gatherings too often. That got Uncle Joe reminiscing about old Sheriff Chalou from Donaldsonville, who got him to join the police department when he was 19. Sheriff Chalou had gone to my grandparents' house on Lessard Street to talk to Paw Paw Tony (I was named after him) to ask if it was alright for Uncle Joe to come and work for him. After a couple of years on the Donaldsonville force, he went on to be a policeman in New Orleans, where he met his wife.

"Chalou told my daddy not to worry, that he would teach me everything I needed to know about policing," Uncle Joe told me for the umpteenth time. "I tell you, I was headed in the wrong direction before Chalou hired me. He turned my life around 100 degrees."

That's more than a quarter of the way around, I thought to myself, but I didn't even bother to say anything. I just let him ramble a bit more because we were almost at Frank's by that time.

Frank's parking lot was packed. One of the chemical plants must have been having a big breakfast meeting in the large back room to talk about how environmentally friendly they were and that theirs was the safest plant to work at and that there was absolutely no truth to the rumor of them killing thousands of people in Bangladesh.

I dropped Uncle Joe off at the front door while I drove around waiting for someone to leave so I could park. It wasn't long before someone at the very end of the parking lot pulled out, and I backed into the spot. I always back in or find a pull-through space to use. Darlene used to rag me about doing this, but I think she's finally seen the wisdom of backing in. Or she's just given up in complete frustration. I can't tell.

Of course, as I walked the 100 yards or so to the restaurant, someone pulled out right near the front door. It was a big wide spot too. I chalked it up to another example of Murphy's Law.

Some of the MOSS were already at our table drinking coffee, and Uncle Joe was flirting with Wendy, who was clearly super busy but too nice to brush him off. I grabbed him and we said hello to everyone and sat down. In a few minutes, we had a pretty full table and everyone had had at least one cup of coffee and had told Wendy what they wanted to eat. I called the gathering to order.

"Guys," I started, "we have a situation. The Oak Harbor Estates HOA folks would like us to act as an arbitration panel, sort of like we did over at Elms on the Hill. This one has to do with solar panels. Most of y'all already know a little about this. Any comments or suggestions?"

Slim offered that at least it was a step up from dog crap. Several others wondered if No Neck Lalonde's jambalaya was a possibility this time. Alden reminded everyone of the complete lack of wisdom – one of the few traits we required for membership in MOSS – we showed by continuing to deal with HOAs, veritable incubators of lawsuits.

Dr. Dart, who is typically very quiet and reserved, cleared his throat and raised his hand. No one had ever raised his hand in our gatherings unless it was to get Wendy's attention for more coffee. He was looking in my direction, so I looked behind me to see if Wendy was lurking, but she wasn't. I said, "Dr. Dart, do you have something you want to say?"

"Yes, thank you, Tony, I do. I know that you spent some considerable time studying the subdivision restrictions, and I commend you for that, but don't you think that it would be wise and prudent to know more about solar panels before taking on this assignment?"

I was embarrassed to admit that I hadn't even given this any thought. "Well, of course, Dr. Dart, I planned on spending some time in the next two weeks at the main library sharpening my understanding of the solar panel industry. I'm sure that more knowledge could be very useful."

Dr. Dart cleared his throat again. That's not a good sign. "Tony, I am a loyal patron of the Parish library system, and I'm certain that your time there would be well spent. I suggest that you also do some internet research for the very latest trends in renewable energy."

Uncle Joe, only partially listening as usual, chimed in with, "I don't believe in that reusable energy crap. That's just another step to Communism." Several of the guys grinned at that but nodded in agreement to appease him.

Dustin sarcastically asked, "When will the happy arbitration event take place?"

"About two weeks from this past Monday, if the HOA Board over there got the notice out," I responded. "They have to give a minimum two-week notice of a meeting to the residents."

Then I asked Alden if there was some way the MOSS could protect itself from some sort of legal complaint.

"Yeah," he said. "I can get you some boilerplate hold-harmless language for their HOA Board to sign like I had suggested to you for the Elms on the Hill stuff, which you ignored. That won't guarantee anything, but it would make it a little more difficult for anyone to come after you."

"Great! That makes me feel a little better about the whole thing," I said. I had forgotten about doing that for Elms on the Hill. Luckily, nothing happened, I guess.

"Well, don't get too comfortable," Alden replied. "Like I said, it's no guarantee that some fool won't try to sue you anyway."

Nevertheless, I was still comforted by having something in writing to protect us. I just had to get Maynard to sign it. Then I got to thinking that I would just send it to Clara and ask her to get Maynard to sign. She seemed to have a pretty chummy relationship with him. She probably baked him a lot of gingerbread muffins.

No one else had any objections to us going forward with this, in spite of Uncle Joe complaining about having neither payment nor jambalaya to look forward to. He was absolutely dead set against doing this as a public service. "That sounds like Communism to me," he complained.

It was decided that the same guys that sat on the first arbitration panel would sit on this one – me, Ronald, Jack, and Slim. At least that way we could say we all had experience doing this. We were all set.

Nobby called me later on Friday to confirm that the notice was sent out on the Monday after we met, and the meeting was set for 7:00 p.m. on the Tuesday following the required two weeks. I told him that I would check with the guys but that I was pretty sure it wouldn't be a problem. Unlike Elms on the Hill that had to use a local church for a meeting place, Nobby told me that Oak Harbor had its own community center with a meeting room that could accommodate 150 people without violating the fire department's limits. He didn't think we'd get that many people, because there were really only a few that had, as he put it, "a dog in the fight."

Chapter Nine

I spent Saturday cutting the grass and edging, cleaning out my box garden of all of the stuff that failed to grow or to produce any of the "bountiful harvest" that was promised on the seed packets, and generally puttering around. I was always told that as men got older, they puttered, and I didn't understand that until now. I had definitely become pretty adept at puttering.

On Monday, Jack, Slim, Ronald, and I met for coffee at Ye Olde Antique Coffee Shoppe on Burnside, a block away from the Irma Street library. I thought that Ye Olde Antique Coffee Shoppe was a very presumptuous name considering it had been open for all of 6 months. It was decorated with antiques, though, and the tables and chairs were, if not authentic antiques, at least looked old and decrepit.

The owner/manager/barista/waiter was a youngish man with a beard and long hair and explained that he had plans of franchising. He originally wanted to call the place Ye Olde Coffee Shoppe, but that name was already taken. His name is Travis Parmenter, nephew of our MOSS member Terry. We were trying to help him out and besides, he served Community Coffee New Orleans Blend among other varieties. He also had fresh blueberry scones.

The four of us sat there at the rickety table on rickety chairs and plotted our path forward. We would find, with library staff help, as many books and magazines about solar panels as we could. Slim, Jack, and Ronald would pore through those and jot down pertinent information while I would hop onto one of the many computer terminals there and see what I could find on the internet. I got this assignment not because I was so adept at using computers and exploring the internet – I was just better at it than the other three.

We finished our coffee and scones, paid Travis, and headed to the library. With a lot of help from the library staff, and after about two hours of research, we gathered on very stable wood chairs at a large very stable wood table to compare notes. It was a lot of information, much of which was related to the invention and development of solar panels, the average cost of purchase and installation, the impact on the power grid, companies that manufacture panels, and other facts that were of little help to us. Here's what we found that we thought might be useful:

1. *In the northern hemisphere, the ideal angle to install solar panels is between 30 degrees and 45 degrees, as close to perpendicular to the sun as possible.*

2. *Solar panels facing true South are the most efficient at harnessing energy.*

3. *Panels facing North are the least efficient.*

4. *Panels facing East or West are not perfect but can work.*

5. *There are federal and state tax incentives for having solar panels.*

6. *Solar panels can provide significant energy cost savings.*

7. *Most property owners can see a return on investment in less than 10 years.*

8. *They work well even in winter, especially in the South.*

But on the internet, I also found information about the environmental impacts of manufacturing and ultimately disposing of solar panels, such as:

1. *Producing the panels requires a large amount of water and industrial materials.*

2. *Coal is the primary energy source in the production process.*

3. *Hydrofluoric acid and sodium hydroxides are toxic wastes used in the process and have to be disposed of.*

4. *The workers employed in producing the panels are exposed to these and other potentially dangerous chemicals and wastes.*

> 5. *Solar panel glass contains Cadmium and Lead, which are carcinogenic and can be released into soil and groundwater when old panels are disposed of in landfills.*

I was really sorry to find out about the Cadmium and Lead thing because it might mean that Uncle Joe was at least partially right about solar panels causing cancer, and we had all either ignored him or made fun of him. He'd never let me hear the end of it.

The information about the environmental impacts was scarce. I just happened to stumble upon it because I didn't have very narrow search criteria. There was 50 times more information about the benefits of solar energy than there was about the downsides. I guess that's because solar panel manufacturers were the ones publishing or sponsoring the books and articles about the environmental benefits and cost savings of "clean energy."

The library staff were, without exception, excited by and supportive of clean energy concepts, especially solar panels. When I asked one of them, a young man named Nick, what he thought about the potential environmental impacts, he shrugged and thought that even if it were true, it was still a very good long-term trade-off and that the source of this negative information might not be completely trustworthy. He didn't come out and say "conspiracy theorists," but that's how I interpreted his comments.

The four of us felt like we had spent a pretty productive morning and were well and properly educated about solar panels and renewable energy sources in general. Our knowledge might be a mile wide and an inch deep, but we still knew more than the average citizen. We were as prepared as we were going to be for the arbitration meeting. We headed to our respective homes.

When I got home and checked my email, I found that Alden, out of character and taking me completely by surprise, had sent me the "hold harmless" agreement that he had recommended at our last Friday gathering. This gave me enough time to look it over, print two copies, sign one of them, and call Clara to explain what it was about before sending it to her to get Maynard's signature. Before calling Clara, though, I thought that I should run the thing by the MOSS group on Friday. I didn't want to take the blame alone.

Ronald, Jack, Slim, and I and a few of the other guys gathered as usual on Friday morning and I showed them the hold-harmless agreement with my signature. They knew less than I did about such things, and I didn't know much, so their nodding approval didn't give me a lot of comfort. Nevertheless, I called Clara after we left Frank's.

"Clara, this agreement is pretty standard in our arbitration business," I began, having no real idea what was standard in our arbitration business, "so I hope you can get Maynard to sign it for us. I'll scan it and email it to you. We'd feel a lot better about doing this as a public service."

"Oh, you don't worry at all about that now, Tony," she assured me. "That man will sign anything I put in front of him. He's so busy. You go ahead and send it to me. I have your cell phone number, so I'll text you my email. Is it okay if I give you the agreement at the meeting?"

"Will you be at the meeting, Clara? I didn't realize – well, sure, that would be okay, as long as I have it before we get started," I said. Then I thought to ask her, "Clara, do you think that we ought to have some security for the meeting? There's someone we used at the last arbitration hearing we conducted. I can check to see if he's available."

"Oh Tony, don't you fret about that," answered Clara. "Maynard will have Yolanda and Big Boy there in case there's any trouble. They can handle it, believe me."

Big Boy, I thought to myself as we said goodbye and hung up. What other name could possibly fit better? In terms of sheer size, Big Boy would give Wide Load Morales a run for his money. I was a little worried, though, that Yolanda and Big Boy would be the ones to cause the trouble.

I got home and scanned the agreement, then sent it as an attachment to the email address Clara had texted me. In the body of the email, I just said, "Clara, thanks in advance for getting Maynard to sign this before the meeting next Tuesday. We appreciate it." I signed it *Tony Campachi, MOSS Founder*. I was going to add "Chief Arbitrator," but I wasn't sure that was even a word, and I didn't want to take the time to Google it.

Darlene and I then headed out to look for pickleball paddles. I don't know what possessed us to think that we'd want to start playing pickleball. Maybe it was because a bunch of our friends were into it; also, the courts were a lot smaller than the tennis courts we were used to playing on and, the older we got, the bigger the courts seemed. Dr. Fontenot told me at my last checkup that I should lose weight, but I explained that I needed the extra stomach weight to lower my center of gravity for golf and tennis. I don't think he bought it. That low center of gravity would come in even handier on the smaller pickleball court. Let those young skinny people run around like crazy. My strategy was to be solid and stationary.

We checked out several sporting goods stores and couldn't find a paddle for under $65. I guess all of the cheaper ones were snatched up by our cheap friends. We went to CC's for coffee and a chocolate scone, and since they had free Wi-Fi, I checked out what Amazon had to offer. I found a deal that offered two paddles, four balls, and a carrying case for $63. Dang! Not only that but they would be delivered the next day!

I'm a big believer in shopping locally, and I dread the possibility that Amazon will put other local stores out of business. Still, it's hard to ignore the savings and the convenience. And Amazon can't yet deliver hot coffee and chocolate scones, so we'll still go out for that. Uncle Joe believes that Amazon is just one more giant step to Communism and he refuses to use it. He's even more old-school than me. I know that his wife, my Aunt Millie, orders stuff from Amazon behind his back by having it delivered to her neighbor next door. What he doesn't know won't hurt him, I guess. I sure hope he doesn't find out that his wife of fifty-plus years is a Communist.

Chapter Ten

When Tuesday rolled around, I called Jack, Slim, and Ronald and suggested we go together because I didn't know how much parking there would be. I also thought that we go early to get a lay of the land. So we met up in the parking lot of what used to be the Farmer's Market grocery store and all got in Ronald's SUV for the five-mile ride to Oak Harbor Estates. We chit-chatted about various things along the way, including the suggestion that I was nuts for taking up pickleball at my age.

"You're only as old as you feel," I said, in my defense.

"Well, it's a good thing you're not as old as you look," answered Slim. Smart-ass.

We found Oak Harbor Estates easily enough, but we had not been there before and didn't realize that it was a gated community with a guard house and everything. Ronald pulled up to the door of the guard house and rolled down his window as a uniformed young man approached the car.

"Can I help you?" he politely asked. The name on his badge was "Dillon."

"We're here for the HOA meeting," replied Ronald. "We're the arbitration panel. We're a little early, I guess."

"That's not a problem," Dillon assured us with a smile. "We were expecting you. You'll be meeting in the Community Center main building." He handed Ronald a map and pointed out the building, which seemed to be in the center of the subdivision. "Take this first right, follow the road around, and take the second exit of the roundabout. It's pretty easy to find. There will be a young woman in this same kind of uniform there to greet you."

We thanked him, and Ronald handed the map to Slim, who was riding shotgun. We took a right turn and followed a wide, winding road for a while, noticing that the huge homes looked as though they were all on at least one-acre lots, maybe more. We finally came upon the roundabout. I've seen roundabouts before, but never one with a giant four-tiered working fountain in the middle, complete with a fleur-de-lis top. Having little experience with roundabouts, Ronald took the first exit instead of the second, but we decided to explore a bit since we were early. What we saw was impressive. Tree-lined sidewalks, manicured lawns, gardens, and spotlessly kept common areas were everywhere we looked.

It was dusk by now, and streetlights began to come on. They were domed lights hanging out from black, highly decorated wrought-iron poles. The lights cast a muted circular glow onto the ground. We saw two couples walking their dogs, which, of course, reminded us of our last arbitration venture. This place was so ritzy that I was surprised that no hired hand was following them to pick up the dog's poop. But maybe these high-classed dogs thought pooping in public was beneath them.

"Time to get back on course," I suggested. The road was wide enough for Ronald to make a U-turn in his SUV without having to go into someone's driveway to turn around. We got back to the roundabout and took the next exit. In about half a mile, we found ourselves at the Community Center. There was a large building in the middle and smaller, similarly designed buildings on either side. To the right of the three buildings were an Olympic-size swimming pool and a large well-equipped playground. To the left of the buildings were a number of tennis courts and – what do you know – several pickleball courts, all under lights! There was a mixed doubles match getting started on one court, and it looked like lessons on another.

Money may not be able to buy happiness but, apparently, it can buy stuff that makes people seem happy, and I wondered what the difference was. I also wondered if I could swing an invite to get pickleball lessons, but then realized that it might constitute a conflict of interest. Or at least someone would see it that way.

Ronald parked and we walked over to the main building. The front doors were huge, with beveled glass panels and massive door handles. As we approached, a young, uniformed woman opened the door from the inside and greeted us. "Welcome," she said. "Dillon let me know you were on the way. Did you get turned around? I expected you about 10 minutes ago."

"Ronald took the wrong exit on the roundabout," offered Slim, the navigator. "I tried to tell him."

"It's not a problem at all," she said graciously. Her name badge read "Denise." "Follow me, and I'll show you to the meeting room."

Denise led us through the large foyer, in the center of which was a highly polished dark wood table that must have been 10 feet in diameter. The table featured a large glass centerpiece of dried grasses and a variety of colored flowers. Over the table hung a chandelier almost as wide as the table. We walked around the table toward a large set of double doors. A tripod supporting a professionally lettered sign stood on one side of the doors to inform us there was an "HOA Meeting In Progress."

Denise let us know that we were the first to arrive and that we were to make ourselves comfortable. As we entered the meeting room, we all looked around to get our bearings. To the left was a hallway that led, according to discrete signage, to the restrooms. To the right, against the wall, was a long, narrow table covered with a black cloth and decorated with flowers. In the center of the table were coffee urns, one with a small sign that read "regular" and the other "decaf." There was also a large bowl of ice cubes with an ice scoop, real glasses (not plastic), and assorted soft drinks and water neatly arranged to the side.

Just then, a man and woman came in from a door to the rear of the room, and each was carrying a large silver tray – one with sandwiches and one with cookies, brownies, and little muffins. A third woman appeared just then with a tray of what appeared to be assorted cheeses, crackers, and other niceties. I felt like I was at a wedding reception – a really nice one. I began to wonder if there would be an open bar.

The tray carriers all had similar shirts, on the back of which was the logo and name of a local catering company. *Wow,* I thought to myself, *A catered HOA meeting.* We may not be getting No Neck's jambalaya, but we would at least eat. I think Ronald, Slim, and Jack had similar thoughts.

We walked to what appeared to be the head table, toward the rear of the room. It was covered with a white tablecloth and had small vases of flowers near either end. This was clearly where it was intended that the arbitration panel and the HOA Board sit. There were eight chairs at the table, all facing the audience, with one microphone in front of every other seat. People were beginning to arrive. It was almost 7:00, and very few people had shown up. There must have been about 100 seats in the place, arranged with a center aisle from the entry door to the table where we were to sit. I had just realized that I didn't bring my gavel, which I had repaired with a liberal amount of wood glue, when I saw that there was a very nice gavel and board already at the table, obviously for the HOA President to call the meeting to order, and to bang on when folks got unruly. Nobby came in as we were contemplating grabbing some coffee and a sandwich. He was still on crutches with a large stiff brace on his right leg. He was followed closely by Yolanda and Big Boy. Yolanda had held the door open for him.

"Hello, fellas," Nobby said in greeting. "I should have warned you that nobody comes to these HOA meetings on time. Most of the people that live here like to arrive fashionably late."

"Yes, we were wondering about that," I said. "Do you suppose the place will fill up?"

Nobby chuckled. "Well, it never has in the past, and we've had some fairly controversial issues come up on occasion. I expect we'll only see the people who are requesting to be allowed to install solar panels and the residents on the same street that object. If people aren't directly affected by something, they usually don't show up."

Slim was eyeing the sandwiches and asked Nobby, "Do you think we have time to grab a bite to eat and maybe some coffee before we get started?"

"Well, we can't start without the President, that's for sure," Nobby said with a grin. "He's usually one of the fashionably late ones. Say, Tony, would you mind grabbing me a cup of black coffee, decaf?"

I had to work my way around Big Boy, who was munching down a brownie and eyeing the cheese display. I got coffee for Nobby and myself and went back for sandwiches and a cookie. Nobby told us that he and his wife had already had their usual early supper. We sat at the head table with Nobby on the end so as to be able to stick out his braced leg.

A few more people trickled in, some waving a greeting to Nobby and asking about his leg. Jack, Slim, and Ronald were standing around the food table deciding what to put on their plates. I took the opportunity to ask Nobby something.

"Nobby, the people that live here are obviously well off…" He stopped me to let me know that it was his wife with all of the money, not him. He described himself as a regular working stiff.

"Don't get me wrong, I'm not being critical of people with money," I said. "I wish I was one of them. I just wondered why some of your residents want solar panels. I mean, it can't be because they're trying to save money, right?"

"You are probably right. They're not doing this primarily to save money – that's just an added benefit. They're doing it because they think they're saving the planet," Nobby said sarcastically. "Some of them are tenured professors at LSU, one couple is the daughter and son-in-law of one of the professors, and the rest are just wealthy and feel guilty about the size of their carbon footprint."

"But how did they get on the solar panel bandwagon to start with?" I asked. "I mean, did someone convince them to do this?"

"There's a lady's group here that organizes social events, shopping trips, and such," Nobby began. "Don't tell my wife I said this, but these ladies are of the snobby variety. Maynard's wife, Nadine, is the head of the group. I don't think that it's a formal thing like she was elected head or something, but she appears to have a lot of influence on the rest, including my wife, Frankie. Nadine had her brother Vinny come and speak to the group about the wonderful benefits of solar panels."

"Well, that explains how Vinny Voisin got his nose under the tent," I thought out loud.

Nobby continued. "The word got back to the various husbands who, I'm told, discussed it over drinks at the Clubhouse bar, and that got the ball rolling. They contacted Vinny, who, I believe, either told them outright that the ACC had already signed off on the installation of solar panels or he presented it in such a way that they were led to believe that the ACC had okayed it."

I picked up the story from there. "So Vinny put thirteen of these homeowners under contract and collected a substantial down payment from each."

Nobby concluded, "I think that Vinny would be 'in the wind,' as they say, if he hadn't been afraid that Maynard – or Nadine – would kill him. You see, this group that wants the solar panels is actually like Maynard. Maynard bought Nadine a Prius. They think he's a tree hugger because he has a recycling facility as part of the garbage collection business. They all happily pay extra to have these blue recycling bins picked up. I suspect Maynard just throws the stuff in the bins in with the rest of the garbage."

It was at this time – 7:25 p.m. – that Maynard strolled in with Clara and several gentlemen and one other woman in tow. The residents that had previously arrived were milling about the food and drink table, but when they noticed Maynard, they started making their way to seats. He and Clara strode to the head table and, grinning broadly, greeted us with a booming "Hello, fellas!" One of the men and the woman who arrived with Maynard took seats at the head table. Yolanda and Big Boy stood at parade rest on either end. The rest of the group that came in with Maynard found seats together on one side. It wasn't that crowded. I estimated that more than half of the 100 or so seats were empty.

Clara sat down next to me, and Maynard stood behind his chair – his place was indicated by a nameplate that read "Maynard Krebs, HOA Chairman" – and addressed the audience. He clearly did not need the microphone. "I'm sorry for the delay in getting this thing started. I hope you all enjoy the fine food and beverages I was happy to provide for this important meeting."

So Maynard hired the caterer, I thought to myself. I would like to know if that constitutes a bribe. That might be true if he came right out in the meeting and supported the approval of solar panels openly.

Maynard continued with, "I'd like to introduce our two other HOA Board members for those of you who might not know them—our Vice-President Lawrence Penhetty and our Treasurer Pamela Smythe. The Chairman of our Architectural Control Committee, Nolan Narcisse, is at the other end of the table. Clara, next to me here, is my assistant. I also want to take this time to introduce and thank Tony Campachi, head of this arbitration panel. His group is very well known in Ascension Parish as being unbiased and fair when it comes to resolving disputes. Tony, why don't you introduce the rest of the panel?"

I pulled the microphone near to me and cleared my throat – a habit that Darlene has tried in vain to break me of – and it sounded like an explosion. I then introduced Slim, Ronald, and Jack. I started to explain how this arbitration session would be conducted when Maynard, still standing, interrupted me.

"Folks, Tony here will explain how we're going to do this arbitration thing. Everyone will get a chance to give their opinion about solar panels in our subdivision. I just ask that y'all be patient and open-minded about this. Go ahead, Tony. By the way, our Board Secretary couldn't be here tonight, so Clara here will be taking the meeting minutes."

"Thank you, Mr. Krebs," I started. I thought it best to keep everything formal. "Ronald here will be passing around two clipboards. One is labeled 'In Favor Of' and the other 'Opposed.' Please sign one or the other if you wish to speak tonight. We will first hear from the petitioners – that is, the residents who have requested permission to install solar panels. Then those residents opposing the installation of solar panels in Oak Harbor Estates will speak. Each speaker will be allowed as much as five minutes to present their case, but please keep your comments as brief as you can, as we may have a lot of speakers. The petitioners will then be given two minutes for rebuttal, and likewise, those in opposition will be given two minutes. Oh, and if anyone has their comments written out and would like to submit them for the record, just hand them to Clara here after you've spoken." I decided when we accepted this gig to forego the whole coin toss thing and just dictate how this would go. I envisioned somehow hitting Clara in the eye again.

As the clipboards were being passed around and there was general murmuring in the seats, Clara put both of her hands on my forearm, pulled her chair up close to mine, and whispered, "Tony, you are so good at this! This is exciting! I hope I can take good notes. I don't know shorthand or anything. I brought a little recording thingy, but I don't know how to work it."

I took a look at the "recording thingy" and passed it on down to Jack to see if he could get it to work. In about ten seconds, he said that it looked like the batteries were dead. I looked at Clara and said, "Just do the best you can with your notes." Then I looked at Jack, Slim, and Ronald and suggested that we all take notes and compare later.

Ronald and Slim collected the two clipboards, and after making sure that everyone who wanted to speak had signed one or the other, I called on the first person from the "In Favor Of" list, on which there were only two signatures. And right off the bat, I was stuck.

"Mr…uh..uh…Norman…or is it…Normal? Normal Kramer?"

"Thank you, Mr. Campachi; it is Normal Kramer," Mr. Kramer answered as he stepped up to the microphone stand that was positioned in the aisle. "I've been asked to speak on behalf of a number of our residents – in fact, nine residents – who are petitioning the Architectural Control Committee to approve the installation of solar panels at their private residences."

I interrupted Mr. Kramer. "Pardon me, but are you an attorney?"

"It happens that I am, in fact, an attorney, but I'm not here in any sort of legal capacity. I'm one of the homeowners who wish to install solar panels, and I offered to informally represent other such homeowners who either could not commit the time to be here or would rather not speak themselves."

I feared at this point that Alden was right. We had barely gotten started and already had a lawyer setting up shop on the ground floor.

"Okay, Mr. Kramer," I said, "please proceed."

"Thank you," he responded. "I'll be brief. I also have a transcript of my comments to provide to your panel when I've concluded. And please keep in mind that my comments represent the positions of nine homeowners, all of whom are of the same mind with respect to their belief that solar panels should be approved."

Mr. Kramer continued by first naming the nine homeowners, including himself, represented by his presence. He then enumerated a number of reasons for approving the installation of solar panels in Oak Harbor Estates, as follows:

1. *As a renewable energy source, solar panels play an important role in reducing greenhouse gasses and mitigating climate change.*

2. *Solar energy is known to improve air quality and reduce water use from energy production.*

3. *Solar panels are known to increase home value.*

4. *There are currently tax breaks and financial incentives to install solar panels.*

5. *Prices have come down considerably in recent years, making solar energy a viable option.*

6. *Solar power gives the homeowner control over their electricity by avoiding peak electricity rates.*

7. *Making use of this renewable energy source is what every good citizen who cares about the environment should support.*

He concluded with the following: "The positive environmental impacts should be reason enough to approve the solar panel installation and use, but there is also another overriding reason for doing so. Each of the petitioners that I named earlier, including myself, has made a $5,000 down payment for the purchase and installation of solar panels with the understanding that the Chairman of the Architectural Control Committee, in taped conversations with our sales representative, Mr. Voisin, verbally approved the installation of the panels, and is now, for some unknown reason, denying that fact!"

There were audible gasps from the audience. Nobby Narcisse immediately yelled, "Why you lying son-of-a..." and jumped up, or at least tried to, but having forgotten about his leg brace in his excitement, he succeeded in knocking over the entire table, tripping Yolanda, who was standing next to him. She fell onto her back, and Nobby then proceeded to fall, in slow motion, face down on top of her.

"Man, get off me, get offa me!" she screamed, slapping at his head with both of her two-inch long-fingernailed hands. "Get off me, man; I mean it! Help me, Big Boy!"

The audible gasps were largely replaced by even more audible laughter. Nobby managed to roll off of Yolanda, one crutch in his hand flailing around dangerously, hitting Big Boy in the crotch as he came to Yolanda's rescue. Big Boy went down to one knee with his left hand on the floor and his right on his privates. He was breathing hard. He looked like a football player kneeling down at midfield to pray after a loss.

Maynard tried to restore order, but when the table went over, his gavel and board, microphones, glasses of water, papers, and everything else flew towards the people sitting in the front row just a few feet away. No one was hurt, but a couple of folks got pretty wet. Lawrence Penhetty had instinctively grabbed for the tablecloth with one hand and was left holding it like a magician completing a trick as the table and everything on it disappeared. With the table gone, Clara no longer had cover and was pulling frantically down on her short skirt in a futile effort. Someone had been filming Normal Kramer's presentation, probably at his request, caught the entire fiasco, and would later show it to several attendees who would be greatly amused all over again. It was certain to be an internet sensation.

Normal Kramer, who had every reason to believe that Nobby, before his tryst with Yolanda, had intended to brain him with his crutch, slowly crept to the back of the room. Jack and I, after our initial shock subsided, went over and helped Nobby to his feet. Slim and Ronald were checking on Big Boy, who was not yet ready to stand up. Pamela Smythe tried to calm down Yolanda, who had stopped screaming but was crying pretty loudly and trying to readjust her purple wig that had come askew during the melee.

Someone had returned the gavel and board to Maynard, and he held both over his head, banging the board for order. The caterers came out from the kitchen and put the table back in place and picked up the debris. A new tablecloth was brought out and installed, pitchers of water and glasses replaced, and order was restored. Someone in the audience brought over chairs for both Big Boy and Yolanda, who gratefully sat.

Nobby, still visibly shaken, insisted to Maynard that he be allowed to immediately refute the "spurious and unsupported lies" of Mr. Kramer. Maynard promised him that he would give him the floor after both sides had presented their positions.

"Mr. Kramer, are you done?" Maynard yelled to the back of the room.

"Oh yes, sir, I'm finished presenting," Kramer yelled from the back row.

"Well, don't go away; the panel here might have some questions later," Maynard told him. "Isn't that right, Tony?" I mutely nodded. Maynard didn't appear to be flustered at all by the recent events, whereas the four of us MOSS members didn't quite know what to say or do.

People settled back down, and Jack found the two clipboards, both wet and with smeared names. He gave them to Maynard, who decided to take over this aspect of the meeting and called out the only other name on the "In Favor Of" list – Mrs. Gladys Summerville. Mrs. Summerville, a smartly dressed and coiffed mature lady, approached the aisle microphone. As she was no more than five feet, two inches tall, she struggled for a moment, trying to adjust the mic stand until someone sitting nearby helped her with it. She seemed to be looking at a spot just over our heads as she spoke without notes in a soft Southern accent.

"I am Gladys Summerville of 15152 Harbor Lights Drive. My husband, Marvin, had an important Elks Lodge meeting tonight and apologizes for not being here. We decided to represent ourselves, so we are not represented by Mr. Kramer. My husband and I built the first home on Harbor Lights almost 19 years ago. Had we known more about solar panels at that time, we might very well have had them installed when the house was built. We have always, always been sensitive to environmental concerns, and have raised our three children and encourage our grandchildren to treat Mother Earth with the care she deserves."

There were a few snickers at the "Mother Earth" statement and someone said something about Father Time, to more snickering. Mrs. Summerville ignored the comments and, with stoic dignity, carried on.

"We wish to set an example to our children and grandchildren, and soon to our first great-grandchild, of care and compassion for our beautiful state, which is quickly disappearing with the sea level rise caused by the melting of the polar ice caps, all due to climate change.

There is so little that we can do individually, but every little bit helps. We wish to do our small part by installing solar panels on the roof of our beautiful home and we trust that you will allow us to do this small thing to help future generations. Thank you for listening."

With that, she turned gracefully and returned to her seat to a smattering of applause. Nobby, who had regained his composure, had been jotting down notes during Mrs. Summerville's soliloquy and now slid them over to me. As Maynard picked up the "Opposed" clipboard from the table and tried to make out the first smeared name on the list, I read Nobby's notes.

"Marvin Summerville, retired multi-millionaire, made his money in the oil business. His company is responsible for several oil spills in the past and for cutting hundreds of canals through the marshes in south Louisiana, which of course, resulted in increasing saltwater intrusion. He owns a gas-guzzling jet and an 80-foot long yacht. He's actually catching hell from his grandchildren, several of whom are at west-coast liberal arts colleges and are active in protesting companies just like their grandfather's."

I looked at Nobby when I finished reading, and he just snickered and shook his head. I whispered to him, "If the Summervilles think that they can appease their liberal grandkids with a few solar panels after all of the damage his company has done, they may want to re-think that strategy." Then I got to wondering whether the grandkids would stand on their environmental principles if granddad promised them each millions in his will. Tough call. If I were one of his grandkids, I just might have to stop hugging my tree long enough to be able to grab the money with both hands.

Maynard finally figured out the name and asked me if I'd like him to call up the next speaker. I said, "Sure," and Maynard called out, "Mr. Wade Moore – if you'd still like to speak, please come up to the microphone."

A bald gentleman of about my age, I guessed, approached the microphone. He wore a navy blue sport shirt, white shorts, a knee brace, and tennis shoes. I'm pretty sure he was the guy I saw on the pickleball court earlier. After readjusting the microphone a few inches higher, he began to read with a slight stutter from prepared notes.

"My name is Wah-Wade Moore, and I live at 15169 Harbor Lights

Drive, across the wah-way from the Summervilles. I'm a retired Chemical Engineer. My wah-wife Doreen and I are concerned about several aspects of the proposed solar pah-panel installations, nuh-not the least of which has to do with the aesthetic nature of the panels and the puh-possibility that the sight of them will simply be an eyesore. As a Chemical Engineer, I am also aware of the toxic by-products in buh-both the manufacturing and eventual disposal of solar panels. I believe that this Mr. Voisin, who I see failed to make an appearance tonight, has sold some of our residents a 'buh-bill of goods' with regard to the environmental benefits of solar panels."

I wondered if anyone would bring up the stuff we found out during our library research. I liked this Mr. Moore, him being a fellow engineer and all.

Mr. Moore continued: "It may be t-t-true that there is, in the long term, a financial benefit for the homeowner, but I find it hard to believe that anyone who lives in this de-development needs to save a few pennies on their electric bill. If you want to leave a better environmental legacy for your grandchildren, I cuh-can suggest any number of better ways to do so. Doreen and I are opposed to allowing solar panels in this development puh-primarily because we fear they will be an eyesore and devalue our home. I guess that's all I have to say."

With that, Mr. Moore returned to his seat. Five other people, all of whom lived on Harbor Lights Drive, spoke in opposition to solar panels. All were opposed for about the same reasons – they thought the panels would really look ugly and probably devalue their homes. One woman, Mrs. Van Wagener, spent her entire five minutes complaining about the pool company that parked their cars and trucks all over the street, blocking mailboxes and leering and whistling at her teenage daughter walking the family dog. I guess she was concerned about the crew that would install the solar panels, but she never really made that connection, so everyone was a bit confused by her complaint.

Having gone through all of the names on both clipboards, Maynard was ready to call on the "In Favor Of" folks for their rebuttal, but Nobby banged his crutch on the table and got his attention. "Oh, right, uh, Mr. Narcisse, our Architectural Control Committee Chairman, would like to say a few words before we continue. Go ahead, Nobby."

Nobby started to stand but then thought better of it as he caught Yolanda's wary eye. He decided to speak from his seat and, grasping the microphone on the table in front of him, brought it closer. "I am Nolan Narcisse, Chairman of the Oak Harbor Estates Architectural Control Committee. I have been in this position for almost 10 years now, and I've endured countless ridiculous requests and complaints from homeowners, but never – NEVER – have I been insulted and demeaned as I have tonight by Mr. Kramer and the people he represents. I promise you that I DID NOT tell Mr. Voisin that my committee approved the installation of solar panels. In fact, I have neither met nor spoken to Mr. Voisin about this matter or anything else. I challenge Mr. Kramer to produce the taped conversation that he claims to have because I can tell you that it's a complete fabrication!"

Nobby's neck was getting redder and redder as he spoke. He paused and took a drink of water before continuing in a somewhat calmer tone. "I want to make it clear that neither I nor the members of my committee are personally opposed to solar panels. It is simply our belief that our subdivision restrictions are written in such a way as to encourage us to err on the side of caution when it comes to allowing any visible additions to homes or property. We believe that this arbitration panel is the best way to resolve this matter, and we will abide by their ruling."

Nobby turned to Maynard and nodded, indicating that he was done. Maynard banged down the gavel to quell the murmuring in the audience and then asked if anyone from the "In Favor Of" list had any comments in rebuttal. Mr. Kramer made his way from the back of the room to the microphone.

"I just wanted to clarify that I have not personally heard the recording that Mr. Voisin told me that he made of his conversation with Mr. Narcisse. I had hoped to hear it before the meeting tonight but, as you can see, Mr. Voisin isn't here. I had no reason to doubt Mr. Voisin's claim regarding this recording but, since he failed to produce it, I think it's best that we just forget about that aspect of my previous comments. I and the nine residents that I represent tonight are likewise willing to abide by the ruling of the arbitration panel. We trust that the panel will see that the environmental benefits of solar panels far outweigh any aesthetic or other concerns. That's all, thank you."

As Normal Kramer headed back to his seat, Nobby called out, "I didn't hear anything like an apology for calling me a liar, Mr. Kramer!"

Normal Kramer, possibly fearing a reprisal, turned back and said, "It certainly was not my intention to suggest that you were lying, Mr. Narcisse. I thought it possible that you had either forgotten your conversation with Mr. Voisin or that Mr. Voisin might have misspoken."

"Misspoken my butt!" Nobby yelled in a cutting rejoinder. "Your Mr. Voisin is the one who's lying! You can tell him that I said that when and if you ever find him!"

"Now hold on there, Nobby," Maynard cautioned. "There's no need to get nasty about this, accusing someone who's not even here to defend himself. You've had your say; now let's move on." I guess Maynard felt obligated to protect the reputation of his brother-in-law just in case this exchange got back to Nadine.

Maynard asked if anyone else wanted to comment on behalf of those who were in favor of allowing solar panels, but no one else wished to say anything. He then asked if anyone on the "Opposed" list wished to speak. After a moment, Mr. Moore rose and approached the microphone.

"Wade Moore again. I huddled with the other fah-folks who are generally opposed to installing solar panels in our subdivision, and here's wha-what we want to say. We don't care if you want to throw your money away on solar panels. If they are installed in such a way as to nuh-not be visible from the street, and if the next-door neighbors who can see them don't ob-ob-object, then we don't really care. We just think that you're being muh-misled about the environmental benefits, that's all."

No one else in the audience had anything to add. Maynard told the assembly that the arbitration panel would talk this over and make a decision tonight if possible. It was a few minutes before 9:00 p.m. The pressure was on. I asked Maynard if there was a "private room to which the arbitration panel could convene to deliberate." I thought that sounded really official. He led us to a small conference room adjacent to the entry foyer. The four of us grabbed a soft drink, a glass of ice, and a snack. We could be a while.

I started off with, "Guys, let's just talk first about what we think about this in general. Does anybody want to share their thoughts?"

Ronald asked, "Do you think we need to get Clara's notes before we start?"

"I sat next to Clara and saw what she was writing. I don't think her notes will help," I answered. "We'll have to rely upon the notes we took. I don't think that she was hired for her secretarial skills."

Jack said, "I think it was an important statement that the last guy made – what was his name, the one who stuttered? – about not objecting if the panels weren't visible from the street and so forth."

"Yeah, that was Mr. Moore," offered Slim, looking at his notes. "Yeah, I agree with Jack. It didn't seem like the folks who were against the solar panels were all that excited – like, they really didn't care all that much."

Ronald asked, "What about that woman who talked about the pool workers catcalling her daughter? What the heck was that about?"

"I think she was worried about who would be installing the solar panels – you know, letting strangers in this high-class subdivision without knowing what kind of people they are," I guessed. "I don't know if you've noticed, but there might be a few snobs in the place."

"Yeah, I guess we're lucky they let us in without a background check or a body cavity search," offered Slim.

"I think that's only because Maynard vouched for us," I suggested. "Look – all kidding aside – we have to make a recommendation pretty soon. So what do y'all think?"

After discussing the arguments made during the meeting, we decided we had to ask Nobby a couple of questions. So Jack went back to the meeting room and asked Nobby to come in.

"So what do you think, fellas? Have you decided anything?" Nobby asked as he hobbled in with one crutch. He may have broken the other one on Big Boy's privates.

"I think we're close, Nobby," I said, "but we have a couple of questions for you."

"Okay, go ahead, shoot," he replied.

I started with, "First of all, we drove down only one of the streets, but we noticed that the homes were pretty far apart, on really big lots, and all of the ones we saw backed onto either woods or a big lake. Is that typical of the whole development? I mean, do any of the homes back onto other houses?"

Nobby thought for a moment and replied, "No, in fact, no house backs onto any other house in the development. We really have a lot of privacy, especially in the backyards. A lot of the homes – most, in fact, have pools, even though we have an Olympic-sized pool at the clubhouse."

"What about neighbors on either side?" Jack asked. "We didn't see any houses that were very close to one another."

"No, the lots are between two and three acres," Nobby said. "Besides for that, most people have high brick privacy fences around the back. I know that we can't see anything our neighbors are doing, even if we want to. I mean, we really don't want to, you know…see what they're doing."

I asked, "Nobby, just out of curiosity, you said that all of the folks who were asking to be allowed to install solar panels were on the same street, right?" He nodded. "Do you happen to know in which direction the houses face? I mean, north, south, east, or west?"

He thought for a minute. "Well, it varies because the roads aren't straight at all. They meander quite a lot. Why does that matter?"

"It matters only because solar panels are most efficient if they face south," I answered. "I wonder if Mr. Voisin told the people he was dealing with anything about how these things worked."

"Ha! You're assuming that he even knows about how they work," said Nobby. "Also, you're assuming that the people he's dealing with even care how efficient they are. They're just trying to impress their green friends. They're still going to have so-called carbon footprints larger than 99.9% of the people in the world."

With that, we thanked Nobby and let him get back to the meeting room.

"Here's what I think," I began. "We suggest that solar panels be allowed under certain conditions. One is that they are installed on the rear roof of the home and can't be seen from the street. Two, that any adjacent neighbors on either side who might be able to see the panels have no objections. Anything else?"

Jack offered, "Yeah, three, that the company that installs the panels has to be licensed and bonded and promises not to whistle at young girls walking dogs."

I said, "Okay, maybe we'll word that a little differently, like, the installers must be respectful of property and people, or something like that, or else they'll be run off and not allowed to do business here. Anything else?"

Slim suggested that the residents who have signed up for solar panels be told by Vinny Voisin about how the solar panel efficiency varies with the direction they face, plus be made aware of the negative side of solar panels manufacture and disposal. I said that I doubted that Vinny would voluntarily offer up that sort of information.

Jack suggested, "What if we just give Nobby the information we found and he can include that with the conditions as sort of an informational package?"

We all agreed that this was a good plan. We wrote down our recommendations, played with the wording a bit, and then felt as though we were ready to get this over with. We headed back to the meeting room.

Everyone was milling about, drinking coffee, and munching on sandwiches and such that had apparently been replenished by the catering staff. Maynard greeted us as we returned and asked if we'd come to a decision. We said that we had and he muttered, "I sure hope it's the right one," as he found his gavel and banged on the table and everyone began slowly getting to their seats.

As soon as everyone was seated and quieted down, Maynard announced, "Folks, the arbitration panel has arrived at a decision. Everyone involved here has agreed to abide by the decision of this panel. Okay, Tony, let's hear it."

I thanked Maynard and the Board and Nobby and started with, "After careful consideration, we recommend the following," and then I read out what we had come up with. I didn't know what to expect, but what I didn't expect was no reaction at all, and that's what we got. I asked if there were any questions and there was just one, from Mr. Moore, who asked, "So are we done then? My friends are waiting for me at the pickleball court." I said that if there weren't any other questions, then yes, we were done. Maynard banged the gavel and adjourned the meeting, and that was it. Not exactly Robert's Rules of Order, but no one complained.

"I sure want to thank you, boys; I think you did the right thing," Maynard said, offering his hand. "That was a good decision. You okay with that, Nobby?"

Nobby, who was getting to his feet, looked tired and a little beat up. It looked like Yolanda might have scratched his face with her long fake nails. "Sure, I'm happy with it. Like I said, my committee isn't really opposed to solar panels. I think that the stipulations Tony and his group put together will ease the minds of the folks who were concerned about them being an eyesore. I'll prepare something for the Board to get out to the residents about the requirements for putting in solar panels."

Clara came up and gave me a big hug. "Tony, y'all were great! I told Maynard that you'd do the right thing." Then she whispered, "He's very happy about this decision. It gets him out of the doghouse with Nadine."

I didn't ask her why Maynard was in the doghouse with Nadine in the first place – none of my business. I'm sure it must have had something to do with her no-account brother, but I didn't want to know the details. At the time, I was worried about what Darlene would say when she smelled Clara's perfume all over me.

Chapter Eleven

By the time I got home after the wild HOA meeting, I was too tired to send out an email to the MOSS. I'd take care of that on Wednesday. Darlene let me know, however, that I was not too tired to give her a blow-by-blow account of the event, including why I smelled like a "French whore" – her words. I told her how the evening progressed – or regressed – and suggested that she might even see some of the more interesting action if she explored Facebook. Darlene found the Oak Harbor Facebook page, but there was nothing exciting on it except for Mr. & Mrs. Marvin Summerville winning the Garden of the Month.

I suggested she try YouTube or Tic-Tac-Toe or whatever it's called. After searching for "Oak Harbor HOA," she found the video that was posted right after the skirmish. Seeing it from another perspective for the first time, I had to admit it was pretty entertaining. The guy who took the video was a pro. He captured everything – Normal Kramer's presentation, Nobby knocking over both the table and Yolanda, then falling on top of her, Big Boy getting whacked in the crotch, and Clara trying to pull down her skirt. He even zoomed in on her pink panties. This guy was so good he hardly even wavered, even when you could hear him laughing hysterically. The video already had over 1000 views. The only part of any interest to Darlene was why "that woman" was sitting next to me and why I was sitting there like a deer in the headlights instead of getting up and helping someone. I explained that right when the video ended I was with Jack helping Nobby and Yolanda get to their feet.

Darlene was less than completely mollified and went on for a bit about me being an idiot for turning a harmless group of old men having breakfast once a week into a "I don't know what to call it" group of old men just looking for trouble. I swear she must have been talking to Alden Roussel. I got her off of the subject by mentioning that there were pickleball courts at Oak Harbor and that I saw some couples playing, but then she reminded me that "we can't afford to live in Oak Harbor, so what's your point?" I gave up and retreated into the shower.

The next morning I sent out an email to the MOSS giving a brief recap of the events of Tuesday evening and suggesting that if anyone wanted more details, to come to breakfast on Friday. At my Rotary meeting at noon, I discovered that most of the club members had already seen the video and told me that I was "tagged" or something, whatever that means. I began to yearn for the days when we communicated by handwritten letter that took several days to arrive if it ever did. Simpler times.

Darlene had signed us up for pickleball lessons at the YMCA on Thursday morning. It was fun and less work than tennis. I still suggest, as in tennis, that husbands and wives not play on the same team. In fact, it's best if they don't play on the same court. We had a pretty good time and learned the complexities of pickleball scoring and not volleying the ball in the "kitchen." The best part of lessons at the Y was going to Another Broken Egg for brunch afterward, during which Darlene, a better tennis player than me, proceeded to instruct me on the finer points of pickleball. I acted as though I was listening as I ate my Salmon Eggs Benedict. At least she had apparently forgotten, at least for now, about Clara and her pink panties. Darlene never really forgets about anything, and I mean never.

We had a pretty good turnout on Friday morning at Frank's. I had picked up Uncle Joe on the way, and Dustin, Kevin, Slim, Terry, Dr. Dart, Rodney, my brother T-Joe, Ronald, Jack, and Alden were all there. One thing I was pretty confident of – none of these old guys would have seen the online video. I was mistaken. Dustin's daughter had seen it and showed him how to find it on his phone. By the time Uncle Joe and I showed up, all of the guys had already seen it on Dustin's phone at least twice. Ronald, Jack, and Slim, who were present at the now-famous event, hadn't even realized that they were now part of local history. Dustin showed the video to Uncle Joe, who thought it was great fun but asked Dustin why he didn't record the whole meeting. Dustin explained that he wasn't even there and that he didn't record the video, someone else did, but Uncle Joe said, "What do I look like, an idiot? It's on your phone, so I know you recorded it. Why do you want to lie about it?" Uncle Joe wouldn't drop it until Dustin admitted that, yes, he took the video and was really sorry he didn't record the whole thing. Uncle Joe accepted his apology and sat down to his coffee. It's no wonder I leave Frank's with indigestion most of the time.

It was another of those dreary wet mornings with scattered

showers, so I half-expected Jed Wally to show up again. Sure enough, just as we had finished giving our orders to Wendy, Jed made his grand entrance.

"Hello, boys; good weather for you old ducks today, huh?" Jed said in greeting.

"Not playing today, Sheriff?" asked Slim. In Ascension, once the Sheriff, always the Sheriff.

"No, I depend too much on a good roll. Can't get much roll on a day like this," Jed responded. "So I thought I'd come and see what kind of trouble y'all have gotten into lately."

"Well, I was just about to tell everybody about our arbitration meeting at Oak Harbor Estates on Tuesday," I said. "You know, that solar panel thing with Vinny Voisin."

"Oh, yeah, but let me order something first," Jed said. "I don't think I want to hear this on an empty stomach."

Wendy took Jed's order, Jed sat next to me, and I started in on the story. I was giving the background of how we ended up serving as an arbitration panel for Oak Harbor when Uncle Joe interrupted and said that we didn't have all day to get to the good stuff. I would have ignored him, but several of the guys backed him up on this, and Darlene always tells me that I have a bad tendency to ramble on, so I got to the good stuff. When I reached the part about Normal Kramer insulting Nobby Narcisse, Dustin shoved me aside to show Jed the video, telling me that "a picture is worth a thousand words," so why don't I just let the video do the talking? Several of the guys who had already seen the video twice or more still tried to look over Jed's shoulder as he held Dustin's phone. Jed got a big kick out of it.

"Dang, that's hilarious!" Jed said with tears in his eyes. Then he watched it again and asked, "Who took the video?" Of course, Uncle Joe told him that obviously Dustin took the video – that it was his phone after all – but he didn't seem to want credit for it. "Look, it's got almost two thousand views!" Jed noticed.

After the novelty of the video wore off a bit, I finished telling everyone about what happened, including our panel recommending the approval of the solar panel installations with certain restrictions.

Jed asked, "Was Vinny Voisin there at the meeting?"

"No," I said, "he was a no-show. I guess Maynard has given him the good news by now."

"Hmmm…I'm not sure Vinny would necessarily think that it's good news," Jed offered.

"Well, why not?" I asked. "He can go ahead and complete the sale of the solar panels. How can that not be good news?"

"Because I was told by someone who, let's say, knows Vinny's dark side," Jed responded. "Vinny took down payments from everyone, but I'm told that there's a clause in the contract that they all signed, probably without reading it, that stipulates that the down payment is non-reimbursable if the HOA fails to approve the installation of solar panels."

I pondered this for a moment. "You mean Vinny was hoping that Nobby's committee would not allow the solar panels? But that's crazy! Surely he would make more money going through with the sales and installation. And it was pretty clear that Maynard wanted the solar panels approved."

Jed shook his head and said, "You're assuming two things; one, that Vinny's company is legitimate and actually sells and installs solar panels, and two, that Maynard was in on the deal. He wasn't. As far as Maynard knows, his brother-in-law's business is on the up-and-up."

Jack jumped into the conversation and said, "Wait a minute. One of the guys who was representing nine homeowners, that guy Normal Kramer, he said that he was an attorney. You mean he didn't even read the contract himself?"

"I guess not," replied Jed. "He probably knew and trusted Maynard and Nadine."

"You know, it was when Normal Kramer said that Vinny told him he had a recording of Nobby approving the solar panels that started the whole thing on the video," Slim suggested. "It's pretty clear that Vinny lied to Mr. Kramer about that, so don't they have a case against him?"

"They'll have to catch him first," said Dr. Dart.

"What do you think is going to happen now?" I asked Jed.

"I don't know," he replied. "I suspect Vinny will do like Dr. Dart said and make a run for it and leave Maynard and Nadine holding the bag."

"But why doesn't he just fess up and return the money?" I suggested. "No real harm done."

Jed shook his head at me again. I was getting pretty tired of that. "Because he probably already spent it, gambled it away, or paid off his old gambling debts. Plus, if he still had the money and returned it and admitted that he couldn't honor the contract, he could get sued for breach. And if Maynard is, as I suspect, a partner in the business, he'd be the one with deep pockets."

What a mess. I just have a hard time understanding how people like Vinny Voisin can be so dishonest. I've never met him, but he must be pretty smart and personable to get thirteen homeowners to slip him $5000 each. I guess it's like my Pastor says about the wickedness of Man in almost every Sunday sermon – "people always do what they want to do." I guess that people like Vinny have no conscience. They just do what they think is best in their own eyes – best for them, anyway.

A couple of weeks later, Nobby called to tell me that Maynard, with his brother-in-law on the lam, found a legitimate solar panel company and put up the $65,000 down payment that Vinny took. The thirteen homeowners were going to get their solar panels after all, and at a price cheaper than Vinny quoted them. Also, Nadine left to visit her sister in Sarasota for a month or until Maynard cools off.

Part Three

Chapter One

Dustin, Ronald, Rodney, and I play golf at Santa Maria most every Tuesday at around 10:00 a.m. or so. If the weather is nice, we walk nine holes for the exercise, then go to lunch. When I say "if the weather is nice" I mean if the weather is not too hot, not too cold, and not too wet. We get that sort of weather about 30% of the time. When I say we "walk nine holes" that is assuming none of us have a bad knee or some other debilitating condition that day. In that case the afflicted player or players ride the nine holes and the rest walk, pulling our clubs on hand carts and generally wishing we were riding also.

The 70% of the time that the weather is not to our particular tastes, we still go to lunch. We generally go to the nearby BurgerSmith, where the staff has come to know us over the years and lets us in anyway. We have been fixtures at BurgerSmith longer than all but one of the current employees. We feel an ownership there, or at least a kinship. We thought about going somewhere else, like Gemaine LeBlanc's Chicken Shack, but BurgerSmith has these frequent diner cards and, once you've accumulated five stamps, you get your bill knocked down by the price of a regular Smith Burger. So we're stuck; we can never leave the place. Unless we all have five stamps on the same day – which has never happened – then maybe we can quit cold turkey.

About three weeks following the Oak Harbor Estates debacle, a Tuesday came up that was a promising golf day. Dustin got a tee time for us every Tuesday, but we hadn't used one in a while. This would be the first time we played in a couple of months. We dusted off our clubs, or, in some cases, wiped off the mildew, and headed out to Santa Maria.

After we hit our best drives on the driving range and took our best putts on the putting green, we headed to the first tee, where our games went quickly downhill. We separated, crisscrossing the fairway, spent a good deal of time looking for lost balls, and eventually met up at the green where we were generous with gimmes and frugal with scores. We followed this scheme throughout the morning without a whole lot of talk. We were pure concentration. Our concentration didn't always appear to be about golf though. I usually thought about the things I needed to do around the house instead of wasting time on this stupid game.

But on occasion – mostly on rare occasion – someone got a birdie, and it made the entire otherwise grueling adventure worthwhile. Whoever got that rare birdie got his lunch paid for by the other three. We yearned for a time when two of us would get birdies on the same day. What joy that would be. As it is, most of the time we all paid for our own lunch, and the wait staff at BurgerSmith would snidely say, "What, no birdies today?" We just want to one day be able to say, "In fact, there were two birdies today!" I just want to see the shock on their smug faces.

On this particular Tuesday, with no birdies for anyone to brag about, we began to talk about the MOSS business.

"I tell you, guys," I said with resignation, "I've had my fill of HOA problems. I do not want to take on any more of those HOA arbitration hearings."

Dustin laughed. "According to what my daughter tells me, social media thinks that HOA problems are the MOSS's specialty."

"Yeah," added Rodney, "Sharon told me that her teacher friends said that we're blowing up Facebook, whatever that means."

"That doesn't sound good," offered Ronald. "I think we need to check out the social media stuff and see what they're saying about us. Our names and pictures are all over the place now. I don't like it. It's not good for my business."

"Hey, you know what they say," I told him. "All news is good news."

"That's not what they say," corrected Dustin. "They say 'No news is good news.'"

"Oh yeah, that's right," I admitted.

"Maybe you mean 'What's good for the goose is good for the gander'," offered Rodney.

"What? No, that's not it," I responded.

"What about 'Beauty is in the eyes of the beholder'," suggested Ronald.

"Or 'One man's trash is another man's treasure'," was Dustin's entry.

"You guys are idiots. I'm talking about how no one will remember why your name and picture were there, they'll only remember seeing it. I think it's like 'any press is good press,' or something like that."

"I don't think that's true," lamented Ronald. "People always think the worst."

Rodney tried to comfort Ronald with "I don't see how having your name and picture on Facebook or whatever is going to hurt your urgent care business. What, if someone gets a nail in their foot they're not going to go to urgent care because they saw your picture on Facebook?"

"Yeah, I guess you're right," agreed Ronald. "I'm probably worried about nothing, as usual. I mean, really, what's the worst that can happen?"

"The worst that can happen is we keep getting calls and emails from HOAs to help them with stupid problems," I answered. "Like an idiot, I put my email address in those e-newspapers."

"If that happens," suggested Dustin, "then just say 'no'."

Rodney looked at me and said "Tony, when you started this thing, you called us 'Ascension Parish's premier think tank.' I don't think doing this arbitration thing is what think tanks do."

"No, it's probably not," I responded. "You're right, we have to get back to basics. I'll come up with an agenda for this Friday's gathering, and we'll get back on the right track."

The week following the Oak Harbor Estates HOA meeting, I received quite a few emails. Some were almost complimentary.

"I hear your think tank approved solar panels for that swanky subdivision. What kind of bribes did y'all get for that?" – Anonymous.

"I am considering joining your MOSS group. I sometimes identify as a 60-year-old man and consider myself very wise. I saw your group at Frank's one Friday morning, and I sense that you lack diversity. I can help you with that." – Patricia "Pat" Sigura

"If you want to do something useful instead of dealing with that HOA crap, come over to Bayou Manchac Retirement Home and talk to some men and women who are older and wiser than you. You might learn something." – Raymond Sedgewick, resident, Bayou Manchac Retirement Home.

"I know you from Donaldsonville, but I never see you over here. I do not know how a bunch of old men could help this town, but we need help! Why don't you do something?" – Lanny "LaLa" Pourciau, Donaldsonville resident.

"If y'all eat at Frank's every Friday then you must be rich. If you got that much money to throw away, I can't afford to pay my electric bill this month and they going to cut me off. I can't afford groceries neither. I can barely buy beer and cigarettes. I need some help. I take Venmo." – George "Skillet" Waring, Venmo address attached.

"My boyfriend is a friend of Vinny Voisin and he told me that Vinny said that you're the reason he had to leave town, and that he's going to make you sorry for what you did. I don't like Vinny so I'm telling you this so you can be ready." – Anonymous.

I called Maynard's office about that last one and spoke to Clara. She got with Maynard and called me back to tell me not to worry, if Vinny came back into Ascension Parish, Maynard would kill him before he could get to me. I felt a lot better, I guess.

Chapter Two

I began to realize that I may have been too glib when suggesting that MOSS was the premier think tank of Ascension Parish. What I had in mind when I labeled us as a think tank was, I discovered, not exactly the same as how Wikipedia defined think tank – to wit, a think tank might do the following:

Perform research concerning things like:

Social policy

Political strategy

Economics

Military technology

Culture

Publish articles and studies

Draft legislation on policy or society

I felt like I was out of my depth here. What I had advertised was that the MOSS was "…ready to lend their brainpower to the study of any problem, big or small, presented to them. If you have a problem you'd like the MOSS to analyze… contact tony.campachi@gmail.com." I never said anything about serving as an arbitration panel, but we got sucked into that anyway – twice. I guess that in the end, though, we did help some people solve a problem they had, so what can I say? We might not meet the Wikipedia definition of think tank, but they don't know everything. I don't know exactly how Wikipedia works, but someone told me that people just upload stuff onto the site. As far as I know, somebody had their own idea of what a think tank was and put it up on Wikipedia. Heck, I could do that! Actually I didn't know how to do that, but if I did know, I could put up my own definition.

I decided that I needed to get a consensus about what our think tank would do from the MOSS members, so I sent out an email on Thursday and asked everyone to show up Friday morning. I said that the think tank idea seemed to have taken a turn in the wrong direction, and so we had one item to decide on: What is the purpose of the MOSS think tank? I guess you could call this my "share the blame" strategy.

I picked up Uncle Joe on Friday morning and we headed to Frank's. Man, did I get an earful from him. I got enough "I told you so"s for the year. Also, "Why can't we just eat breakfast and talk about LSU and Saints football?" and "We're just a bunch of old men, nobody expects us to be useful or anything," and "You know just because you're a Civil Engineer doesn't mean you know more than me. I got my education in the streets of New Orleans when I was in a patrol car by myself. Now that's a education. You never seen anything the whole time you were at LSU like I saw in one weekend in New Orleans." Actually, I could believe that.

Most of the regulars showed up for this gathering, including Dustin, Slim, Rodney, Kevin, Donnie, Dr. Dart, Terry, Ronald, Jack, Alden, and my brother T-Joe. I knew Jed wouldn't be there because the weather was, for once, pretty nice. Uncle Joe quickly went around the table to tell everyone hello and remind them that he said this think tank thing was a bad idea from the start, and why wouldn't anybody listen to him?

Everybody got their coffee except for Ronald, who always drank iced tea, the weirdo, and Wendy took orders, telling us that the deep fryer was out, so no chicken-fried steak with sausage gravy this morning. I don't know why she bothered to tell us that because no one in our group had ever ordered it, but just because she told us we couldn't have it I all of a sudden had a craving for chicken-fried steak smothered in sausage gravy. I had to settle for biscuits with sausage gravy, but it just wasn't the same.

After everyone gave Wendy their orders, we got down to business. I reminded everyone what we were talking about at this gathering and asked their thoughts about how our think tank should operate. What I got from them made me question the wisdom of a democracy. These are the comments that I could remember, in no particular order:

Dustin: "As long as we don't have to deal with HOAs anymore, I don't care what we think tank about."

Donnie: "Marlene asked me to tell you 'Hi' and that she always thought you were smart in high school. What happened?"

Terry: "You know what we used to say in the wastewater

business? Business stinks, but business is business. If all we can get is HOA business, what's wrong with that?"

Uncle Joe: "Why should I tell you what I think? You won't listen anyway."

Ronald: "The biggest problems in Ascension Parish have to do with flooding and traffic. But I don't think that the Parish wants ideas from a bunch of old men."

Dr. Dart: "Lack of education is a big problem here too, especially early childhood education, but also adult education. We have a lot of illiterate adults here who don't have a high school diploma and can't read well enough to get a GED. Maybe we could come up with ideas on how to help with that."

T-Joe: "Are those biscuits with sausage gravy good? Are you going to finish that?"

Alden: "Several of us are from Donaldsonville, and there are more problems there than I can count. I think we could take a look at doing something there."

Kevin: "My wife Janice wants to know why we think we can solve all these problems when we can't even fix a leaky toilet. Does anyone know how to fix a leaky toilet?"

There might have been more comments, but at some point I zoned out. I asked the Board members to stick around for a few minutes when breakfast was done so we could summarize the suggestions and decide something. Uncle Joe wasn't happy about this, but I was his ride, and he hated to call Aunt Millie to pick him up.

When everyone else had left, Dustin, Kevin, Uncle Joe, and I moved over to a small, clean table, thus aggravating the wait staff. It wasn't Wendy's table, so if we wanted more coffee we had to start a new tab. I said that if anyone wanted anything to go ahead and order, I'd pick up the bill since this was my idea. Everyone wanted more coffee, and Uncle Joe, who had eaten only raisin toast, ordered a cajun omelet. He was going to literally make me pay for this.

I was prepared with a notebook this time and, among the four of us we came up with the following suggestions that had been tossed around by the group:

Address the drainage problems

Address the traffic problems

Focus on helping Donaldsonville

Address the problem of illiteracy in adults

Focus on early childhood education

Continue to accept requests from HOAs if appropriate

We realized that the traffic and drainage problems in Ascension Parish were all on the east bank of the river. Donaldsonville and the west portion of Ascension Parish were not plagued by these issues. Although adult illiteracy and lack of early childhood education were problems on both sides of the river, there was definitely a higher concentration of these problems on the Donaldsonville side.

"I don't think we can look at traffic and drainage," I offered. "There are consultants working for the Parish studying those things already, including the firm I do some work for."

"Consulting! What a racket!" was Uncle Joe's comment. "All they ever do is study, study, study, but they never do anything!" I thought briefly about defending my noble profession, but that would just be a waste of breath. Besides, what Uncle Joe said was at least partly true.

Dustin suggested, "You know, most of the MOSS members have college degrees and a couple have advanced degrees. Plus, I'm a retired teacher, Dr. Dart runs the community college, and Donnie used to teach shop. I think we could help adults who didn't finish high school get a GED."

We all liked this idea, even a reluctant Uncle Joe. It felt like a big problem to tackle though.

"So do we concentrate on Donaldsonville to do this?" asked Kevin.

"I think so," I answered. "How do we get started though? I mean how do we even find people who didn't finish high school?"

Kevin quoted a line from one of my favorite movies: "'If you build it, they will come.' If you open a store, people will come to it. If you open a night school to help people get a GED, the people that need

GEDs will come." That sounded too easy.

Dustin suggested that we meet with Sheriff Pepper because a lot of the men and women who didn't finish high school ended up being guests of his at the Donaldsonville jail. "I think that we should meet with the mayor too, if we're going to be doing something in his town."

We gave ourselves some assignments. Kevin, who had supported Mayor Strong of Donaldsonville in his last election, would contact him and tell him what we had in mind. Dustin would talk to Dr. Dart to see if the community college could be involved somehow. I would talk to Sheriff Pepper to see if any of his guests would be interested in getting a GED and how that might work. Uncle Joe would aggravate me until I called Rob Pepper and otherwise offer moral support.

That night Darlene and I went over to Dustin and Connie's for cocktails and snacks. Actually, 'snacks' is the proper description of what Darlene and I have when we host cocktail night. Connie has a different definition of snacks. Her definition is a three-course event beginning with an impressive selection of crackers, cheeses, olives, dips, spreads, and such expertly arranged on a large platter, with each of us having our own plate. Not a paper plate, by the way, but a glass hors d'oeuvres plate. Connie puts this out while I act as bartender, and we enjoy our first cocktails with this course. Our second cocktail is served with the main course which consists of a complete meal that might be stewed chicken (Dustin's specialty), or spaghetti and meatballs, or steaks, or gumbo, accompanied by a vegetable and a salad with no less than twelve ingredients. This is all followed by a dessert of homemade brownies with a side of Blue Bell Moo-llennium Crunch ice cream. This is all followed by Dustin falling asleep in his recliner and me dozing on the sofa in a fat-calorie-induced stupor, while Connie and Darlene, who each ate a quarter of what we did, gab away about who knows what. And so, we enjoyed another relaxing Friday night, some of us slumbering and drooling just a little.

Chapter Three

Late Monday morning I called Sheriff Pepper's office, but he was out so I was routed to his assistant, Lieutenant Cory Mahony. I gave a detailed description of what the MOSS was thinking about doing, and it happens that Lieutenant Cory was very interested in the plan and promised to get with Sheriff Pepper as soon as possible and get back to me.

I got a call from Dustin right after lunch. He had a good conversation with Dr. Dart about the educational needs of Donaldsonville, a matter with which Dr. Dart was quite familiar. He had, in fact, been in discussions with the local Chamber of Commerce, the Donaldsonville Downtown Development District, and the mayor's office about the possibility of locating a branch of the community college in the town. He apologized for not having said anything about it because it was early days and he didn't think it was his news to spread until details were worked out.

Toward evening on Monday, Kevin called with interesting information. The mayor was happy that we wanted to be involved in helping Donaldsonville in some way. He mentioned that something was in the works related to adult education that he couldn't discuss at this time. Since we wanted to help, though, he had an old friend he wanted us to meet. He was sure the man could use our help. His name was Thaddeus Toombs and he and the mayor had shared an apartment for his last year at the University. Kevin got Mr. Toombs' phone number and promised the mayor that we'd give him a call. We were thinking that he must have something to do with adult education.

As you know if you've been paying the least amount of attention, I was born and raised in Donaldsonville, the Parish seat of Ascension. La Ville de Donaldson was originally founded by William Donaldson in 1806 on land he purchased for $12,000. Donaldsonville later served as the State Capitol for a short time in 1825 or so in order for the state legislators to hide from their wives, but the structure built to house them was poorly constructed and there were no paved streets or sidewalks. More importantly though, the entertainment afforded to the legislators consisted of sitting on the bank of the river looking at boat traffic and watching locals catch catfish. You would think that the lack of distractions would be of great benefit to the legislators who wanted to focus on State business. You would be wrong. In 1831 the whole bunch went back to New Orleans from whence they came, apparently discovering that they were able to focus on their work much more intently when distractions abounded. I guess it's why my grandkids can study only while listening to hip-hop.

Prior to the completion of I-10 from New Orleans to Baton Rouge on the east side of the Mississippi River in Ascension in the mid-to-late 70's, Donaldsonville was a bustling small town with lots of thriving businesses, a theatre, car dealerships, the oldest family-owned and operated department store in Louisiana, and small Italian grocery stores scattered on corners throughout town. Growing up there seems in hindsight to have been idyllic but, as we all know, the sharp edges of our memories are ground down and blunted by time. Once I-10 was completed between New Orleans and Baton Rouge, growth began to develop on the east bank and Donaldsonville slowly faded into the background, where it remains today. Large chain grocery stores drove out almost all of the small corner groceries, and the large chain stores were later driven out by Walmart.

Many of the Donaldsonville residents moved to subdivisions on the east bank. Kids who left town to get a college education, like myself, rarely returned. I would have gone back, but Darlene, who visited Donaldsonville when we were dating, made me sign a pre-nup that I would never make her live there. The town has suffered for a long time now from lack of investment, a scarcity of industry, and White-flight to the east bank. A local resident famously described Donaldsonville as "the town of endless impossibilities." But things are starting to look up. There is, lately, a growing interest in investing time, money, and resources in the town. I wondered if Thaddeus Toombs was a part of that interest.

Kevin called Mr. Toombs on Tuesday morning, and he agreed to meet us for lunch at noon at the Grapevine, a gastronomical blessing on Railroad Avenue in Donaldsonville. Kevin, Dustin, and I were free to make the lunch meeting, so we met at Dustin's house and rode the 25-mile trip together.

Dustin parallel parked on Railroad Avenue just a few cars away from the Grapevine entrance. We were lucky to get the last table for four in the place, which was, as usual, full of local working folks from the nearby chemical plants. We didn't know what Mr. Toombs looked like, but there was no one seated alone, and no one at the bar, so we got iced teas, looked to see if there were any new Alvin Batiste paintings for sale hanging on the walls, and waited. About fifteen minutes later a well-dressed distinguished-looking Black gentleman with a gray goatee and dark fedora walked in, scanned the room, and spotted the table with the only old-looking people in the place. He walked over to the table and we stood to greet him.

"I'm Teddy Toombs," he said as he reached out his hand. "Happy to make your acquaintance."

"Hello, Mr. Toombs," I responded. "I'm Tony Campachi and this is Kevin Farmer and Dustin Sonnier. We're glad to meet you. Any friend of Mayor Strong is a friend of ours."

"Now you just call me Teddy," he instructed us. "Surely you've heard of Teddy Toombs? Hasn't Sidney bothered to tell you who I am? Why, I'll have to reprimand him for that!"

"No, Teddy, the mayor was in a hurry and just gave me your name and number," explained Kevin. "He didn't have a chance to tell us very much about you, except that y'all were college roommates."

"We just assumed you had something to do with adult education," I added.

Teddy laughed at that, and pulling on his goatee he replied, "Oh yes, if you count that I single-handedly got Sidney Strong through his senior year at Grambling, then, yes, I have something to do with adult education!"

We sat there for a minute, a little confused, while Teddy Toombs ordered a Bloody Mary. Finally I asked, "Teddy, the mayor said you might be able to use our help. What is it that you do? I mean, what do you need help with?"

Teddy laughed again and said, "The mayor thought that since some of you gentlemen were from Donaldsonville, you could help me in my latest venture. You see, I know people. I know a lot of people in high places! High places! Very high places!"

"You mean in D.C.?" asked Dustin.

"D.C.! I should hope not! I'm talking about Hollywood boys!

Hollywood!" Teddy said with exuberance. "Not those imposters in Washington! I have no use for those fools. The Stars are whom I'm referring to! The rich and the famous!"

Now we were even more confused. "But Teddy, what's that got to do with us and Donaldsonville?" I asked.

"But don't you know?" asked Teddy. "We are going to make a movie here. A movie! A blockbuster! This movie is going to put Donaldsonville on the map, you hear me? On the map!"

Around this time the waiter came around and we hadn't even looked at the menus yet, so we took a few minutes to do that while Teddy ordered another Bloody Mary. I was beginning to think that alcohol might be called for at this time. Teddy told the waiter to just bring him the usual, which gave us a hint that he might have eaten here a few times. After we ordered, Teddy said that he would tell us what this blockbuster movie was going to be about. He pulled a pickled okra out of his drink and pointed it at each of us as he told us, "Gentlemen, you don't know what you have here in this absolute gem of a town. Well, I'm going to tell you a little story. It might be a true story, or it might not be. I'll leave that up to your imaginations. All I'll say is this – the idea for this movie came together when Sarah St. Pierre, the best friend of the – let's call her the heroine – was left all of her possessions when she passed on, including a cedar hope chest. In the hope chest was, among other memorabilia, a diary. Out of respect for her privacy, the friend did not read the diary. Some years later, when Mrs. St. Pierre also passed away, her granddaughter Emma, who she raised, found the diary and, having fewer scruples than her grandmother, read the diary and immediately recognized its potential pecuniary value. This young woman knew of me by way of her friendship with Sidney Strong's daughter Stacey and made contact. The diary was sold to a producer that I recommended to her. The content of that diary forms the basis – the theme, if you like – of this movie."

Teddy Toombs took a large swig of his Bloody Mary and began. "In 1954, a young singer, a 19-year-old boy, sang a song on the Louisiana Hayride radio show in Shreveport. When he was done, his manager wanted to take him to New Orleans so that he could listen to some of the jazz in the French Quarter, maybe pick up some ideas. They drove down toward New Orleans and, by chance, they stopped in a small town on the way for dinner. That town was Donaldsonville. While at a local restaurant called The Tavern, the young boy and his manager were waited on by a young girl who was a 16-year-old junior at Donaldsonville High School, working part-time for her uncle at the restaurant. Her name was Rosemary Rizzo. It is her diary that we have in our possession. The boy's name was Elvis Presley."

We sat there with our mouths open, as the waiter delivered our food. Teddy ordered his third Bloody Mary and, as the waiter walked away, I asked, "Wait a minute, Teddy. Is this supposed to be a true story?"

He answered, "It's like I said, it might be a true story, or it might not be. Some of it is certainly true – we have corroboration of certain details. Whether it's all true depends on whether or not you give credence to the information in the aforementioned diary. But who's to say it's not true?"

Then I said, "Do you realize that The Tavern you're talking about was in this very building that we're sitting in?"

Teddy winked and smiled and said, "Yes, I do."

I added, "My grandmother on my mother's side was a waitress at The Tavern. I remember that my daddy brought me there to meet Billy Cannon – it must have been right after he won the Heisman in 1959. I was nine years old."

"Isn't that something!" Teddy responded. "You see, that's why Sidney wanted you boys to be involved with this. You have a history here – you know things, you remember things that are important for the back-story. Your group is going to be a great help to me! A great help!"

Teddy continued with his story: "Well, Elvis was completely smitten with Rosemary, and Rosemary had never met anyone like Elvis, certainly not in Donaldsonville – or in Baton Rouge, the only other town she had ever been to. Elvis' manager at the time, Bob Neal, discouraged young Elvis from having any romantic entanglements. He wanted him to focus on his music, you see. But Elvis flirted with young Rosemary and managed to get her address and promised to write to her. She didn't really expect to hear from him again. Elvis wrote down his mama's address in Memphis on a napkin and asked

Rosemary to please write to him, it would mean a lot. She said she would, but the napkin later got wet and the ink smeared so she couldn't make out the address. She didn't think any more about it."

"The story goes that Elvis did write to Rosemary, but it is believed that Bob Neal, who handled all of the correspondence and bills and so forth, didn't mail the letter. After a while, Elvis was so busy with his career, he put Rosemary out of his mind. Bob Neal was busy also – so busy that he didn't feel as though he had time to manage young Elvis. Sometime in 1955, Colonel Tom Parker took an interest in the young singer and began to manage him full time."

At this point Teddy stopped and asked us, "Do any of you know how Tom Parker, who was not in the military, got promoted to Colonel?"

We were clueless. He was happy to tell us. "Tom Parker helped Jimmie Davis's campaign to become the governor of Louisiana in 1944. Governor Davis gave him the honorary rank of Colonel in the Louisiana State Militia!"

We were all pretty sure he was pulling our collective legs and that it was the Bloody Marys talking at this point. Besides, we wanted to hear more about Elvis and Rosemary. Teddy complied.

"In March of 1955 Elvis made his first appearance on the television version of the Louisiana Hayride, with Colonel Tom Parker as his agent. Colonel Parker had lined up other appearances for Elvis in Baton Rouge and New Orleans, so they rode on down from Shreveport. The Baton Rouge show was to be in an outdoor venue, and it was storming that night, so the show was canceled. When Colonel Parker told Elvis that they were going to head down to New Orleans in the morning, Elvis recalled the young girl he met in Donaldsonville, and suggested that they should stop at this restaurant there – he had forgotten the name – on the way down. That was okay with Colonel Parker, so they left Baton Rouge at about 10:00 a.m. the next morning, parked the car in Darrow, and got the ferry over to Donaldsonville. From the ferry landing they walked the few blocks to The Tavern. They strolled in at around noon and there to greet them was 17-year-old Rosemary, who had graduated to hostess."

This was getting good. The waiter cleared away our plates and we all ordered coffee and bread pudding with rum sauce.

"Now this event must have made quite an impression on young Rosemary, because her diary contained considerable detail about this meeting," Teddy explained. "Here's what happened – of course I'm paraphrasing the conversation. Before Colonel Parker could say 'Table for two,' Elvis shoved him aside and said 'Rosemary! You remember me? Elvis, Elvis Presley!'"

"Then Rosemary said, 'Well of course I remember you. I remember that you didn't write to me like you said you would.'"

"A contrite Elvis replied, 'But I did write to you, just as soon as I got back to Memphis. Why didn't you write to me?'"

"Rosemary responded, 'Well, if you did write, I never got your letter. I was going to write, I promise I was, but I couldn't make out the address you wrote down. I'm real sorry.'"

Then Teddy said, "This might have gone on for a while, so Colonel Parker told Elvis he'd be at the bar and that Elvis and the girl should go sit down and hash this out. Rosemary led Elvis to a table in the back corner, but she was busy seating people because it was right around noon and the place was hopping. So Elvis sat in the corner and Colonel Parker sat at the bar and neither one of them was too happy."

At this point the Grapevine had pretty much cleared out. Teddy pulled out a pocket watch, looked at it, jumped up, and said, "You gentlemen will have to excuse me. I have a very important call to make. Very important. Very important." He pulled out his iPhone and headed out to the sidewalk. A minute later he stuck in his head and told us that he was sorry but he had to leave and that he would get back in touch with us soon. And he stuck us with the bill.

Dustin, Kevin, and I talked about what had happened in the last two hours as we headed back across the Sunshine Bridge. The bridge that was, by the way, named to recognize Governor Jimmie Davis and his song "You Are My Sunshine," or possibly to recognize his horse, also named Sunshine. The same governor who, according to Teddy Toombs, promoted Tom Parker to the rank of Colonel in the Louisiana State Militia. We couldn't figure out what parts of the story Teddy told us were true, what parts were made-up, what was historical fiction, and what was pure fantasy. More importantly though, what did Teddy Toombs need from the MOSS?

Gasper A. Chifici

And I'm pretty sure on the ride back all of us were quietly thinking to ourselves, *I wonder what happened with Elvis and Rosemary.*

Chapter Four

Kevin tried calling Teddy Toombs on Wednesday morning but got a message that his voice mail was full. Next, he called the mayor's office and had this conversation:

Kevin: "Mayor, we can't make heads nor tails out of your friend Teddy Toombs. He told us a wild tale about making a movie, about Elvis falling in love with a Donaldsonville girl, all kinds of stuff we had a hard time swallowing."

Mayor Strong: "Yeah, that boy is something, ain't he? He's a wild man! Dresses good though. I don't know how I got him through Grambling. After graduation he went off to Hollywood and got even crazier. So he told you about the movie, huh?"

Kevin: "Yes sir, but he didn't tell us what we're supposed to do to help him. He had to make a phone call and ran out without finishing his story. I tried calling him but he didn't answer and his voice mail was full."

Mayor Strong: "Oh yeah, that sounds like Teddy alright. He's always got a bunch of balls in the air, you know what I mean? He had some business in Biloxi and he's supposed to be back here early next week. I'll make sure he calls you when he gets back."

Kevin: "Well look, Mayor – is this story he's telling us about Elvis – is it supposed to be true?"

Mayor Strong: "Hell, I don't know, Kevin. You boys lived around here all your life. I just came here from Back Vacherie 'bout 20 years ago. Y'all would know better than me. But I tell you, Teddy tells a very compelling story. I don't know where he's getting his information, but he sure tells it like it's true."

We had our usual gathering on Friday morning at Frank's with the regulars in attendance. We got our coffee and shot the bull for a while about the weather. We were well into June now, and it was getting mighty warm. Of course, you wouldn't know it was summertime judging by Frank's back room, which was kept at about 60 degrees. Donnie always brought a sweater with him. The rest of us should have, but if we did then we couldn't make fun of Donnie. So we sat there shivering with both hands around our coffee mugs. We asked Frank about maybe raising the thermostat, but he said something about that room being connected to the kitchen and the kitchen would get too hot if he raised it. Sounded like nonsense to me, but it was his money paying the electric bill.

Kevin and Dustin pulled me aside and said that they thought I should tell the rest of the guys what went on in Donaldsonville on Tuesday with Teddy Toombs and his Elvis story. I said that I wondered if we were supposed to keep all that about the movie and Elvis confidential. But we all agreed that no one, not Teddy Toombs or Mayor Strong, told us we couldn't say anything about it. So I got everybody's attention and told them about Teddy Toombs, Elvis and Rosemary, and the blockbuster movie – interrupted occasionally by Kevin or Dustin to correct me on the finer points or to add embellishments.

Everyone, especially Uncle Joe, was incredulous.

"The only part of that story that's true is that Rosemary worked at The Tavern," said Uncle Joe with conviction. "Her name was Rosemary Rizzo and she was a looker, I'm telling you. Every boy in town wanted to go out with her, including me, but I was a year or two younger than her and, besides, she wouldn't have nothing to do with boys from Catholic High. She ended up marrying a White Castle boy. But that stuff about Elvis is crazy. Don't you think we would have known if Elvis had visited Donaldsonville?"

Dustin responded, "But this was when he was about 19 or 20 years old or so. He wasn't well known yet. We wouldn't have known who he was. I was only five years old when this was supposed to have happened. How old were you in 1955?"

Uncle Joe said, "Let me see…. I made 15 in January of '55. You know, people thought that I looked like Elvis when I was in high school. I was good looking, I can tell you. I had the hair and everything. I could shake a leg, too. Elvis didn't have nothing on me. He just had a agent, that's the only difference."

"Could you play guitar and sing?" asked Slim.

"No, I played the trumpet in the high school band. Same thing," he replied.

No one bothered to tell him that maybe it wasn't the same thing.

Then Jack asked, "Well what are we supposed to do? What does this have to do with the MOSS?"

"To tell you the truth, Jack, we don't really know," I told him. "At least we don't know yet. Teddy Toombs is supposed to be back in the Parish next week. The mayor told us he'd have him call us."

Dustin asked, "I wonder where Teddy Toombs is staying? Maybe with the mayor. They look like they're pretty chummy, being old college roommates and all."

Kevin said that he bet Teddy was staying at one of the bed and breakfast places in Donaldsonville, but I said that anybody that ran out on a restaurant bill probably wouldn't want to pay to stay anywhere. I agreed with Dustin.

During Friday night cocktails, Dustin and I reminisced about growing up in Donaldsonville, the things we did, part-time jobs we had, the teachers we harassed, and the girls we liked. We talked about the friends and classmates that have passed on and the quirky characters that made Donaldsonville interesting. This completely bored Darlene and Connie who were both from New Orleans, so they started in on how they saved a couple of country bumpkins from certain ignominy. We had already told them about how Elvis came to town and fell in love with a girl named Rosemary, but they blew that off as complete nonsense. After Dustin had his two scotches and I had a couple of gin martinis, the whole story was not only plausible to us, but no doubt completely factual.

Chapter Five

True to his word, Mayor Strong had Teddy Toombs call Kevin on the following Wednesday. He was back in town and anxious to talk to us. Could some of the MOSS meet him at the Grapevine for lunch on Thursday? The mayor would join us. This meant that we would be picking up the tab for two lunches, but Kevin agreed and roped in me and Dustin.

We got to the Grapevine just before noon and found Mayor Strong and Teddy Toombs at two tables pushed together toward the rear of the restaurant near the bar. With them were City Councilman Elmer Thibaut and Chamber of Commerce President Camille Ardoin, two more mouths to feed. Teddy was already enjoying his first or maybe second Bloody Mary and the mayor, Councilman Thibaut, and Camille Ardoin were each having some concoction of a reddish color in martini glasses. There were also plates of fried eggplant and crawfish cornbread on the table. They had started without us and started well.

Dustin and I had known Elmer Thibaut since he was born. His daddy, Thomas, was in our high school graduation class. Kevin supported his last campaign, so he knew him also. We knew Camille Ardoin from her presenting the status of the Donaldsonville Chamber to our Rotary Club once a year. No introductions were necessary and after a bunch of "hello, how are ya?"s," we sat down.

Apparently, our entrance interrupted Teddy regaling Camille and Elmer with the meeting he had in Biloxi with some "very important people in the industry, very important," so he ignored us and picked up the thread of his account and shortly concluded it with a punch line and a flourish. His audience was enthralled. Then Teddy turned his attention to us.

"Gentlemen," he began with solemnity, "you are going to play a very important role in this project, very important – vital, even. We can't get this extravaganza off the ground without your assistance."

I was thinking to myself that this was nice and all, but can you please finish the story about Elvis and Rosemary?

Dustin broke in with, "What role are you talking about? You mean you want us in the movie?"

Teddy and his entourage enjoyed a pretty good laugh at this. "No, that's not what we have in mind for you all. Of course, anything is possible in the movie business. No, what we need your group to do is to help us to reconstruct the look and feel of Donaldsonville in the mid-1950s – or parts of it at least – and to perhaps line up a few locals for extras and bit parts. You see, Sidney, Camille, and Elmer feel that it is very important for the image of the town to have some of its residents intimately involved in this movie. I think that they are spot on with that assessment. Now of course we will have a casting director to screen these people and make the final decisions, but it is our intention to use as many locals as we can."

While we were mulling this over, the waiter walked up and took our drink orders. As much as I felt like I could really use a double martini, I thought it prudent to remain sober for this and so asked for lemonade. Dustin and Kevin must have felt the same as they ordered

Arnold Palmers.

I was about to ask Teddy how this was going to work when he pointed at me with yet another pickled okra and said, "Now let me tell you how this will work. We will advertise in the Donaldsonville Chief and in the various local papers in Gonzales and so forth – we want to limit this to Ascension Parish – for people who would like to try out for minor roles and extras in the movie. We're going to tell you gentlemen what we're looking for and ask you to do a 'first screening' with applicants. In this way, hopefully, our casting director will not have to interview hundreds of people."

We got our drinks, Teddy got his second or third Bloody Mary – but who's counting – and we gave the waiter our food orders. While we were having our first course of salad, we asked Teddy to please tell us the rest of the Elvis and Rosemary story. We reminded him that he left us with Elvis simmering in the corner, Colonel Parker at the bar, and Rosemary seating customers.

"Well, there's not much more to tell. Rosemary sat with Elvis when the lunch crowd slowed down, but no one knows the exact topic of their conversation. You see, Rosemary failed to provide a verbatim account of their dialogue in her diary. She only alluded to certain things that are, shall we say, subject to interpretation. She did document that about an hour later Elvis and Colonel Parker left for New Orleans."

"Wait a minute!" I exclaimed. "That can't be the end of the story! I mean, what kind of movie would that be?"

"Oh, it's not the end of the story – at least not the end of *our* story," Teddy said with a grin. "I'll tell you all the rest over dessert."

We chatted about Donaldsonville and its storied past over lunch, then ordered coffee and bread pudding.

"Now what I'm about to tell you," began Teddy, "is based largely upon young Rosemary's diary which she kept faithfully for years, and also upon a certain amount of second and third-hand knowledge, rumors, and speculation, so you may not necessarily accept it all as factual, but what a movie it will make! Think about it as a very credible version of what may have happened."

We were captivated. We grew up watching Elvis movies at the

Grand Theater in Donaldsonville, which was, until it was demolished some years ago, across Railroad Avenue and just up the block from The Tavern/Grapevine. Dustin and I, Alden, and other friends all worked at the Grand when we were in high school. We watched *Blue Hawaii, Girls Girls Girls, King Creole, Girl Happy* – really every movie Elvis made, on the Grand Theater's single screen. We bought all of his albums with our meager earnings and knew all of his songs.

Teddy continued: "According to her diary, we know that, for a couple of years, Elvis stayed in touch with Rosemary. He would call her and write and she would write back. None of the letters from Elvis to Rosemary survived, at least not as far as we know. They certainly liked each other, but nothing could come of it. Elvis was well on his way to stardom and Rosemary, who was quite lovely, was being heavily courted by the local boys and was being pressured by her parents to forget about that wild-looking boy she hardly even knew. The relationship, if you want to call it that, between Elvis and Rosemary seemed doomed.

"In September of 1959, when Elvis was in the army and stationed in Germany, Rosemary wrote to tell him that she was engaged and was to be married the following June. No one knows how he took this news, but he wrote back and said that he was very happy for her. Rosemary married a young man from nearby White Castle, Emile Doiron, in June of 1960. As a wedding gift, we believe that Elvis bought them a brand-new car from the Capone Pontiac Company right here in Donaldsonville. Little did he know that about three years later Emile would be killed when he flipped that car while drag racing on the river road on the same day Kennedy was assassinated."

Teddy then told us that the details of the following account were relayed to him by Mr. Jordan Levy, an army buddy of Elvis who was found by Teddy and his research team after considerable effort. "Elvis was 24 years old and in the army by the time he quit writing to Rosemary, but while serving in Germany he met 14-year-old Priscilla Beaulieu, an air force brat, at a party. According to Mr. Levy, when Elvis saw her he couldn't believe his eyes. He thought it was this Rosemary girl that he'd been telling his friends about. Bewildered, he ran up to her and asked, 'Rosemary, what are you doing here?!' He had to be convinced that she was not, in fact, Rosemary. But she could have been her identical twin. She even sounded like her. Priscilla, who was very mature looking for her age, told Elvis that she was only 14 and in the ninth grade. Mr. Levy told us that Elvis soon realized Priscilla was just a child but he told her not to worry, that he would wait for her to grow up. We think this demonstrated how taken he had been with Rosemary. He knew she wasn't Rosemary, but he figured he'd lost the Donaldsonville Rosemary forever, so he began this very strange relationship with 14-year-old Priscilla.

"It has been publicly documented that people who knew Priscilla at that time said that she swore their relationship was, let's say, platonic. They spent a lot of time together over the next seven years, but the word is that Priscilla remained a virgin until she married Elvis in May of '67, before she turned 22. Elvis on the other hand, as his fame grew dramatically, was anything but platonic with any number of young women for all those years."

At this point the waiter refilled our coffees and we took a restroom break. The wait staff was cleaning up and setting tables for the dinner crowd and I wondered if we'd still be there by then. We couldn't leave until we heard the rest of the story. But it turned out that the rest of the story had to wait. The Mayor and Councilman had to prepare for their City Council meeting later in the evening and Teddy Toombs would be introduced at the meeting as the potential savior of Donaldsonville. Along with Camille Ardoin, they stood up to leave, shook hands all around, and again left the three of us with a hefty check. No matter, I thought. This would surely be good for Donaldsonville. It wasn't what we had in mind when we brainstormed on helping, but we were caught up in this movie idea and didn't feel like we could back out.

Chapter Six

The next morning Dustin, Kevin, and I were back at Frank's for our usual Friday gathering, trying to explain to the rest of the group how we went from the idea of helping folks in Donaldsonville get their GEDs to working on a movie. We couldn't verbalize the almost hypnotic affect Teddy Toombs had on us. We tried to convince them – and ourselves – that this was a good thing. This would be good for Donaldsonville, good for Ascension Parish, and good for the residents. Like Teddy said, it would put Donaldsonville on the map. One thing that Dustin, Kevin, and I did agree on – we would try to avoid lunch and dinner meetings with the Mayor and Teddy Toombs. This was starting to be an expensive venture.

There were, as expected, some questions from the MOSS.

Uncle Joe asked, "You don't think this will be one of them Hallmark movies, do you? Those must be the sappiest movies ever made. I hope it's not a Hallmark movie."

Now this was a touchy subject for me, because it was well-known in my circle of family and friends that I was a sucker for Hallmark movies, especially the Christmas movies. I was known to cry even when watching them for the third or fourth time. I told him, "I hope that it *is* a Hallmark movie, but I honestly don't think it is. At least Teddy Toombs never mentioned it. I get the impression that it's some kind of independent film."

"Well do we at least know how we're supposed to be helping with this?" asked Ronald.

Dustin responded, "It looks like they want us – especially those of us from Donaldsonville – to help them to recreate portions of the town that might be in the movie. We know The Tavern will be an important part. I was thinking that Ferris' grocery store and soda fountain right across the street might be good to have."

"And what about the Grand Theater?" I added. "That was right down the street, along with the X-Ray Pharmacy."

Alden, also from Donaldsonville, added, "What about the Club Bar? Wasn't that LaLa Regira's place? It was right across the street from The Tavern, I think." Alden's father had a business nearby on Railroad Avenue right across from the Grand Theater.

"LaLa's place was on Mississippi Street," Dustin corrected him. "You must be thinking about Tom and Babe's Club Bar. That was on Railroad Avenue right next to Ferris'. Where the library is now on the corner of Mississippi and Lessard used to be the Belaire Bar, and then next to that was LaLa's place, then Hotel Donaldson."

They argued over this for a few minutes until Kevin broke in with, "But that's not all they want us to do. We're supposed to help them find people to be in the movie, like extras and such."

Just as Kevin finished his remarks, his cell phone buzzed. He glanced at the screen, pointed to it, and mouthed to us, "It's Teddy," and went to a quiet corner to take the call. He was back a few minutes later. "Teddy says that he's emailing me a list of the characters in the movie that they'd like to hire locally. Each character will have a description of the qualities they're looking for – you know, like age, sex, looks – stuff like that. He says the advertisement for the parts will be in the paper next Wednesday."

I began to panic. "We're not ready for this. Where are we supposed to be interviewing the applicants? Do we have some paperwork we have to do? Do the characters have lines we can have the applicants read?"

Dustin broke in. "It's called 'screening.' We're going to screen the people who show up for certain roles. I'm sure they'll set up something in Donaldsonville for us to use." Unlike his father, Dustin's son is talented and is working in New York as an actor, so Dustin knows something about the process – at least, more than the rest of us do.

"Okay, fine," I said. "So who wants to do this screening thing? Any volunteers?"

Dustin shot up his hand. I figured he would. He not only had a son who was an actor but he was also involved with helping the Ascension Community Theatre – I think he was the treasurer or something. Dr. Dart minored in Performing Arts at LSU, so he was excited about it. No one else appeared anxious to be involved, so I said that I'd help, since I thought there should be at least three of us.

That evening I decided to do some internet research on Elvis to see if the web version bore any resemblance to Teddy's recounting of the story. The internet did confirm a few things – that Elvis was 24 and in the army in 1959. By the end of the prior year he was already a big name in entertainment. He met Priscilla as Teddy described, but there was nothing about him thinking that she was Rosemary. In fact, there was nothing about Rosemary in anything that I could find. It was even suggested that Priscilla may have reminded Elvis of his recently deceased mother, Gladys, and that's what attracted him to her. Following a lengthy courtship of sorts, Elvis married Priscilla in 1967, when she was 21, and had a child, Lisa Marie, on February 1, 1968, exactly 9 months later.

Priscilla left Elvis after four years together and their divorce was final in 1973. Six months prior to the divorce being final, Elvis took up with Linda Thompson. She was still with him when he died on August 16, 1977. They were never married. There was information about Elvis appearing on the Louisiana Hayride at the beginning of his career, but nothing about him going to Donaldsonville – and of course nothing about him meeting a young girl there.

Chapter Seven

Kevin called me on Monday afternoon to say he had the list of characters from Teddy and would send it to Dustin and me. I asked him to send it to Dr. Dart also. He also sent us the advertisement that would be published on Wednesday. Here's what it said:

ACTORS WANTED!

The City of Donaldsonville and Teddy Toombs Inc. are seeking cast members and extras for a major motion picture to be filmed in Donaldsonville. Acting experience a plus, but not a necessity. Preference given to Donaldsonville and Ascension Parish natives and permanent residents. Try out for the following speaking roles:

Bartender, Waitress, Hostess, Busboy, Car Salesman, Policeman, Newspaper Reporter, Restaurant Proprietor, Soda Jerk, others.

Extras are also needed for various non-speaking roles.

A phone number was provided for applicants to call for interview times and location. It looked like Teddy had someone putting a schedule together for the MOSS group to use for the initial screening. Kevin said that we were supposed to meet Teddy in Donaldsonville on Wednesday afternoon to go over our assignment. We would meet at 2:00 p.m. at the Ascension Catholic High gym, our old stomping grounds. Maybe then Teddy would tell us the rest of the Elvis/Rosemary story, if there was any more. At least we didn't have to buy lunch again.

Dustin, Dr. Dart, and I drove together to Donaldsonville on Wednesday. During the ride, Dr. Dart told us that the plans for establishing a branch of the community college in Donaldsonville were coming together nicely. There would be financial help from the state legislature and a temporary building provided by the town for the college's use while a new campus was constructed on property donated by a local benefactor. There would soon be new opportunities for adult education in my hometown – with or without the help of the MOSS.

When we arrived, we followed the signs to the Principal's office, bringing back fond memories of my time there when Brother Eldon

Crifasi was the Principal. Teddy was already there, meeting with Principal Teri Crocket, when we were shown in by her administrative assistant. After introductions we headed over to the gym to meet with Remy Bourgeois, drama teacher and head of Social Media for the school. On one end of the gym was a stage used for high school productions. Mr. Bourgeois explained that it was currently being transformed into a set for the school's upcoming September production of Oscar Wilde's "The Importance of Being Earnest," one of my favorite plays. Rehearsals, Remy told us, would begin in early July during summer break. I wondered if the coon-ass kids from here would try to affect a British accent. Remy Bourgeois was pretty excited by what we were doing and I strongly suspected that he would show up at our screening and read for a part. Teddy explained that, depending upon how many people called for appointments, screening could begin as early as the following Wednesday.

We talked for a few minutes about the setup for screening, where applicants would wait until they were called, where we would sit, the questions we would ask of each one, and other general stuff. We decided that microphones would not be necessary as the acoustics on stage were pretty good and, besides, Teddy said that the prospective actors needed to show that they could "project" their voices. I wondered why that was important for a movie, but I didn't ask. We reconvened in the Principal's small conference room where Principal Crocket and Mr. Bourgeois excused themselves and left the four of us to go over some of the details. That's when I told Teddy about the research I'd done on Elvis' life and that I could find no reference to Rosemary anywhere.

Teddy was unfazed. "No, I wouldn't expect that you would find anything about Rosemary when researching Elvis. The only information we have is in her diary and the corroboration of his army buddy. You gentlemen can be a big help in verifying other details from the diary."

Dustin asked him to finish the story for us. Teddy explained, "Now you have to understand that the writers are still working on some of the details of this movie, you know, the finer points. But I can tell you the gist of it. Now where did I leave off?"

I quickly said, "Rosemary got married, Elvis gave her a car, her husband got killed in it three years later, Elvis went into the army and met Priscilla who was 14 years old and the spitting image of Rosemary. They got married when she was 21."

Teddy chuckled, "I seem to recall that I embellished the story a bit more, but you captured the gist of it. Well, as your internet browsing suggested, Elvis and Pricilla had a child, then were separated a few years later and eventually divorced. Elvis was then with Linda Thompson – and here's where the story gets interesting."

I'm thinking, *This is where the story ends – Elvis dies.*

For the first time since we met him, Teddy got a rather serious look in his eyes and spoke to us in a whisper – which is not good since I wear two hearing aids and whispers don't usually do it for me. He said (or at least I think he said), "Gentlemen, I'm going to share something with you that only a few people know, a very few people. What I've told you so far about the relationship between Elvis and Rosemary has been, for the most part, verified as factual. However, we have been unable to independently corroborate the rest of the story, which is pieced together from Rosemary's diary entries."

Teddy paused for a moment, leaned back in his chair, and continued. "Now, according to Rosemary's godchild, Emma St. Pierre, her grandmother, Sarah, on her deathbed, verified the validity of the final diary entries. According to Emma, Sarah had never read the diary so, if Emma is to be believed, this would be independent evidence, but it is hearsay. The people I'm working for, the ones that are financing this venture, are willing to go forward with it on the strength of Emma St. Pierre's word and the final entries in Rosemary's diary."

"But how do you feel about it?" I asked – and added, "And what in the heck is in the final diary entries?"

"Personally," Teddy replied, "I'd like to know more. I've met Emma St. Pierre and I don't trust her. I thought that she was somewhat elusive in her answers to our questions, somewhat shady, if you know what I mean. But I'm not the one making the call on this. I'm afraid if we go forward with the story and it's found to be less than truthful, we could be open to litigation by Elvis' estate."

I repeated, "What in the world is in the final diary entries?!"

Teddy looked down and shook his head from side to side,

replying, "Gentlemen, I'm bound by a Confidentiality Agreement not to share the diary entries with anyone except with those working on the movie who have a specific 'need to know.' But I'll tell you what I'll do. I'll talk to the money people, who will in turn discuss the situation with their attorneys, and see if I can release to you a copy of the last few diary entries. I'll tell them that you're working on corroborating the information contained in the diary. You'll have to be patient, because this may take a while. Of course, you, too, will have to sign a Confidentiality Agreement."

That was it. We would have to wait for Teddy to do his magic if we wanted to know anything more. We thanked Principal Crocket and Remy Bourgeois and headed back to the other side of the river.

Chapter Eight

I got busy around the house on Thursday with grass cutting, flower bed weeding, and the never-ending task of cleaning the I occasionally glanced at my phone to see if I had received an email from Teddy Toombs. Nothing came all day and by nightfall I was too tired to think about it. I showered, shaved, and went to bed. Friday morning would bring our regular gathering at Frank's.

I picked up Uncle Joe the next morning and filled him in on the events of the previous Wednesday. He had also attended Ascension Catholic High about ten years ahead of me.

"You know that I was a football standout at Catholic High," he told me for the umpteenth time.

"Yes, I know," I replied. "I remember going to games to see you play. I also remember wondering why you had a towel sticking out of the back of your pants."

"That's because I played center, and the quarterback would dry his hands on the towel," he said impatiently. "I thought everybody knew that."

"Well, I was a kid. I didn't know about that back then. I didn't even understand the game," I explained.

I guess that was an adequate explanation because he changed the subject. "I also played linebacker on defense. We all played both ways back then. Those were the days."

I could see him quietly reminiscing, but then he broke the silence with, "You know I almost died when I was a kid."

"What, from playing football?" I asked.

"No, no, I had really, really bad asthma. I couldn't breathe, I couldn't go out and play or nothing," he told me, "until this lady momma knew – I don't remember her name – she came over and laid her hands on my chest and prayed over me and the next day I was cured! That's the only reason I was able to be an outstanding football player. It was a miracle. That lady should have been canonized."

I had heard the story before, but he loved telling it, so I listened patiently and said stuff like "Wasn't that something" and "She was a saint all right" until we got to Frank's.

Once there and seated, Dr. Dart, Dustin, and I each filled in the MOSS with parts of the events of Wednesday. Neither of them had yet received any word from Teddy. Some of the guys said that they had seen the advertisement on Wednesday and knew of certain people who were interested in trying out for a part. I was pretty sure they were talking about their own kids or wives, but no one admitted to it. We'd find out soon enough.

Later that day, as Dustin, Connie, Darlene, and I were just beginning cocktail night at our place and were in the middle of a game of bourré, my iPhone vibrated. It was an email from Teddy. In it he mentioned that he had called the producer and warned him that, if the last entries in the diary were not verified, a lawsuit was almost a certainty, and that he trusted the MOSS group to get to the bottom of this in short order. The producer called the other money people and they called their attorneys, and to Teddy's surprise they quickly complied with his recommendation. Attached to the email was a Confidentiality Agreement that Dustin, Dr. Dart, and I were to sign and return. We would then, presumably, be provided with a copy of Rosemary's diary, or at least the last few pages of it.

I ran upstairs, pulled up the email on my laptop, and printed a copy of the agreement. After reading the details, Dustin and I signed and dated it and Dustin offered to bring the original to Dr. Dart at the college on Monday. We hated to wait that long, but Dr. Dart and his family were visiting relatives in Pascagoula for the weekend. Darlene and Connie were not amused that we were interrupting cocktail night with what they snidely referred to as "that Donaldsonville nonsense." Their attitude stung us to our cores, not that they cared. I shot back with a clever "I don't like bourré anyhow," but it was less than satisfying.

At our wives' insistence, we resumed the game and, in our excitement about the possibility of getting to the bottom of the Elvis and Rosemary affair, Dustin and I may have imbibed more than our usual two drinks. I regretted the three martinis for many reasons, not the least of which was that Saturday morning was a Men's Bible Study at 7:00 a.m., followed by a workday at my church. I never sleep well after drinking that much, which seems counterintuitive, so it was something of a struggle to get up at 6:00 a.m., get dressed, pick up two dozen donuts, and head to the church, some 18 miles away in Baton Rouge. The smell of the donuts in the cab of my truck was nauseating. I ate two anyway, though.

Sunday morning found me heading back the same 18 miles to my small Baptist congregation while Darlene traveled about two miles to St. John Catholic Church. I went up to the choir loft where our church computer and recording equipment was kept, adjusted the sound of the clavinova during the hymns, and recorded the Pastor's sermon, which would later be uploaded to Sermon Audio. Included in his sermon on this day was about how most people believed, when asked, that they were "good enough" to get to heaven, perhaps on a sliding scale and relative to other people they knew. When considering Jack the Ripper and Adolph Hitler, most of us by comparison lead rather sedentary and altogether fruitful lives.

But it's also true that you can't make assumptions about people's faith – or lack of it. It reminded me of something I'd read about Elvis when researching him. Elvis had a step-brother who wrote a book about him. The book revealed that, while Elvis was seen as a rock-and-roll idol by his fans, he was said to be a deeply devout Christian. He recorded a number of Gospel songs during his career. He prayed quietly before every show, read the Bible, and relied upon God to give him the strength he needed to perform well. This seemed to be in conflict with his reputation as a consummate ladies' man and flagrant philanderer.

It reminded me of the time when Darlene and I were staying in the French Quarter for our anniversary and took a taxi to a restaurant. This was before Uber was a thing. I noticed that the driver had a statue of the Blessed Virgin, a small Buddha, and a Star of David on the dashboard of his car. When I commented on this strange combination of religious icons, he explained that he was "hedging his bets." I know that my Pastor would not have supported that strategy.

Chapter Nine

By noon on Monday we had obtained Dr. Dart's signature and scanned and returned the Confidentiality Agreement to Teddy. We hoped we'd hear from him right away but figured it might not be until the end of the week at the earliest. Late afternoon on Tuesday, Teddy Toombs called Kevin to tell him that his assistant (apparently working remotely because we never met anyone else) had lined up interviews for our advance screening sessions. Hundreds of people had called in to take their shot at fame and fortune. We would begins at 10:00 a.m. on Wednesday. We were provided with suggestions on how to proceed with the screenings, forms with which to document everything, and instructions to take everyone's picture using an iPhone – a full-length frontal shot and a close-up of the face. Prospective actors hoping to land speaking roles were to read certain lines for a particular character of our choosing and we would record each session.

We were also instructed not to tell anyone what the movie was to be about, except that at least part of it was set in Donaldsonville. But, of course, the word was already out. Discussions at the MOSS gatherings had quickly spread to our wives and then to the rest of Ascension Parish with the speed and indiscriminate behavior of a California wildfire. By the time word had reached the nether regions of the Parish, the inaccuracy of the facts – as we would soon discover – was astonishing.

According to the schedule provided, we were expected to interview and photograph eight to ten applicants a day, with a break for lunch. Those that we, by consensus, thought were good for a particular role would be sent to the movie's casting director for his/her consideration. I figured that we three might have a difficult time turning anyone down, especially if we knew them. We were all admitted pushovers.

Applicants were instructed to arrive at least thirty minutes in advance of their interviews in order to fill out some necessary paperwork. They were to wait in a designated classroom until called into the gym for their screening. They could elect to provide their own acting portfolio if they had one. We were not given the list of names until Wednesday morning. The very first two names on the list were the identical twin sisters Cora Givens and Clara McManus. I mean, what are the odds?

Clara's name was first and the three of us chatted about her before we called her in. This was when it struck me that Clara, if she demonstrated any talent at all, would make a perfect 1950's waitress. We only now realized that she looked just like a younger version of Flo from Mel's Diner, but with more makeup and a fuller figure. We sent for her via our runner, a summer student lent to us by Mr. Bourgeois. Two minutes later, Clara walked in. She was sporting an outfit similar to the one I'd seen her wear at Maynard Krebs' office – short, hip-hugging red skirt, frilly low-cut white blouse, and red patent high heels. Her blond hair was like a large cloud above her head. She was smiling broadly.

"Tony Campachi!" was her opening line. "I heard y'all were in charge of this thing! I'm so excited! It's so good to see you all again. I gave my acting portfolio to that nice young man over there."

Our runner, whose name was Chad, handed me a two-inch binder. "Well it's good to see you again too, Clara. I didn't realize that you'd done any acting," I responded.

"Oh, you know, bits here and there," she said modestly. "Most of it was in high school. I was the lead in *The Glass Menagerie* and in *A Streetcar Named Desire*."

"Your high school drama teacher must have really liked Tennessee Williams," Dr. Dart suggested. "Did you do *Cat on a Hot Tin Roof*, too?"

A frown interrupted Clara's smile. "My sister Cora got that lead, but only because I came down with strep throat. Of course, Cora was a natural in a role that requires a wife to beg a man to sleep with her."

Hmmm, I thought to myself. *I might have to re-read that play.*

"Hey, are y'all looking for the lead actress? I have really good experience in the lead role,. Then she added quickly, "but I'm very versatile – that's what my drama teacher always said. That I was a very versatile actress." She pronounced versatile with a long 'i' sound.

"Actually, Clara, a couple of big Hollywood stars are already cast in the lead roles," I said, totally making this up. "But there are a number of very important speaking roles that the casting director would like to fill with local folks."

"Oh my goodness!" Clara exclaimed, her heavily mascaraed eyes wide with excitement. "Do you know who they are? My Bunko group heard Denzel Washington was going to be in it. I just love Denzel!"

"I can neither confirm nor deny that," I continued to fabricate. "It's a closely guarded secret. But if you are selected for a role, you may very well be working with the lead actors."

"I'm sure I'm going to faint any minute now!" she said, faking a swoon. "Are you looking for someone to play the role of the jilted lover? Or maybe 'the other woman'? I have some experience playing those."

I smiled and said, "Clara, we envision you as the very attractive restaurant waitress who actually interacts with the leading man and woman."

"Oh my goodness," she responded breathlessly. "Do you know that many people have told me that I look just like Flo on Mel's Diner? That would be a perfect part for me! Do you think I can get that part?"

"Well, let's see. Why don't you read these lines…" I said, handing her lines given to us for the prospective waitress to read, "…and we'll see."

"Oh my goodness! Oh my goodness! Give me just a moment to get into character." Clara took a few deep breaths, causing the ruffles shielding her ample breasts to shudder. She held up the paper, studied the lines for a minute, and recited from memory in a perfect, if somewhat affected, Southern accent, "Well, how are y'all today? Would you like a table for two? Let me find something real nice for y'all by a window. Can I get you started with a nice cocktail?" She embellished the speech with hand gestures and head tilts and I thought she was perfect.

The three of us clapped, which we certainly should not have done. It was very unprofessional of us but, then again, we're not movie people. "Clara, that was just wonderful," I said. "My only concern is that you'll steal the spotlight from the stars!"

She beamed with pride. "Oh, go on now, Tony. You'll make me

blush!"

I said, "Clara, we'll recommend you for the waitress role, but it's ultimately up to the movie's casting director for the final say."

Then Dustin just had to ask, "Say, Clara, did you know that your sister signed up to try out for a part?"

"Yes, I saw her go into the classroom as I was leaving," she said with undisguised disgust. "If you need someone to play a frigid, heartless bitch, she's your girl. She wouldn't have to act, just be herself."

Apparently, we had touched a tender spot. Dustin quickly changed the subject and asked Clara to pose for a couple of photographs. Clara suggested using the professional photos that were included in her portfolio and we readily agreed. I walked her to the door and before leaving she gave me another one of those perfume-laden hugs. Darlene would not be happy.

Since the three of us were in agreement regarding Clara McManus, we put her portfolio and other paperwork in the "Yes" box provided by Principal Crocket, which was a cardboard container from the cafeteria that previously had held gallon cans of tomato sauce. We then had Chad go and fetch Cora Givens.

Unlike her twin sister, Cora was conservatively dressed in a dark blue pants suit, white blouse buttoned at the neck, and what I would call "sensible" shoes. Her red hair was done up in a stylish French twist, and her makeup, while a lot more than Darlene would have worn, was minimal compared to her sister's. She was really very attractive.

"Mrs. Givens," I greeted her. "Thank you so much for coming this morning. It's nice to see you again."

"Oh, please call me Cora, Mr. Campachi. It's nice to see you all, too," she responded.

"And you can call me Tony. I think you know Dustin and Dr. Dart, right?" I just realized that I had no idea what Dr. Dart's first name was. We had always just called him Dr. Dart.

"I've met you and Dustin of course, but I haven't met Dr. Dart before," she said quietly, shaking hands with him. "My son Otis Junior – he goes by 'O.G.'- is taking courses out at the community college, so I know who you are."

During this exchange, Chad, hovering in the background, handed me Cora's paperwork. Unlike her sister's, it consisted only of the paperwork she was asked to fill out, and a one-page resume of her acting experience. She provided no photos, professionally taken or otherwise.

Included in her resume was "Starred in a local television commercial." Dustin asked her to expand upon that description. "Well," she said, "I did a commercial for Givens' Mortuary, my husband's funeral home business. You know it takes a very sensitive approach to talk to someone about preparing for the inevitable. You have to possess the ability of being both sympathetic and empathetic."

Dustin asked Cora to tell us a little more about the roles she took on in the several plays listed.

"They were high school plays, almost all Tennessee Williams plays, except for 'Guys and Dolls', the one musical I was in during my first and only year in college," she answered. "I played Sister Sarah Brown, the lead female. I have a very good singing voice. I sing soprano in my church choir and I'm asked to sing at a lot of weddings. This will be a musical – I mean, the movie we're auditioning for – I heard that it will be a musical, right?"

"No, this won't be a musical as far as we know," I answered. "But I think that there will be some music in it. Excuse me for a minute while I confer with Dustin and Dr. Dart."

I huddled with the other two and quietly suggested that we have Cora read for the newspaper reporter role.

"Why not for the waitress or the hostess? I thought the newspaper part was for a man," whispered Dustin.

"Because I'd like to avoid a serious confrontation between Cora and Clara auditioning for the same part," I responded. "They're already at each other's throats. I just don't want them at my throat."

Dr. Dart agreed with me and we turned back to Cora and I said, "Cora, we'd like to consider you for a particular role. It's a newspaper reporter." I handed her the lines. "If you would just read these lines – take all the time you need."

Cora looked at the lines, pursed her lips, then closed her eyes for a few seconds. "Okay, I'm ready," she said.

The three of us sat there with copies of the lines of script in front of us that Cora was to read. The idea of the script, I think, was for the reporter to introduce herself to someone she was to interview, ask for a few minutes of their time, and then ask a couple of probing questions. While Dustin and Dr. Dart had some experience, if limited, in the theater and understood the idea of ad libbing, my engineering brain told me that the auditioner should be reading the lines verbatim.

Cora began – and she did not read the lines verbatim. What she did was so very much better. Even my "by the book" brain realized this fact. When she finished, she looked at us, smiled warmly, and asked, "How was that? I hope that it was okay that I strayed from the script. I just felt that it was very flat and not engaging at all."

"And you were right," offered Dustin. "Your delivery was really very good." Dr. Dart and I readily agreed.

"Thank you so much!" Cora replied. "Is it true that Julianne Moore is going to star in this movie? I'm often told that I look a lot like her."

I gave Cora the same "closely guarded secret" spiel that I had given her sister. We then took the requisite photos, thanked Cora, and told her that we would recommend her for the reporter role but that the final decision was up to the casting director. She thanked us and walked gracefully out and we put her paperwork into the tomato sauce box with her sister's.

Before calling in the next applicant, we mused on the stark differences between the twin sisters. Clara and Cora were both attractive, but in completely different ways. We agreed that Clara was someone you'd take to a casino and a karaoke bar, while a date with Cora would consist of dinner at a fine restaurant, and perhaps ballroom dancing.

Chad, still hovering in the background and, like most of his generation, not wearing a watch, held up his phone to show us the time, in a not-too-subtle hint that we were already well behind schedule. We instructed him to usher in the next person on the list, a

Mr. Egdar Morvant. Dustin, upon hearing the name, mentioned that he knew of Edgar from his connection with Ascension Community Theater.

"Do you think I should recuse myself, since I know Edgar?" Dustin asked.

"No, I don't think so," I answered. "We all knew Clara and Cora, but we didn't recuse ourselves. I think it's an advantage that you know him. It might save us some time. Is he an actor?"

Dustin smirked. "He's a wanna-be actor, that's for sure. I've never met him, but friends of mine at the theater mentioned at our last Board meeting that there was this guy named Edgar who tried out for every part that came up, male and female, in the last three seasons. This has got to be him. The different directors always gave him a tryout but he was never cast in any role except very brief non-speaking spots, like someone in a crowd or a bystander – that sort of thing. He mostly helped out with props, set construction, painting – that's about it."

We had Chad go and fetch Mr. Morvant. He returned ushering in a nice-looking, somewhat overweight, middle-aged dark-haired gentleman sporting a moustache and goatee, wearing black slacks, white shirt, and black loafers. He introduced himself as Edgar Morvant as he shook hands with each of us. Chad handed us Mr. Morvant's paperwork and portfolio. We had him take a seat while we glanced through his information.

Dustin began with, "I see you've been with the Ascension Community Theater for several years. I happen to be the treasurer for the ACT. I really appreciate everyone who's connected to that group. It's great to have such an active community theater here. Thanks for being a part of it."

Edgar Morvant nodded and said, "You're welcome. I'm happy to be involved with the theater. I really enjoy it."

Dustin followed with, "I see you've played various roles in several plays. I'm sorry, I don't recall seeing you in anything."

"I've had only bit parts," he offered. "I help with props, painting, building, maintenance. You know. I haven't had a chance to play a lead role yet."

Dr. Dart suggested in an aside that we have Edgar read for the bartender role. We agreed. He looked like a bartender. Dustin pulled out the script written for that role and handed it to him. "We'd like to consider you for the bartender role," Dustin told him. "Would you please read these lines?"

Edgar glanced at the script, stood, and read, "Hi, what can I get you? Our thpecial today ith a Thatherac. We altho have a thrimp appetither." He put down the script and looked embarrassed. He had the absolute worst lisp I'd ever heard.

"I apologize," he said. I was glad that he didn't say "I'm thorry." "I have a little problem with thertain words."

"Oh, that's okay Edgar," replied Dustin with sympathy. "It's not that bad." This was a flat-out lie. The only role I could see Edgar playing was Winthrop in *The Music Man*, except that it was a part for a kid.

Dustin, Dr. Dart, and I huddled together for a few minutes and came up with an idea. A few more minutes later, we asked Edgar to read the handwritten script we revised.

Edgar cleared his throat and read, "Hi, what can I get you? We're offering a two-for-one deal on a Kettle One vodka martini. And we've added crawfish cornbread to the bar menu – if want a light bite." Edgar smiled broadly as he finished and looked up at us. "How wath that?" he asked.

I almost said "Thuper," but stopped myself. "That was great, Edgar. We'll just take your photo and recommend you for the bartender role." Chad stepped over and mentioned that Mr. Morvant had provided professionally taken photos with his portfolio. We thanked Edgar and decided to break for lunch. Like I said, we were pushovers.

Chad declined our invitation to join us for hamburger steaks at the First and Last Chance. The Grapevine would have been closer, but nothing is very far away in Donaldsonville. Also, we didn't want to risk running into folks for whom we'd feel obligated to buy lunch. But, as the poet Robert Burns once opined about "The best laid schemes o' Mice an' Men Gang aft agley," the mayor and Teddy Toombs were standing there waiting to be seated when we walked in.

They had walked over from the Mayor's office, less than a block away.

The Mayor smiled at us and told the waiter, "Table for five, please."

The First and Last Chance bar and café, located at the southern end of Railroad Avenue, is a landmark of Donaldsonville and the turn-around point for teenagers cruising the avenue back in the day. Patrons who didn't wish to go inside could park in the back, blow their horns, and a waiter would come out and get their order. You could even order drinks from your car. Any teenager with a driver's license could get a rum and coke or a Tom Collins because the waiter couldn't actually read, so, if you had a license, that was good enough. There were also huge banana trees in the back where teens could park and smooch undisturbed – or so I've been told.

As we sat down, the Mayor turned to Teddy and said, "You are now going to experience some of the best food this town, this Parish, or this State has to offer!" We all agreed and recommended several of the dishes, including the amazing fried chicken, spaghetti and meatballs, and the shrimp po-boy. Dustin, Dr. Dart, and I ordered the hamburger steak special from the lunch menu because it would be served faster and we had people scheduled for screenings right after lunch. The Mayor got a po-boy and Teddy ordered the catfish lunch special and a Bloody Mary. I wondered if he ever drank anything else.

While waiting to be served, I let the Mayor and Teddy know how the initial screenings this morning went, adding that there was a surprising amount of talent in Ascension. Teddy admonished us that we must be tough and only approve those for additional screening for speaking roles who were exceptional. As far as he cared, anyone we didn't like could still be a non-speaking extra. We assured him that we would be highly selective and that only Broadway-star-quality folks would get through our gauntlet. Ha.

When we finished our meal, I called the waiter over for the check and, as I did so, Teddy directed him to put another Bloody Mary on it before closing it out. I had been considering making Teddy an honorary member of the MOSS but now I was having second thoughts. I paid the check, and Dustin and Dr. Dart promised to get the next one. I was pretty confident that there would, in fact, be a next one – and one after that, ad nauseam.

Chad looked at us with what I can only describe as bitter disappointment when we returned, pointing out that we were running at least an hour late. He might have pulled it off more convincingly if he hadn't been a pimply 16-year-old. Nevertheless, we acted appropriately reprimanded and asked Chad to send in the next candidate.

As we promised Teddy, we tried to be much more selective in the afternoon interviews. Of the five screenings we got through, we put only three candidates in the "yes" tomato sauce box. Of the interviewees we rejected, one was a four-year-old brought in by her mom. Without any prologue or prompting, the mom pressed "play" on a recorder she brought in and the kid broke into a rollicking rendition of Joan Jett's "I Love Rock and Roll," all while performing a well-choreographed dance routine. We thanked them but told the mother that we didn't think that there was a need for her daughter's considerable talent for this film. It broke our hearts to say "no."

The other rejected applicant thought that we were interviewing people for the school janitor's job. We liked him a lot and said that we'd recommend him to Principal Crocket.

Chapter Ten

We muddled through nine screenings on Thursday and couldn't find it in our hearts to reject any of them. Teddy would not be pleased, but Teddy didn't live here and wouldn't be running into these locals for the rest of his life. Neither Dustin, Dr. Dart, nor I wanted to be responsible for someone local missing out on perhaps their one shot at stardom.

Thankfully, no screenings were scheduled on Friday, giving us a three-day reprieve. Our Friday morning gathering at Frank's was very well attended. Everyone knew about the screenings we'd done and wanted details. Uncle Joe grilled me about it when I picked him up on the way to the restaurant.

He started with, "Did y'all find anybody worth a lick? Your aunt Millie told me that Camella Langois brought her little daughter Olivia to try out. Millie said that the little girl sang the National Anthem at the bowling tournament in Gonzales last week and made people cry, she was so good."

"Yep," I said. "That's one talented little girl, but there isn't a call for children in the movie."

"That's a shame, ain't it?" Uncle Joe lamented. Then, after an uncharacteristic pause, "Millie thinks that I should go get screen tested. She thought that maybe I could play the old Elvis because I looked so much like him when I was young."

I doubted that Aunt Millie said any such thing. "But Uncle Joe, Elvis was only 42 when he died. There wasn't an 'old Elvis'."

"Oh," was his response. "I don't know if I can pass for 42, what with my autharitis and all." Then, when it appeared to him that I wasn't going to say anything, he said, "I don't want to be in a sappy Hallmark movie anyway."

"Look, why don't you come and sign up as an extra?" I offered. "They say they're going to need a lot of extras."

"I don't know, maybe," he said sullenly. "I'll see what Millie says. Maybe we'll go to the Chance for lunch one day next week and we can go by the high school and see what y'all are doing."

We walked together into the side room at Frank's and were slapped in the face with arctic air. Some of the guys were already there sitting around our table, including Donnie Ourso in a LSU sweatshirt, and even he was shivering. I'd have to talk to Frank again. Maybe he could put in some of those portable heaters that they used out on the patio in the wintertime.

Wendy was pouring coffee as quickly as she could and we sat down and wrapped hands around our steaming mugs. In a few more minutes the rest of the regulars came in and grabbed a seat, complaining about how cold the room was when it was already 80 degrees outside at 7:00 a.m.

Dustin and Dr. Dart already had the guys laughing about Clara and Cora being the first two people screened and I heard Jack asking, "Cora is the redhead, right? How did she look? That's one fine-looking woman." Dustin showed Jack the photos we took of Cora on his phone and he whistled appreciatively. I silently commended them for not saying anything about Edgar Morvant. That would just be mean and they weren't mean guys. I thought about talking with a lisp for a second but then thought better of it.

After we filled in everyone on the screenings, Slim asked, "Well what's next? When do they start filming this movie?"

Dustin answered, "We still have a bunch of people signed up for screen testing for next week. I don't think they'll start filming for weeks or even months yet."

"Also," I added, "we're supposed to try to verify the truth about Rosemary's diary if we can. They haven't sent copies of the diary to us yet. We had to sign an agreement saying that we wouldn't blab what's in the diary all over town."

"Yeah, but you'll tell us, right?" asked Terry.

"No," I said. "I think that would be the very definition of blabbing."

Discussions went on about screenings and the diary and Elvis all through breakfast. Ronald asked Wendy if she was going to try out for a spot in the movie. After all, one of the characters is a waitress and she was already experienced in the role. It turns out that, as comfortable as Wendy is with us old guys after all of these years, she's actually really, really shy around normal people. She blushed crimson and walked away. It took us a while to get our checks.

Just as we were paying at the register, I felt my phone vibrate in my pocket. It was a text from Teddy to me, Dustin, and Dr. Dart telling us that he would have one hard copy of some of the last pages from Rosemary's diary for us this afternoon. Could we meet him at the Mayor's office in Donaldsonville at 3:00 p.m.?

The three of us were still at Frank's, so we quickly agreed that one of us should go and pick up the copy. Dr. Dart had meetings in the afternoon and Dustin would be helping Connie clean the house and pick up something exotic for our cocktail night later. It was down to me, so I agreed to go. Maybe I would take Darlene to the Grapevine for a late lunch. She wasn't crazy about Donaldsonville, but she really did like eating at the Grapevine.

Darlene agreed to go with me if, after lunch, she could wait in the car while I went in to meet with Teddy. She had met Mayor Strong on several occasions and liked him, but didn't like what she'd heard from me about Teddy Toombs. She thought he sounded pompous and full of himself, but I said that I liked him and that the only thing he was full of was Bloody Marys. We walked into the Grapevine at about 1:15 p.m. and I carefully looked around to make sure that the Mayor and Teddy weren't waiting there for someone to pick up their lunch tabs.

After a very nice lunch – we each had a salad and split the Mediterranean Pasta – I needed a nap, but it was 2:45 p.m. and time to head to the Mayor's office. Instead of her waiting in the car, I dropped Darlene off at the library on Mississippi Street. She loved the library and was happy to sit there and peruse the Nora Roberts books to see if there were any she hadn't read. Fat chance. Nora Roberts had to write night and day to keep up with Darlene.

I got to City Hall right at 3:00 p.m. and was ushered into the Mayor's office to find Mayor Strong and Teddy sitting on one of the two sofas reminiscing about their college days.

"Well hello, Tony, how's it hanging?" began Teddy. I got the impression that he may have had a three-Bloody Mary lunch without me. The Mayor also seemed to be in a happy place.

"I'm great, Teddy, couldn't be better," I replied. "Looking forward to seeing what you have for me."

"How did the screenings go on Thursday?" Teddy inquired. "I trust that you were most particular when approving an applicant to the next level?"

"Oh absolutely," I lied. "Only the very best got by our scrutiny."

"Well good, that's very good, very good," Teddy mumbled, as the Mayor just sat there smiling broadly.

I cleared my throat and said, "Teddy, Darlene is waiting for me at the library. I wonder if I can get the information you said you had for us."

"Oh yes, yes, yes, of course. I have it right here," he responded as he reached over for a manila package on the Mayor's desk. It was addressed to him and had been roughly torn open. "I checked to make sure it was what I thought you gentlemen needed to investigate the veracity of the contents. Now remember," he cautioned as he handed the package to me, "keep this information close to the vest. No one else is to see this but the three of you who signed the agreement."

I assured him that I would guard the contents with my life, waved goodbye to glassy-eyed Mayor Strong, and walked quickly out of the room. Getting into my truck I realized that I would be picking up Darlene in minutes, so I tossed the package onto the back seat. If she checked out a new book she might be preoccupied and not think about the diary.

"Did you get the diary?" were the first words out of her mouth after "hello" when I called to say that I was on the way.

"I didn't look at what was in the package yet. I assume it has copies of some of Rosemary's diary pages," I said and added, "but you can't look at it. I promised Teddy…and I signed some sort of legal document."

"Right," she said – and I could almost see her smirk over the phone.

Three minutes later Darlene was in the truck and poring over the contents of the package. As much as she and Connie poo-pooed our excitement over the whole Elvis and Rosemary and Donaldsonville story, this was different. Reading someone's diary was better than reading a romance novel.

"Maybe we should wait until tonight when we're at Dustin and Connie's," I suggested.

"No way, José," was her response, not taking her eyes off of the first page of a small stack of what appeared to be black and white copies of pages from a spiral-bound book. Glancing over I could make out neat handwritten script.

I had taken the river road to the bridge since I was already on Mississippi Street and almost went into the ditch in front of the old Goette house. I'd either have to pay attention to driving or pull over somewhere and wrestle the stuff away from Darlene. There wasn't anywhere to pull over.

"Well at least tell me what you're reading," I said with resignation.

Clearly aggravated that I was interrupting her reading, Darlene huffed a bit and said, "The diary pages are small, like a little spiral notebook, and it's copied in the middle of the sheet. The first page of the diary they sent you is dated October 17, 1954 at the top. It's all written in cursive, but it's neat and I can read most of it. This first one says 'Dear Diary, I met a cute boy today from out of town. His name is Elvis something. He wrote his name and address on a napkin but it got wet and I can't make it out. He said he'd write to me. If he does, I'll write back. I called Sarah and told her about him. I wish I could find a nice local boy though.' That's all there is on the first page."

She flipped over to the next page. The pages were stapled together in the top left corner. "This one is dated March-something – I can't make it out – 1955. 'Dear Diary, that boy that I met last year, Elvis, came back to the restaurant today! I shouldn't have talked to him – he never did write to me. He said that he was going to be a big star, that he was on the television, but we don't have one so I don't know…' I can't make out the next few words. It ends with 'said he would write.'"

We were almost to the Sunshine Bridge by this time. I suggested to Darlene that we ought to wait until tonight so Dustin could go through the stuff with me. Her reply was, "Just a couple more."

"This next one is dated November 12, 1955," she continued.

"'Dear Diary, Mr. Big Shot Elvis Presley wrote and sent me a photo of himself. He signed it "To my best girl Rosemary." All he said in the letter was "I hope I get to see you again." I don't know if I want to see him again. I guess I'll write back. I better call Sarah and see what she thinks.'"

Darlene scanned through the next few pages, looked confused, and said, "There are a bunch of diary entries about somebody named Emile. Emile Doiron."

"That's the guy that Rosemary married, in 1960 I think," I explained.

"Wait, here's another one about Elvis," Darlene said with some excitement. And she was making fun of Dustin and me. "It's dated September 22, 1959. Wow, that's years from the last one. Listen to this: 'Dear Diary, Elvis called me today from Germany to congratulate me on my engagement to Emile. Can you believe it! From Germany! That was really sweet of him. He said that he would send us a wedding present. I told him that he didn't have to do that. He'll probably send us autographed pictures of himself in one of those awful outfits he wears. I shouldn't make fun. He's real popular, even around here. He was right about being famous one day.'"

Darlene noticed something else. The diary pages each had a small number on the bottom corner. The numbers were not consecutive – not even close. I explained that Teddy said they would send only the pages that they thought were pertinent, so they probably skipped a lot of pages that had nothing to do with Elvis.

"There must have been a reason to include the pages about Rosemary meeting Emile, though," I suggested. "Maybe it's because Emile died in the car Elvis gave them three years after they were married."

"What?!" Darlene exclaimed in astonishment. "Elvis gave them a car and the husband died in it? You never told me that!"

"Well, you and Connie never were that interested when Dustin and I were talking about this," I said defensively. "Y'all just ignored us." *Just like you're doing now*, I thought, as she buried her nose into the diary pages again.

After a few silent minutes, just as I was passing the Cajun Village and heading to the interstate, Darlene said, "Listen to this – it's dated May 21, 1960. 'Dear Diary, Something really crazy happened today. Emile was over sitting with me on the front porch so we could talk about our wedding vows when Mr. Capone drove up in a new car. He walked up to the porch and gave me the keys! He said somebody bought it for Emile and me as a wedding present, but he didn't know who it was. They just ordered the car, paid for it by Western Union or something, and told him to deliver it to me! I thought it must be from my daddy, but he said no, it wasn't from him. Then I thought "Elvis," but that's crazy! I hardly know him! I called Sarah and she said it must be from him. Maybe – because I don't know anybody else who could afford to do that.'"

Darlene quickly turned to the next sheet. "This is the next day. 'Dear Diary, Emile took the car home with him. I don't have my driver's license yet. Daddy never taught me to drive but Emile said he would. Mr. Capone said that the title for the car has my name on it, but once Emile and me are married on June 18, it won't matter. I thought about writing to Elvis to ask him about if he sent us the car, but if he didn't, I'd feel really dumb. It had to be him though, right?'"

We were just passing the Tanger Outlet Mall when Darlene turned to the next sheet. "I don't think I like this Emile character. Listen to this. It's dated June 15, 1960. 'Dear Diary, My momma told Emile that I kept a diary. I didn't even know she knew about it. Now I wonder if she's been reading it when I'm at work. Emile told me that after we're married on Saturday I couldn't keep a diary anymore. He said that married women don't keep diarys. I don't know, maybe. I hate to stop writing in it. I'm going to ask Sarah what she thinks.'"

We were at our exit now and I offered to go to PJ's for coffee to get Darlene to put the thing down. She agreed. She just loves a honey oat milk latté in the afternoon. Like all real men, I ordered a dark roast coffee, black. I do like those gingerbread lattés they have around Christmas, though. We sat outside on the deck in the back, drank coffee, and talked about what we had read – well, what she had read, and I listened to. She was all of a sudden very interested in the whole Rosemary/Elvis saga and couldn't wait to get to Connie's to tell her about it.

Chapter Eleven

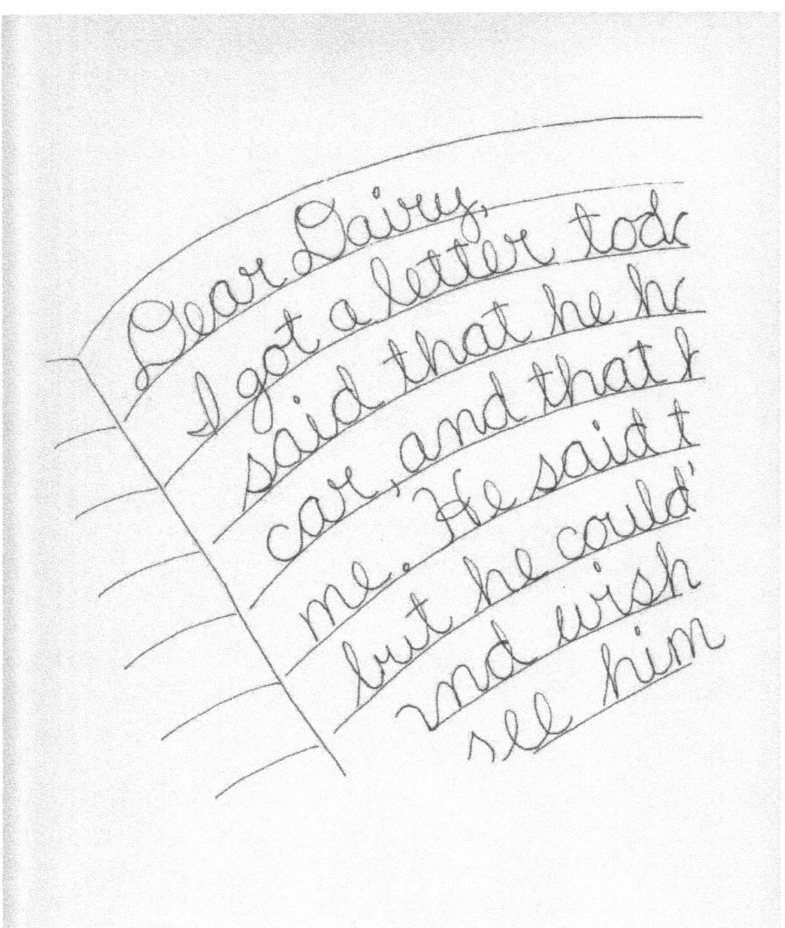

We had a couple of hours before we were supposed to be over to the Sonniers' for cocktail night. We were supposed to bring a dessert, so we stopped at Harvest to get some Moo-llennium Crunch and Darlene made brownies when we got to the house. We left the manila envelope and its contents in the back seat of the truck so we wouldn't be tempted to read any more before we got to Connie and Dustin's. I spent some time weeding my raised vegetable garden then went in and washed up, changed into jeans and an LSU shirt, and Darlene did the same. We left to go to the Sonniers' earlier than usual, which I know Connie hated because she wouldn't be ready for us but, too bad, because we were excited to get to the rest of the diary pages.

After the perfunctory hugs and kisses, I started mixing drinks while Darlene caught Connie and Dustin up on the contents of the package from Teddy, re-reading each page to them. At one point, just when I was bringing in the ladies' Cosmos, Connie punched Dustin in the chest for not telling her about Rosemary's husband getting killed in the car that Elvis bought for them. "You weren't even interested when we were talking about all of this," Dustin reminded her, but his rebuke fell on deaf ears.

I handed Dustin his scotch and I had just started on my martini when Darlene got to new territory in the diary entries. "This next one is dated July 5, 1960. Hey, this is after Rosemary was married to that Emile guy." She said this with some disdain in her voice. She really didn't like Emile Doiron. "'Dear Diary, I got…'"

Connie, looking over Darlene's shoulder, interrupted her. "Look, she wrote 'Dear *Dairy*' instead of '*Diary*'! Ha!"

"Hmmm," Darlene said. "I don't think that she did that before." After a quick check, she confirmed that all of the entries before July 5, 1960 had 'Diary' spelled correctly and all of them from July 5 on spelled it 'Dairy.'

Dustin thought that it didn't mean anything, it was a common enough mistake. I thought that it might be a common mistake using a word processor because spell-check wouldn't catch it, but not if you're handwriting something and you spelled it correctly for – literally – years.

Darlene continued with the July 5 entry. "'I got a letter today from Elvis. He said that he hoped we were enjoying the car and that he misses me and loves me. He said that he was seeing somebody, but he couldn't stop thinking about me and wishes I would come out and see him. Emile would never let me go.'"

The next entry was dated December 22, 1963. In it Rosemary recounted a call from Elvis that morning saying how sorry he was that her husband was killed in an accident, that his heart was breaking for her, and that he would write a song just for her. I told Darlene and Connie that Teddy previously told us that Emile Doiron died while drag racing on the river road on November 22, 1963.

The rest of the diary entries were almost exactly six months apart and they were all similar. Each one recounted a letter or a call received by Rosemary from Elvis in which he pledged his undying love. This went on the whole time Elvis was married to Priscilla, from 1967 through 1973. Finally, the last entry dated August 15, 1977, had the following entry: "Dear Dairy, Elvis called me this morning. He's flying into New Orleans on a private jet tomorrow for my birthday and taking a limo to come to Donaldsonville to see me. He said that he wants to marry me! I might do it! Wish me luck!"

"Is that all?" asked Connie and Darlene simultaneously. "What the heck happened?"

"I'll tell you what happened," I said. "Elvis Presley died on August 16, 1977, the day after this last diary entry."

"So this was a true story after all," said Darlene resignedly.

Dustin responded, "Teddy thinks something is fishy about the whole thing and wants us to see if we can confirm that it's all true."

"How are you going to do that? Is Rosemary still living?" asked Connie.

"No, that's the whole reason we have her diary," I explained. "Rosemary died and left her possessions, including her diary, to her best friend Sarah. According to Sarah's granddaughter Emma, who Sarah raised from a baby – we don't know what happened to Emma's parents – Sarah hadn't read the diary. She may not have even known she had it among Rosemary's things. But Emma swears she confirmed on her deathbed what happened between Rosemary and Elvis. Sarah died sometime later and her granddaughter Emma found Rosemary's diary just a few months ago when she was going through her grandma's stuff."

"I think that we have to find this Emma…what's her last name, Dustin?" I asked.

"St. Pierre," he replied. "Same as her grandmother – unless she got married and changed her name."

"We have to find this Emma St. Pierre," I continued, "to see if she knows anything beyond what's in the diary. If they make this movie, she stands to make quite a few bucks, I imagine. You'd think Teddy and the folks he's working for would have her on speed dial, but he didn't seem to know where she was."

"I wonder if she's on Facebook," suggested Connie. She and Darlene immediately began a search. They found a bunch of St. Pierres, but no Emmas.

"Hey, I just remembered something Teddy told us," I said. "He said that Emma contacted him through Mayor Strong's daughter who's a friend of hers – I don't remember her name – so maybe she knows how to find Emma."

"I don't have the Mayor's number, and it's too late to call him anyway," Dustin added. "We'll have to wait until Monday."

"I tell you what I'll do," I suggested. "I'll send a text to Teddy. I'm pretty sure he's staying with the Mayor. He can get the Mayor's daughter to call us, or at least give us her number. If he checks his phone, he might answer right away."

Teddy didn't answer right away. In fact, he didn't answer all weekend. I kind of like the idea of ignoring my phone all weekend. I've never been able to do it, but I like the idea, so I really couldn't complain about Teddy doing the same. We would just have to wait until Monday to hear from him.

Chapter Twelve

At Principal Crocket's request, no screenings were scheduled for the following week because of some previously scheduled refinishing of the gym floor. So Monday I planned to work around the house and maybe Tuesday would be a golf day if the weather cooperated.

Sure enough, Teddy called me on Monday morning, confirmed that he didn't know where Emma St. Pierre was, and gave me Stacy Strong's number. She was a student at Nicholls State University in Thibodaux, stayed there in an apartment during the week, and came home on weekends.

I called her and she answered right away, explaining that her dad let her know that I'd be calling. I explained that I was helping Teddy out with this movie to be made in Donaldsonville and that I needed to get in touch with Emma St. Pierre.

"I know exactly where Emma is," Stacy said matter-of-factly. "Her butt is in jail."

"What?!" I exclaimed, completely taken by surprise. "In jail where? What did she do?"

"I don't know what the girl did," answered Stacy, "but she's in the Ascension Parish jail near the Sunshine Bridge. I've been once to see her and to put some money into her account so she can make calls and buy stuff she needs, but she wouldn't tell me anything about why she's in there. Oh, and hey, look, don't tell my daddy I gave her money, okay? He would NOT be happy."

I thanked Stacy and promised her that I'd tell her what I could find out. I had the Sheriff's number because he's in my Rotary Club, so I called him but got his voice mail. I knew he was pretty good about returning calls, so I just waited to hear from him.

Sheriff Rob Pepper called me about an hour later, apologizing because he was in a meeting with some of his deputies. I explained why I was calling and asked if he could tell me why Emma St. Pierre was a guest of his in the parish prison. He didn't know off-hand but would find out and get back to me.

I didn't hear from him for the rest of the day, but Rob, Dustin, and

I were all at the Rotary breakfast meeting on Tuesday morning. Sheriff Pepper pulled us aside before the meeting started and he told us what he found out.

"Emma St. Pierre was arrested last week for forging checks. She couldn't make bail, so we're holding her until she goes to trial. She's been meeting with a public defender."

"I wonder if she'd talk to us," Dustin pondered.

"Maybe," Rob replied. "Just go to the jail, check in at the window, and let them know who you're there to see. Of course, that doesn't mean she'll meet with you, though. Does she know either of you?"

"No, she doesn't know us," I replied. "But we know the Mayor's daughter Stacy, and she's supposed to be her best friend, so we can use that to get her to see us."

Rob wished us luck and said to call him if we ran into trouble. It's good to know the Sheriff.

Dustin, Ronald, Rodney, and I had a tee time at 10:06. We thought maybe after playing nine holes at Santa Maria and a Burgersmith lunch, Dustin and I could take a ride to the parish jail to try to visit with Emma St. Pierre. But after walking nine holes in the June heat, we decided to give it a rest until Wednesday. During lunch we filled in Rodney and Ronald on what was going on. Rodney asked a good question about Emma. "Why would she need to forge checks if she sold the diary to the movie people?"

We admitted that we had no idea what kind of deal she made for the diary. Maybe she got paid and squandered the money, or maybe the deal hadn't been finalized. We'd have to ask Teddy about that. That reminded me that we hadn't called Teddy to tell him about Emma being in jail. I'd also have to let Stacy know why Emma was in the pokey. If Stacy was putting money in Emma's jail account, clearly she had no money to speak of.

I called Teddy on the way home. "Teddy, Emma St. Pierre is in jail for forgery. The Sheriff told us that she was arrested last week for forging some checks."

He was so quiet that I thought the call failed. "I'm not that surprised," he finally said. "I told you that I thought something was 'off' with that girl. This is sure to hurt her negotiations for the rights to the contents of the diary."

"You mean she hasn't cut a deal yet?" I asked.

"She was given a small advance just to lock up the diary so that she couldn't sell the rights to anyone else," Teddy explained. After a moment he added, "I'm even more convinced that we must make certain that the last entries to the diary are factual."

"Teddy, how can you be sure that any of the contents of the diary are factual?" I asked.

"Some of it we've been able to check out through other sources," he explained. "For example, the Capone family business records do show that a new Pontiac Ventura was bought by someone who paid cash and had it delivered to Rosemary Rizzo. Now, we can't prove it was Elvis, but still…" Then he added, "And I told you about Elvis' army buddy, Jordan somebody, who specifically remembered Elvis talking about a 'Rosemary' the night he met Priscilla."

"Well then, what exactly *aren't* you sure about?" I asked.

"Tony," he sighed, "the story about Elvis meeting Rosemary is intriguing, but the possibility of him proposing to her, planning to fly in to see her, and then dying on her birthday was what sold the story. Oh, and we were able to confirm from courthouse records that August 16 was Rosemary Rizzo's birthday. And everyone knows the date Elvis passed. That is quite a coincidence."

"What about Elvis' daughter, what's her name? Or Priscilla Presley. Can they confirm anything?" I asked.

"You mean Lisa Marie," Teddy said. "We contacted her, but she was only nine years old when her father passed. She didn't remember anything useful. And Priscilla wouldn't talk to us."

After another pause, Teddy said, "The thing is, the producers of this movie want to believe that everything in the diary is true. They want to go ahead with this movie, but I want to make certain that they're not going to be taken advantage of financially – or worse, be exposed to legal action. That would reflect badly on yours truly." By this time, I was parked in my driveway, still talking hands-free.

"Look Teddy," I said, "Dustin and I are going to visit Emma at the jail tomorrow. I'll let you know what we find out. Oh, one more thing. Did y'all by any chance do a handwriting analysis of the diary?"

"No," he answered. "Why would we do that? My concern is that Rosemary, for some reason known only to her, made up some of the last entries. Wait – are you thinking that Emma forged part of the diary?"

"Well," I answered, "forgery seems to be one of her talents." Then I told him about 'diary' being consistently misspelled as 'dairy' beginning in July 1960. "Would your movie folks be willing to spring for a handwriting analyst?"

"Tony, money to these gentlemen is not a problem," he quipped. "Go ahead and line something up if you can." This from a guy who enjoyed any number of gratis Bloody Marys. I surely did not want to get stuck with the bill for a handwriting analyst.

Chapter Thirteen

I filled in Dustin on my conversation with Teddy on the way to the Ascension Parish jail Wednesday morning. We agreed that before we'd try to find someone to examine the diary entries for possible forgery we would see what we could squeeze out of Emma St. Pierre.

Both of us had been to this facility to visit an inmate before today. As it happens, we both, at different times and under different circumstances, had mentored young men who ended up spending some time in the Ascension Parish jail. I'm not sure what that says about our mentoring acuity, but you probably won't see it bragged about on our resumés, or in our eventual obituaries for that matter.

We parked in one of the Visitor spots, walked through the glass door that had Ascension Parish Prison stenciled at eye level, presented our IDs at the window, and told the attendant who we were there to see. We were told that Emma would be escorted into room C and we were directed where to go. We waited in a small room that had two metal folding chairs and a phone hanging on the wall next to a reinforced glass partition. On the other side of the glass partition was a larger room with a door through which, just as we sat down, Emma St. Pierre was brought in.

In spite of the prison garb and dark hair pulled back into a tight ponytail, it was clear that Emma was an attractive young woman, maybe about 5'6" tall and thin. She sat across from us and picked up the receiver on her side. Dustin did the same and held the phone between us so that we could both hear Emma and ask her questions.

"Who are you guys?" was Emma's predictable question.

"We're friends of Mayor Strong and his daughter Stacy told us where you were," I answered. "How are you doing?" That sounded pretty lame, but what else do you say to someone in jail?

"I'm alright," she replied. "It's not that bad in here. I'm eating more than I did on the outside. Are y'all here to help me? I could sure use some money in my account here."

I looked at Dustin and we silently agreed to put something in Emma's account. We'd done the same thing before for the kids we mentored, probably out of guilt for not doing a better job.

"We'll add funds to your account when we finish talking to you," I told her. "We just wanted to ask you some questions about your godmother, Rosemary Rizzo...I mean, Rosemary Doiron."

"You mean Aunt Rosemary?" she asked. "I mean, she wasn't really my aunt, but that's what I called her. I was only about 8 years old when she died."

"Yes," I said, "your Aunt Rosemary. We've been working with Teddy Toombs on a movie based mostly on your aunt's diary. We understand that you found the diary among your grandma's things after she passed away."

"Yeah," Emma replied, "I was going through her cedar chest a few years after my Memaw died and I found this diary. I thought at first that it was Memaw's, but after I read some of it I realized it belonged to my Aunt Rosemary." Then she added, "Say, can you talk to Teddy about getting me more money or maybe bailing me out? I don't know when I'm supposed to go to court. I might be here a while."

"Sure," I said, "I'll talk to him. He didn't know you were in jail until yesterday. Maybe he can do something for you. We'll ask him."

Then Dustin asked, "Emma, do you remember your grandmother talking about your Aunt Rosemary having anything to do with Elvis Presley?"

"Oh sure," she said confidently. "Memaw had lung cancer and was on oxygen most of the time. I would sit with her and read her the newspaper and People Magazine and stuff like that. One day I read to her something about Elvis' daughter being a singer somewhere in Vegas, I think, and Memaw said, 'Do you know that Elvis almost married your Aunt Rosemary?' I said, 'What are you talking about, Memaw?' And she told me about how Aunt Rosemary met Elvis and how he said he loved her and wanted to marry her. Heck, if he hadn't died, he might be my uncle!"

She chuckled at that and so did we. I asked her, "Emma, how did you come to be raised by your grandmother?"

"Memaw and Papaw only had one son, my daddy, Jacques – but he went by Jack," she answered. "He got my momma pregnant when they were both 16. They wanted to put me up for adoption, but my Memaw took me. My momma and daddy split up right after I was born. I didn't know any of this until I was 12 years old. I don't know where momma is. Daddy works offshore, three weeks on, one week off. He stays in Chalmette."

Dustin asked, "When did your grandmother pass away?"

"She died in 2010 when I was thirteen, right after my birthday," she replied. "She left the house to my daddy, so he comes here when he's off work sometimes."

"So you've been pretty much living alone since you were thirteen?" I asked.

Emma said, "I have friends stay over sometimes and daddy comes in once in a while. It's not bad. It's a nice house and all out on the 308 on Bayou Lafourche."

Then Dustin asked her, "Emma, what did you get arrested for?"

"Oh, they said I forged some checks but that's not true," she said defensively. "That lady owed me some money for some housework I did for her, but she didn't have any cash so she wrote me a couple of checks. Then she denied doing it and said I stole checks out of her purse or something."

"Well," I said as we got up to leave, "like I said, we'll talk to Teddy and maybe he can do something for you."

Emma stood up also, waved to us as she turned around, then Dustin asked her, "Emma, can you read and write okay?"

"Oh sure," she said. "I finished the 10th grade. They said I can work on getting a GED in here, but I hope I'm not in here that long."

Dustin then asked, "Can you spell something for me?"

Emma looked at him quizzically and said, "What?"

"Can you spell the word 'diary,' as in the diary that your Aunt Rosemary kept?" he asked her.

"Why?" she wanted to know.

Dustin replied, "Just wanted to see if you really finished 10th grade."

She looked peeved but answered, "D-A-I-R-Y. Is that good enough for you?"

"That's perfect," we said in unison and left the building and headed back across the river.

Chapter Fourteen

Dustin and I were now pretty convinced that Emma had forged at least the last few diary entries, but to prove it we'd need a handwriting expert to compare Rosemary's earlier entries with the latest.

"How do we go about finding an expert to analyze the handwriting in the diary?" I thought out loud.

Dustin snapped his fingers and said, "I'll bet Alden knows how to find one. They must use them all the time in court as expert witnesses."

"Let's give him a call right now," I suggested. I was driving, so Dustin looked up Alden's mobile number and called. Alden surprised both of us when he answered the phone. We were expecting to have to leave a message.

"What can I do you for?" was Alden's classic reply.

We told him about Emma being in jail for forgery and our suspicion that she was the one to write the last few diary entries but that we needed to prove it.

"A handwriting analyst can't prove anything. He or she can only give their opinion about whether or not the handwriting is forged," Alden told us.

"That's good enough for me," I said. I didn't know if it would be good enough for the movie people. "Do you know somebody?"

"We don't have a lot of need for that sort of expert around here very much," Alden replied. "The forgery cases we've had in Ascension have involved people stupid enough to get caught for other reasons. But I have a couple of names for you. I'll text them to y'all."

"Great, thanks a bunch," I said. "See you Friday morning."

A few minutes later, both of our phones pinged.

"He sent us two contacts," Dustin informed me as he opened them. "Looks like one is in New Orleans and the other in Baton Rouge. Both are women. Hey, guess what their titles are. Both of them are listed as a 'Certified Forensic Document Examiner.'"

"Shoot," I said. "A title like that means they're going to be expensive. Let's try the one in Baton Rouge first."

Dustin made the call and, after explaining what we needed to the receptionist, he was put through to Ms. Wanda Peterson. "This is Wanda Peterson," she greeted him. "How can I help you?"

After a detailed explanation from Dustin, she said, "So you want me to determine if later entries in this diary were written by the same person as the earlier entries, right? Can I assume that the person who began the diary is no longer with us?"

"That's correct," Dustin told her. "She died in 2005. We think – we suspect – that the later entries were made in the last few months."

"Comparison of the ink alone may be of some use. In my experience, women who keep diaries – and they're mostly kept by women – use the same pen until it runs out of ink," Wanda informed us. "I assume that you have the original diary."

Oops. We hadn't thought of that. "No," Dustin told her. "We have only black and white copies. Can you do anything with that?"

"Maybe," she answered. "It depends upon how clever the forger is."

Not so clever, I thought to myself. She's in jail.

Wanda told us that her fee for doing such an analysis would be $400, but she warned that we might be wasting our money if we didn't have the original diary. Dustin thanked her and said we'd get back to her about it.

"What should we do?" he asked me as he disconnected from Wanda Peterson.

"We're not going to be able to get the original diary, that's for sure," I answered. "Let's call Teddy and see what he thinks."

By this time we were at the Cajun Village and decided to stop for coffee and beignets. Neither of us had had breakfast. Of course, it was almost 11:00 a.m., so it would be brunch I guess.

We put in our orders for beignets, got our coffees, and sat and waited in the dining area. I gave Teddy a call. "Tony, I was hoping to hear from you," he said. "What did our jailbird have to say?"

"She told a pretty convincing tale about reading to her dying grandmother," I told him. "She says that her grandmother told her that Elvis almost married Rosemary." Then I told Teddy about the spelling test Dustin gave to Emma.

"Isn't that most interesting," was his response. "So, I gather that you two are convinced that Emma forged the diary."

"Yes, we feel pretty sure about it," I answered. "But proving it is another matter. We spoke to a handwriting expert in Baton Rouge and she says we probably need to have the original document to be sure about it."

Teddy responded, "This is a dilemma. I'm afraid that getting our hands on the original diary is not in the cards for us. Is there any other way to resolve this?"

"We can have the handwriting expert look at the copies," I suggested, "but she told us that it might be a waste of $400, especially if the forgery is a good one."

Without hesitation Teddy said, "Let's do it. When can you get your copies of the diary pages to her?"

"I'll have to call and make an appointment, I guess," was my reply. Then I cautiously added, "How do you want to pay for this?"

"Do you think she would bill me for it?" Teddy asked.

"Her website says something about having to pay before getting the results," I answered.

"Tony, if you go ahead and pay for the service, I'll reimburse you in cash," Teddy offered. "Just bring back a copy of her invoice."

I then suggested, "Why don't you tell the people who have the original diary to have it analyzed? That has a better chance of a resolution than having someone look at a copy."

I could almost hear Teddy shaking his head. "As I may have mentioned before, the people I'm dealing with want the story to be true. They are not interested in proving it to be a lie, in spite of my cautions about the possible repercussions."

Dustin called Wanda Peterson's office and she agreed to see us at 9:00 a.m. on Thursday. I met Dustin at 8:15 the next morning at the Starbucks on Hwy 73. I left my truck and he drove us to downtown Baton Rouge. We parked in a lot near Poor Boy Lloyd's on Florida and walked to Wanda's office on 3rd Street. She was in one of the older buildings on 3rd, with a tiny old elevator that we took to the third floor. We were surprisingly early given the amount of traffic and the construction on I-10. We lost most of that time in what must be the slowest elevator in Louisiana. Even when it finally reached the 3rd floor, it was very reluctant to open its doors. When we exited the elevator, the signage on the wall facing us led us to believe that we needed to go down the hall to the right – but that got us to the ladies' restroom. We backtracked and were able to stumble upon the men's room down another hallway.

Our third try found us entering an unmarked door that turned out to be the office of "Madam Morvant, Palmist and Phrenologist." Fortunately, without the benefit of reading either our palms or the bumps on our heads, Madam Morvant was able to show us the way to Wanda Peterson's office. It turned out to be on the second floor. The sign in the lobby had her address wrong. We advised the gum-chewing receptionist as we finally walked into the right office and she said, "No kidding. I'll tell Ms. Peterson that you're here." Then she showed us into a small conference room, snapping her gum the entire time. We could hear her tell Wanda Peterson that "some old men are here to see you."

We sat and I took out the copies of the diary pages sent to us. Dustin and I were looking over some of the older diary entries when Wanda Peterson walked in. She was a tall, jaw-dropping gorgeous brunette, dressed in a navy-blue skirt and matching jacket over a crème-colored blouse. Her very high heels clicked on the hardwood floor as she approached us with her hand outstretched.

"Hi," she smiled and greeted us. "I'm Wanda Peterson. Wanda to you. I'm very glad to meet you."

Stammering, we introduced ourselves. "Tony Campachi, just Tony," and, "Dustin, Dustin Sonnier, nice to meet you also."

"I apologize for my niece," Wanda told us. "My usual receptionist is on maternity leave and Mandy needed something to do for the summer."

"That's quite alright," I said, when I found my voice. "I'm sure she's a sweet girl."

"No," she countered, "She's not. But thanks anyway. I see that you brought the copies of the diary pages you mentioned. Let's take a quick look."

Wanda studied the pages, asking us questions while doing so. She then took one of the early pages and one of the latest, scanned them both, and projected the images side by side on a widescreen TV in the conference room.

"If this page," she said, pointing to the later entry, "is a forgery, it's a very good one. As I mentioned when I first spoke to you, having the originals is always preferable to copies."

"So you can't really tell us for sure if the later one was forged or not?" asked Dustin.

"Not with any degree of confidence," she replied. Seeing the look of dejection on our faces, she added, "Bring me the originals if you can get them. This story is very intriguing. I'd like to hear how it comes out. I'm not going to charge you for looking at these copies today."

We thanked her profusely as we got up to leave, promised her that we'd let her know what happens, and wished her luck with her recalcitrant niece.

Dustin had an idea on the drive back to Ascension Parish. "Hey, do you remember how we resolved the Elms on the Hill dog doodoo problem?"

"Yeah," I answered, "we lied about threatening to get DNA from their dogs. How is lying about DNA going to help us with this forgery business?"

"It's got nothing to do with DNA," he said. "We go back to the jail to see Emma and tell her that we had a Certified Forensic Document Examiner look at the diary pages and that she said they were forgeries. She might fess up if she hears that."

I thought about it for just a minute and agreed that it might work.

The only thing that bothered me, though, is that neither of us is a good liar. "Maybe we ought to get Alden to do it. He's an attorney. He's good at lying."

"No way he'll do it though," lamented Dustin. "He wouldn't take a chance on losing his license."

"I think that if we practiced, we could pull it off," I said with a confidence that I didn't feel.

So we resolved to visit Emma and give her the fake bad news.

Chapter Fifteen

We called our wives on the way in and they met us at Las Palmas in Dutchtown. We ordered and, as we chowed down on chips and salsa, we told them about going to Wanda Peterson's office and about our deceitful plan for the afternoon. They were somewhat dubious, but couldn't find a major flaw except for the fact that we were terrible liars. We promised to practice our spiel on the way to the jail.

"I can tell you what's going to happen when you meet with her, if she has any brains at all," Darlene said, as she lifted her frozen Margarita with two hands. "First, she's going to deny forging the diary. Second, she's going to want to see the report that this forensic person came up with." She then took a sip of her drink.

"And third?" I asked, because it sounded like there was going to be a "third."

"There is no third," she said, "You're dead in the water after "second."

Then Connie added, "She's already in jail for forgery, so what can you threaten her with?"

Dustin and I looked at each other. That was a good point.

"Maybe we could tell her that if she tells us the truth, Teddy would bail her out," I suggested.

"But would he?" Darlene asked.

Dustin responded, "I guess we'll have to ask him."

We paid the bill and Dustin and I left Connie and Darlene at the table to finish their drinks. I offered to drive to Donaldsonville, so we picked up my truck at Starbucks and left Dustin's car. If they ever checked their surveillance cameras they'd wonder if we were casing the joint, selling drugs, or what. Dustin called Teddy as we left the parking lot and headed to the Parish jail and filled him in on the plan.

"I think that your proposed prevarication might very well succeed," Teddy responded, but he clearly lacked enthusiasm. "Perhaps if I join you in the visit and agree that I would bail her out if she was completely honest with us, our chances may improve."

We agreed with Teddy's strategy, picked him up at Donaldsonville City Hall, and backtracked to the jail. It was nearly 2:00 p.m. when we checked in as visitors. We were told that Emma was in the exercise yard along with other female prisoners but that someone would go and fetch her for us as we waited in the visiting room.

When Emma finally walked in and spotted Teddy on the other side of the glass, she smiled broadly, grabbed the phone receiver on her side, and motioned for Teddy to do the same. He obliged and she said excitedly, loudly enough for us all to hear, "Teddy, did you come to bail me out?"

"Well, we'll see about that, won't we Emma?" Teddy replied. "How are you? Why, I am certain that you look much better than when I last saw you! I do believe that this place suits you!"

"I've been eating better in here than on the outside, that's for sure," Emma said, patting her very flat stomach. "So can you get me out?"

Both Emma and Teddy had been standing during this conversation. Then Teddy sat and motioned Emma to do the same. "Emma, I promise you that if you are completely honest with me, regardless of what the truth may be, I will arrange to bail you out. Do you understand what I'm telling you?"

Emma nodded twice.

Then, pointing to Dustin and me, Teddy said, "These gentlemen, at my direction, have taken your Aunt Rosemary's diary to a – Tony, what did you call her?"

"Ms. Peterson is a Certified Forensic Document Examiner," I replied.

"Yes, they have taken the diary to a Certified Forensic Document Examiner," Teddy repeated, "and she has determined, and is willing to testify, that the diary entries from July 5, 1960 on to the end of the diary were, in fact, forgeries."

We were all looking at Emma to see her reaction to this news, but she didn't bat an eye. Completely stone-faced. I bet she's good at poker.

Teddy continued, "Emma, I need to know if you are the person who forged those entries. Be straight with me, now."

Emma looked straight at Teddy without saying anything for what seemed like forever. Then she calmly said, "Yes, I wrote those pages. But all I was doing was putting in the diary the stuff that my Memaw told me before she died."

Pulling thoughtfully on his goatee, Teddy stated, "Emma, you told me that you were about 13 when your grandmother passed. Now we know that these diary entries that you admit to forging were added in just the past few months. Are you telling me that you remembered everything that your grandmother told you years ago?"

"I have a very good memory," Emma weakly whispered to him.

"Do you now! Then do you recall what I said just a few minutes ago, about you being completely honest with me as a condition of your release?" Teddy whispered back.

Emma's shoulders dropped and she lowered her head. "Okay. Okay, okay, I admit I made the stuff up. What else do you want from me? A signed confession or something?"

"I don't want anything else from you, Emma," said Teddy with sympathy. "I'll keep my promise and put up bail for you, but you promise me that you'll make your court date and not skip out."

"Teddy, I got nowhere to go," replied Emma, near tears. "Will they make me give back the money they gave me? I'll tell you right now, I don't have it. It's long gone."

"No," replied Teddy. "I think that I can convince them not to pursue any action against you. I don't think it would be worth their time and effort to do so. My advice to you is to get yourself a job and straighten out your life."

We walked out and Teddy spoke to the clerk about what he needed to do to post bail for Emma. On the ride back to City Hall I asked him what would happen with plans for the movie.

"I can tell you right now that the money people are going to pull out," Teddy told us. "This has not turned out to be the story that they envisioned building a movie around. It might still be an interesting movie, but now filled with intrigue and crime instead of love and tragedy. But, you never know...."

"So, is that it?" asked Dustin. "We just drop everything?"

"For now, gentlemen, for now," Teddy lamented. "I will have to find new backers, ones that believe this story, as it has unfolded, is still sellable. I can tell you this – it will not be a Hallmark movie."

Chapter Sixteen

The next morning found Dustin and me gathering at Frank's with the MOSS, bowed down, beaten, and humbled by our experience. In spite of the fact that we had tried our hardest to prove that Emma forged the diary, we really wanted the story to be true for the sake of our hometown. Because of our efforts in exposing Emma as a liar and the diary as a forgery, the movie that would "put Donaldsonville on the map" was a gone pecan. The town was once again relegated to its has-been status and would wait in quiet obscurity for someone else to resurrect it from the ash pile. We had such high hopes. It was just depressing.

Even Uncle Joe, who had ridden to Frank's with Jack Roussel, tried to cheer me up. "Your Aunt Millie said to tell you that she's real sorry that Emma girl made a fool out of you. She wants you to stop by the house – she made you and Darlene a muffuletta."

That did cheer me up a little. Aunt Millie's muffuletta is serious comfort food. She makes the best one I've ever tasted, and that includes the ones from Central Grocery in the French Quarter. She might be a French girl from Vacherie, but she sure can cook Italian – thanks to my Mawmaw Campachi, who lived with my aunt and uncle for years before she passed away. That muffuletta would go great later for cocktail night as I drowned my guilt and sorrow in gin.

Teddy and Mayor Strong surprised us by dropping in on the MOSS gathering at about 8:00 a.m. The mayor was bringing Teddy to the Baton Rouge airport. Teddy told us that he would have his screening scheduler contact everyone who was to be interviewed next week and cancel due to "unforeseen circumstances." I introduced him to the guys and he told everyone that he was heading to the greener pastures of Tuscaloosa, Alabama, where he would be talking to Nick Saban about doing a movie based on his life in football. That made us even more depressed.

They had some time to kill, so the mayor and Teddy sat with us and had coffee. I offered to get Teddy a Bloody Mary, but he said, "No, I'd better not. I've been having terrible acid reflux lately. I can't imagine why."

"No, Teddy," I said. "Neither can I."

When they were preparing to leave, I assured Mayor Strong that the MOSS was committed to helping Donaldsonville in some way, and that if he had any ideas, please let us know. He looked around the table at our motley group and shook his head. "I don't know what you boys could do," he said resignedly, "unless you have an extra ten million dollars or so to invest."

"I'll pass the hat," I told him as I walked him and Teddy to the door.

Part Four

Chapter One

Sometimes God, in his infinite wisdom, humbles us by allowing the world to kick us in soft spots while we're already writhing on the ground. The failure of the prospects for a movie in Donaldsonville and our part in it, however innocent, was one of those times. Following are emails I received once it was announced that Elvis and Hollywood had left the building:

"I'm glad that your stupid movie died. My daughter Olivia is still crying because you rejected her. I've called Morris Bart and we're thinking about suing you for mental distress, and for the cost of Olivia's therapy. You'll be sorry." – Camella Langois

"Everybody knows it's your fault Lady Gaga isn't coming to Donaldsonville to make that movie. That might have really helped this town. Thanks for nothing." – Anonymous

*"I was thinking about coming back to kick your a**, but it looks like it's gonna get kicked without my help. If you're smart you better watch your back." – Vinny Voisin*

"While we appreciate your business, we think it's best that you don't frequent the Grapevine until things settle down. See you in six months!" – Grapevine Management

"Someone spray-painted 'MOSS sucks' on the side of our gymnasium. We'd appreciate it if you would have it cleaned off before the start of the Fall semester." – Principal Teri Crocket, ACHS

"We cannot reach Mister Teddy Toombs for payment for advertisements for the past three weeks. He suggested contacting you if he couldn't be reached. The invoice is attached. Thank you for your prompt attention." – Editor, The Donaldsonville Chief

"A Miss Emma St. Pierre has listed you as a reference. Please call us or drop by the Gonzales branch at your earliest convenience to confirm your knowledge of her. Thank you" – Manager, Hancock Whitney Bank

"I wish to withdraw my application to join the MOSS. It's not the group I thought it to be. You all need much more than diversity." – Patricia "Pat" Sigura

There were more, but I just don't have the heart to reproduce them. Darlene tried her best to cheer me up.

"Honey, would you hit some with me this morning?" she asked sweetly. "My tennis league is starting up next Thursday and I haven't played in weeks. I'm worried that playing pickleball might have messed up my game."

"Sure," I answered wearily. "I need to get out of the house and away from the computer anyway."

We changed into shorts and tennis shoes, got our stuff together, jumped in the truck, and headed to the courts in Gonzales. It was a warm July Tuesday, but overcast, so it wasn't a bad day for a little exercise. The courts were empty, so we got one close to where I parked the truck, stretched out a little, and started hitting. I didn't even last an hour. My shirt was soaked, I was out of breath, and as soon as we cooled off a little, everything hurt. I am so out of shape.

At least I had the foresight to bring an extra shirt. I changed in the restroom, and we headed just up Burnside Avenue to the Starlight Café for a light lunch. Darlene also had foresight. She brought Advil in her purse. She didn't need any, but I took two and downed them with my unsweet tea.

"I thought that you hit the ball really well," I told her. "I don't think pickleball hurt your strokes at all."

"I guess not," she replied. "I ought to be okay for next week. We're playing at Bocage on clay, so it's slower, and that helps."

"I have to start getting more exercise," I said. "I feel like a slug. Walking nine holes on the golf course once every three weeks or so just doesn't cut it."

"Instead of eating biscuits and gravy at Frank's every week, you should get your MOSS guys to go for a walk," she suggested.

"If I tell those guys that we should go for a walk for exercise, they would tell me to go take a walk alright – a long walk off of a short pier," I responded. "I have to think of something else for the MOSS to do after that fiasco with the movie."

"Don't some of them play tennis? You could always put a senior team together. It would be good exercise for those guys," she said. "Hey, remember when you were Tennis Chairman at Driftwood when we lived in Kenner?"

I remembered. Of course, we were much younger then. I was a mediocre tennis player, but I was pretty good at writing the tennis newsletter. I think that's why I got the job. When we finished lunch and got back to the house, I looked in a file I keep labeled "Things I Wrote." There were some articles in Engineering News and a few other technical magazines, and in amongst everything else were a few copies of the Driftwood Park Country Club newsletter. It was on those pages I first tried my hand at poetry. My efforts, reproduced below, were less than legendary.

"Fuzzy" by Tony Campachi

O fuzzy yellow tennis ball,

Don't you have a brain at all?

I try to hit you on the strings

But then you flap your fuzzy wings

And hit the frame (and oh that stings!)

I hate you fuzzy yellow things.

O fuzzy yellow tennis sphere,

Is that a snicker that I hear?

I try to smash you o'er the net

I swing and air is all I get.

The one thing that I most regret

I haven't killed the darned thing yet.

O fuzzy yellow tennis orb,

What pain and anguish I absorb.

A lesson that I've oft repeated,

To hold my tongue when I'm defeated,

Despite the fact that I've been cheated

By a fuzzy (expletive deleted).

"The Lob" by Tony Campachi

We stride upon the court with grace,

Muscles rippling, stern of face,

Prepared to strike the ball with pace,

Instead are greeted with the dreaded lob.

We grit our teeth and so appear

So confident and void of fear.

We whisper so no one can hear,

"Please God don't let me miss this stupid lob."

We arch our backs and hide the pain

Of muscles tearing with the strain,

Then swing and find we prayed in vain

As we completely swish a simple lob.

I analyzed the thing and saw

That tennis has this single flaw.

I think there ought to be a law

Which bans once and for all the evil lob.

I showed them to Darlene. "Oh yeah, I remember you writing that. Pretty funny," was all she had to say.

"Maybe I should start writing again," I ventured. "You know, funny stuff. I could do a blob."

"Do you mean 'blog'?" she asked. I think she was smirking.

"Yeah, blog, isn't that what I said? I could do a blog," I reiterated.

Darlene shot back with, "Do you even know what a blog is or how to start one?"

"No," I replied, but with dignity. "I don't, but I'm sure I could learn."

"You know," she said, "not everyone gets your sense of humor."

"My daughters like my sense of humor," I shot back defensively.

"They're your daughters," was Darlene's reply to that and walked away, like that was the last word on the subject. I don't know if she meant that the girls inherited my sense of humor or if they were just being condescending because I'm their dad.

I decided that I would explore this blog idea. I'm sure that one of my grandkids would know how to start one. But in the meantime, I had to come up with something else for the MOSS to do. This time it had to be something that would involve all of us. I went back to the emails I'd received to see if we'd overlooked any ideas. I found one from Mr. Raymond Sedgewick, a resident at the Bayou Manchac Retirement Home. He suggested that the MOSS visit the home to talk to people who were older and wiser than we were – and that we might learn something.

I came to the unpleasant realization only recently that wherever I went, except for the MOSS gatherings, I was almost always the oldest person in the room. That was true at my church, my Rotary club, the company that I occasionally represented, and even the parish council meetings. I wouldn't mind NOT being the oldest person in the room somewhere. That somewhere might just be the Bayou Manchac Retirement Home.

Mr. Sedgewick didn't leave his number, so I looked up the place on the internet, found their webpage, and called. Ms. Jennifer 'Jenny'

Landry was listed as the manager, so I figured I'd ask for her. I was expecting one of those automated answering systems that would give me a choice of various extensions, but instead, an actual live person answered, "Bayou Manchac Retirement Home, how can I help you?"

She took me by surprise. I cleared my throat and probably scared the heck out of her, then I said, "May I please speak to Ms. Landry?"

"Do you mean our resident Mrs. Herman Landry, Mrs. Cecilia Landry, or our manager Ms. Jenny Landry?" she politely asked.

"Jenny Landry, please," I clarified. I forgot just how many Landrys are in Ascension Parish.

The receptionist said, "One moment please, I'll see if she's in," and in just about one moment, however long that is, Jenny Landry was on the line.

"This is Jenny Landry, can I help you?" Another really polite voice. I liked the place already.

"Jenny, I'm Tony Campachi, and I represent the MOSS, which stands for 'Men of Sixty Something.' I got an email a while back from one of your residents, Mr. Raymond Sedgewick. He suggested that we might pay a visit to the place and talk to some of the residents."

Jenny said excitedly, "I know about your group! My Aunt Wendy is a waitress at Frank's and, I swear, y'all are all she talks about when I see her. Y'all gave her a really nice present last Christmas."

Every December I start a collection from the guys to give to Wendy for Christmas. Last year it was over $300. "I can't believe Wendy is your aunt! What a small world, huh?"

"It sure is," she said. "Would you believe that there are four Landrys who are residents here, they didn't know each other before coming here, and none of them knows my daddy's family. We're probably all related somehow, though."

"So you're not married to a Landry then?" I asked.

"No, sir, I'm not married yet," she answered. "I'm engaged, though. We're getting married on my 30th birthday next May." *Dang. She's way younger than both of my daughters,* I thought to myself.

"It's funny that you called," Jenny continued. "I asked my Aunt Wendy if y'all would consider coming over here for breakfast – on us – maybe once or twice a month to visit with the male residents. It's a shame, but they don't get many visitors and we always fix extra for breakfast. I think Aunt Wendy didn't want to take business away from Frank's and she would be giving up her tips once a month, too."

"I'll tell you what," I said. "I'll pass the idea by the group this Friday. If they're interested, I'll call you."

"All I need to know is if and when y'all are coming and how many," Jenny said with excitement in her voice. "We serve breakfast in the main dining room between 7:30 and 9:00."

Then I asked her how many of us they could accommodate for breakfast and she suggested no more than six. I was pretty sure I could get six of the MOSS interested in a free breakfast.

Chapter Two

I picked up Uncle Joe on Friday morning and mentioned what I planned to suggest to the MOSS. I would see if there was any interest in forming a senior tennis team that would compete with other such teams in the area. I would also see what the MOSS thought about visiting the male residents of the Bayou Manchac Retirement Home once a month instead of going to Frank's. I suggested that it would be fun.

"I got something to say about your so-called fun ideas," he began, ticking them off on his fingers. "Number one, as you know, I am an athlete. No real athlete would stoop so low as to play tennis. It's a stupid game, it's not a sport at all because you don't ever hit anybody, and the only game stupider than tennis is golf. And B, what was the other thing? Oh yeah, I remember now. The Bayou Manchac old folk's home. I'm pretty sure I know some guys there. We would go for breakfast?"

I said, "Yes."

Uncle Joe followed up with, "How much do they charge for breakfast?"

"It's free for us," I answered.

"I'm in," was all he had left to say on the subject.

We walked into the gathering to shouts of "Look, it's Elvis! Get his autograph" and "We were betting whether or not you would show up today. Odds were 5 to 4 against" and "Wendy told us that one of the cooks is from Donaldsonville and that you didn't let his granddaughter be in the movie." My hopes that the movie thing would be quickly and quietly forgotten were dashed.

Wendy brought me my coffee. She had pre-heated the mug and I loved her for that. She stood behind my chair for a moment and placed a sympathetic hand on my shoulder. She gave me a couple of pats and walked away to refill the coffee pot she carried. She seemed to understand my pain. That's more than I can say for my other friends and even my family.

Once the guys settled down and were served their various

breakfast choices, which ranged from an order of raisin toast to Crab Cakes Benedict and everything in between, I got down to business. To get everyone in a positive frame of mind, I called for attention, and asked Dr. Dart to update us on the status of establishing a branch of the community college in Donaldsonville. I was hoping that good news would deflect other criticisms lurking just below the surface.

"Thank you, Tony," began Dr. Dart. "I really appreciate that. A lot of progress has been made, and I'm excited about what's happening on the west bank. As most of you know, we will set up shop in a building loaned to us until our new building is completed. We are on schedule to start a limited number of classes, including a GED class, in late August. Our architect has completed the plans for the new building, which will be located on Mississippi Street just across from the Ascension Public Library. We expect to advertise for bids soon and have a contractor on site and begin construction in three months or so. Does anyone have any questions?"

There were a few questions regarding the types of courses offered, whether he would be hiring additional staff, whether high school kids from Donaldsonville could take courses there, and other such things. Everybody seemed really interested and excited about how this could help Donaldsonville residents. It established a good mood in the group, hopefully making it easier to pitch my ideas without being shot down in flames in the first minute.

I tapped on my coffee cup with my spoon and, of course, spilled coffee on my ham biscuit. "Guys, I have a couple of ideas I'd like to run by y'all to get your opinions."

Uncle Joe leaned back in his chair and muttered, "Oh boy, here we go," loudly enough for everyone to hear.

"I mentioned these ideas to my Uncle Joe on the way over and I can tell you that he's completely behind me on this." *Way, way behind*, I thought to myself.

"Wait, what?" Uncle Joe exclaimed as he almost tilted over backwards, just catching himself – with the help of Wendy, who happened to be behind him.

I continued, "My wife Darlene suggested the first thing – that those of us who play tennis or used to play tennis put a senior team together and get on a regular schedule. Anybody interested?"

Dustin and I used to play in doubles tournaments many moons ago and he said that he was game to give it a try. My brother T-Joe still occasionally hit balls with his grandson and Terry Parmenter was already in a Saturday morning group, but said that he would join in if we made this happen. So there were four of us, a good start. I glanced at Uncle Joe who was just shaking his head back and forth in disgust. I'm pretty sure I saw him mouthing "sissies" under his breath.

Now came the moment of truth. Visiting the residents at the Bayou Manchac Retirement Home. For this one, I stood up to get everyone's full attention. Kevin said, "Tony, on your way to the restroom tell Wendy that I'm still waiting for my side of grits."

"I'm not going to the restroom, Kevin," I told him.

"Well then, while you're up, would you ask Wendy about my grits?" he asked.

The magic of the moment was gone. I found Wendy in the main dining area and asked her to please bring Kevin his stupid grits. Then I realized that I actually did have to go to the restroom. By the time I got back to the gathering, the guys were all talking loudly in small groups and there was no way to reassemble the herd. I went around to Dustin, pulled up a chair from another table, and sat behind him. He was in a lively argument with Slim and Jack about the school board race and who of all of the sundry candidates he thought would be best suited for the job. They seemed to have reached an impasse and, when they stopped to catch their breath, I got Dustin's attention. He swiveled his chair around to face me.

"Hey, what would you think about a few of us going over to the Bayou Manchac Retirement Home once or twice a month for breakfast to visit some of the men there?" I asked. While I was talking I realized that it might not have been wise after all to suggest this to the whole group while Wendy was hovering. "I spoke to the manager there, Jenny Landry. She said some of the guys there never get visitors."

"I know Jenny Landry, if it's the same one I taught at East Ascension. Eighth grade, I think. About how old is she?" he asked.

"She makes 30 next May," I replied.

"Yeah, that's about right. So she wants us old guys to visit her old guys?" he asked smiling.

"Yep," I said, "and we get free breakfast. Uncle Joe already said that he'd go. He thinks he knows some of the guys there. If it wasn't for Aunt Millie, he'd probably be there himself. If you go, we only need two or three more."

"Sure," Dustin said, "I'll go. Do we start next Friday?"

"I'll just have to give Jenny a heads-up on how many to expect," I answered. "And if next Friday is good for her, we'll go."

I went around the table and quietly recruited Jack and Donnie to join us on the following Friday. Donnie's mother-in-law had been a resident there some years back and he had been there for breakfast and lunch a few times, so he knew the lay of the land. After leaving Frank's I called Jenny from my truck to tell her that five of us would be visiting next week. She was thrilled. We agreed on 7:30 a.m. and she gave me the code to the front door in case she wasn't there to let us in.

I drove Uncle Joe home and stopped for a minute just to say "hi" to Aunt Millie. We filled her in on the plan to spend some time with the men at the Bayou Manchac Retirement Home, with Uncle Joe emphasizing the free breakfast aspect of the venture. She loved the idea and she and Uncle Joe talked about the people they knew who were living there. They had heard that it was a very nice place and expensive – a minimum of $5,000 a month for a small apartment for one person. I'd never been in the place, but I had driven by a few times and it certainly looked really nice. I'd have a chance to check it out next Friday as a possible future home for me, Darlene, or both of us if it came to that – and if we could afford it. It all came down to one gruesome detail – how long would we live? I figured we could afford it, but only if we didn't live too long. What a nice thought.

Chapter Three

I picked up Uncle Joe at 7:15 on the following Friday morning and we made the short trip to the Bayou Manchac home by 7:30. It was just starting to rain as I parked the truck and headed to the covered entrance. Donnie and Jack were waiting at the door and Dustin drove up as I was inputting the code to let us in. I held the door for Dustin and the five of us stood at the reception desk. There was a visitor's log book on the counter, so we all added our names, who we were there to visit, and the time we arrived. Since we weren't there to visit anyone in particular, we all just put "men" in that space.

Just as we were finishing, the receptionist walked up to Uncle Joe and me. She had a plate of food covered with a napkin in one hand and a cup of coffee in the other. She put down her breakfast, looked at us, and said, "Welcome! My name is Sadie and Ms. Jenny will be here in a minute to show you around. I just know you'll love what you see!" Then looking at me she added, "We're very pleased that you are considering Bayou Manchac Retirement for your father's new home."

Donnie, Jack, and Dustin started laughing and I thought that my uncle would have another stroke on the spot. The veins in his neck stood out and he gritted his teeth and said to her, "Do I really look to you like I could be this man's father? I'm barely old enough to be his older brother!"

Sadie's eyes widened and she did her best to recover. "Why no, you surely don't look like you could be his father. It's just that I was told to expect a new resident this morning that would be brought in by his son. We didn't know that your brother was bringing you over."

Well that just about did it. Free breakfast or no free breakfast, Uncle Joe was ready to turn on his heels and walk back out to the truck. The guys were trying not to laugh but trying in vain. Thankfully, Jenny Landry walked up to salvage the situation.

"Sadie, these gentlemen have graciously agreed to come here today to visit and have breakfast with some of our male residents." Then turning to Uncle Joe she said, "Mr. Campachi, we're really grateful to you, your nephew, and your friends for coming today. We prepared a special breakfast for you all. Please follow me and I'll introduce you to some of our residents."

Uncle Joe liked the attention and respect he was getting from Jenny – and the fact that she was really cute didn't hurt. He was appeased for the time being.

Jenny brought us into the main dining room where, in the center of the room, four men sat spread out at a large round table that was set for ten. Apparently it had been suggested that they not sit next to each other to allow the MOSS to mingle among them. Jenny introduced the residents to us as we sat down. There was Raymond Sedgewick, the man who emailed me weeks ago, Fortunada "Tuna" Aguillard, Charles "Charlie" Matherne, and Vincent "Matty" Matassa. Uncle Joe immediately went over to Matty Matassa and sat next to him. They didn't recognize each other at first, both having changed a bit over the years, but they knew each other well from the old days. Matty was also from an old family in Donaldsonville.

The rest of us introduced ourselves while my uncle was occupied with Matty Matassa, lightly punching him on the arm, laughing, and having a good old time. Jenny moved off to give us space and to alert the kitchen to our arrival. We were told by Raymond that, if we wanted coffee, it was self-service at the side table, so we each got up, grabbed Community Coffee cardboard cups stacked next to the thermal coffee dispensers, and helped ourselves. All of us drank coffee black like real men – except for Dustin, who liked all of those flavored cream things.

I sat next to Raymond and told him that it was his email to me that prompted me to contact Jenny and arrange this get-together. I showed him the email on my phone and he laughed and said, "I don't have a computer or anything, but I read the newspaper every day and I saw your thing about the MOSS group. I got Sadie to write that email for me. I didn't know when I said that you should come here to talk to people who were older and wiser than you that y'all were so darn old!"

I laughed at that, but then realized that I shouldn't be laughing. All of us MOSS guys looked like we would fit in here just fine. I found out later that Charlie Matherne was younger than all of us, but he sure didn't look like it. He had hereditary health problems exacerbated by an unhealthy lifestyle that landed him at Bayou Manchac. He was just lucky in a way that, with a combination of his savings, insurance, and kids, he could afford to be in such a nice place.

Our breakfast was brought out by two servers as most of us were getting coffee refills. There were mushroom and cheese omelets, thick-cut maple bacon, grits, toast, and jars of Smucker's Pineapple and Strawberry preserves. Two pitchers of orange juice were put on the table, along with small juice glasses. Tabasco and Louisiana Hot Sauce were brought over, and salt and pepper shakers were already on the table. I'm sure that everything was purposely cooked to be rather bland for so-called health reasons, but the condiments helped to make breakfast as good as can be. We chowed down but continued our conversations between bites.

Fortunada "Tuna" Aguillard had a Vietnam Veteran cap on his head and he was telling Dustin and Jack about where he was from, where in Nam he served, and that he was a helicopter pilot there. Raymond, only a few years older than me, was also in the first draft lottery. My lottery number was 341, so I wasn't one of the ones that were drafted. I was at LSU in Air Force ROTC at the time. Raymond, coincidently, was also at LSU and in Air Force ROTC, but was a senior. His lottery number was 39. He said that when he graduated, he immediately enlisted as a 2nd Lieutenant and was trained to be a fighter pilot. His father was a crop duster from New Iberia and Raymond told me that he had his pilot license before he got out of high school.

"So what did you do after the war?" I asked Raymond. I knew that some veterans didn't really like to talk about their war experiences.

"Oh, I got a job with American Airlines after my four years and two tours in Nam," he answered. "I retired from American when I was 59 with over thirty years."

"Wow," I said, "that's a nice career you had. Did they make you retire – I mean, is there an age limit for pilots – or was that your choice?"

He grimaced a bit at that question. "Funny you should ask," he answered. "I could have stayed on till I was 65, but the company – how can I put this – strongly encouraged me to retire. I flew for FedEx for a few more years after that, before I decided to stay grounded. I miss flying, though."

"Wait a minute, back up a second," I said. "When you say 'encouraged you to retire,' what does that mean?"

"Well, back in those days, there weren't very many protections for whistleblowers and such like there are now," Raymond informed me. "The company didn't appreciate what some of the other pilots and I were making noise about."

"You mean stuff like bad working conditions, long hours, stuff like that?" I asked.

"No," he responded. "I mean telling anyone who would listen about our UFO sightings."

Whoa! Now this visit might turn out to be a lot more interesting than I first thought it would.

"So you – you and other pilots – saw stuff in the sky during your flights that you couldn't identify?" I asked.

Raymond smiled and said, "And that's why they call them Unidentified Flying Objects. Actually, nowadays they refer to these things as UAPs – Unidentified Aerial Phenomena. I guess that sounds more sophisticated and scientific. And, I suppose, using the term UAP is more inclusive. Anything that happens in the atmosphere – or out of it for that matter – that can't be explained can also fall under the aerial phenomena umbrella."

Recalling something that I heard on the radio this morning, I said, "I heard something in the news today about NASA and UFO's but I can't recall what it was about."

"NASA has put a team together to seriously study the nature of these UAPs," Raymond informed me. "They finally have to admit that every sighting can't be a weather balloon or swamp gas. They're not willing to say these UAPs have anything to do with extraterrestrial life, though. I think that if they find out aliens are involved, there's going to be a huge government cover-up."

It was almost 9:00 a.m. by this time and the staff needed to clean up the dining room, so we said our goodbyes and promised to be back. I talked to Jenny on the way out and suggested that maybe a couple of the MOSS guys could come every Friday. We could rotate who came. She loved the idea of someone coming weekly instead of having to wait a whole month. I said that I'd work on it and get back to her. This was my chance to do a spreadsheet! There was nothing I liked better to do on a computer than create a spreadsheet. My oldest daughter

Gasper A. Chifici

Elizabeth occasionally reminds me of how crazy I made her when she was looking at colleges by putting a spreadsheet analysis together with point values for various aspects of each college – such as distance to travel home, cost per semester, scholarship opportunities, academic reputation, friends who were going there, and a myriad of other criteria. Actually, what I was so obviously trying to do was to convince her of the advantages of attending LSU. It didn't work, of course. It didn't put me off of spreadsheets, though.

Chapter Four

That night at Dustin and Connie's we discussed the visit to the Bayou Manchac Retirement Home, as I enjoyed my usual Bombay Sapphire martini with garlic-stuffed olives and the other three had some fancy shmancy drink made with prosecco and some orange-colored stuff called Aperol in champagne glasses. Connie and Darlene thought that, while it was nice that we would visit these men who may not have many visitors otherwise, they both believed that inviting us over for free breakfast was a ploy to get us to consider moving in when the time was right.

"Do you mean to say that you think they consciously have a long-term investment strategy to lure us over there?" I asked.

Darlene responded, "I wouldn't call it long-term exactly. We can't be that much younger than some of their residents."

This was true. Uncle Joe was probably close to the average age of the men there. The women were, of course, older, and there were a lot more of them. Such is life. Women live longer than men. This is not to suggest that women have an easier, less stressful life than do their male counterparts. At least I'm not suggesting that. Nor am I suggesting that women purposely kill off their mates. I would never suggest that. I don't think that they do it on purpose.

"I was talking to this guy Roger Sedgewick," I commented. "He's the one who emailed me a while back suggesting that we ought to go visit the home. He was a pilot with American Airlines and he said that he was strongly 'encouraged' to retire early because he claimed he saw UFOs, and he wouldn't shut up about it."

"And they made him retire because of that?" Connie asked.

I responded, "He didn't say he was exactly forced to retire, just strongly encouraged. And he wasn't the only one. He told me that other pilots also reported UFOs – actually he said that they call them UAPs nowadays – Unidentified Aerial Phenomena."

"Did he tell you what he and the other pilots saw?" asked Dustin.

"No," I replied, "he didn't have a chance to. It was getting late and we had to leave. I talked to Jenny Landry on the way out, though, and she said that they'd love to have a couple of us come every week. I thought I'd see who was interested and put a spreadsheet together."

"You and your spreadsheets," Darlene smirked. "Elizabeth still reminds me about what you put her through when she was looking at colleges." Then of course Darlene had to retell the story to Dustin and Connie, who I'm pretty sure had heard it before maybe a dozen times.

The discussion then turned to UFOs, whether there could be life on other planets, could Satan be behind it all to deceive us, and couldn't most of the so-called sightings be easily explained as natural occurrences or human contrivances?

"Raymond mentioned that NASA was putting a team together to study this stuff," I recalled. "Apparently there are a lot of things that have been seen that no one has been able to explain."

Dustin pulled out his laptop and searched for NASA + UAP and found what Raymond told me to be true. A team of 16 people from all sorts of scientific and academic backgrounds, including even a former NASA astronaut, had been put together to study events in the atmosphere that couldn't be identified as any kind of known aircraft and have didn't have any sort of natural explanation.

This got us talking about movies. *E.T. the Extra-Terrestrial* was the consensus favorite. Dustin and I liked *2001: A Space Odyssey* and our wives hated it. All of us cringed at *Alien* – too scary. Everyone liked the original *The Day the Earth Stood Still* and no one liked the remake. *Guardians of the Galaxy* was a close second to *E.T.* Both the original *War of the Worlds* and the remake with Tom Cruise passed muster, but the blood-sucking machine in the remake was a little much.

The night was young, so we decided to watch *E.T.* since Dustin and Connie had it on DVD. They hadn't used the DVD player in a while, so I fixed another batch of frou-frou drinks for the other three, freshened up my martini, and Connie made microwave popcorn while Dustin figured out how to get the DVD player working. As we watched the 1982 film, we all agreed that Steven Spielberg was ahead of his time back then – and probably still is today. We had all forgotten that Drew Barrymore was the little girl in the movie, making us all feel ancient. All in all, it was a good night.

Chapter Five

The week flew by, as time seems to do at our age, and Uncle Joe and I talked about our time at Bayou Manchac Retirement Home the previous Friday on our way to gather at Frank's. He had had a good time talking to Matty Matassa about growing up in Donaldsonville, playing football together when Matty was a senior and Uncle Joe a sophomore at ACHS, cruising the avenue, going to the Chance, and working for their respective families – both were in the produce business, which means they bought and resold fruit and vegetables.

I was just telling Uncle Joe about my conversations with Raymond Sedgewick as we arrived at Frank's, when he said, "Matty told me to watch out for that guy Raymond. He said that he was crazy."

"He seemed normal to me," I said, somewhat defensively, as I opened the side door and waved Uncle Joe in ahead of me.

"Oh yeah?" Uncle Joe shot back. "Does thinking that some of the other residents there are aliens seem normal to you?"

"I'm sure you must have heard Matty wrong," I responded as we sat down.

"Heard Matty wrong about what?" asked Donnie who was huddled down in an LSU sweatshirt with the hood up. I'll really have to talk to Frank again about that thermostat.

I answered Donnie with, "You know that guy I was talking to the whole time at the home last Friday?" Donnie nodded. "His name is Raymond. He's a veteran and was a pilot in Vietnam. Then he flew planes for American Airlines. Uncle Joe says that Matty called Raymond crazy."

"Well, did he?" Donnie asked, directing the question to Uncle Joe.

"Yeah," Uncle Joe answered. "I did not hear him wrong. Matty said that this guy Raymond sees aliens around every corner at the home. Does that sound normal to you?"

Jack, who was sitting on the other side of Donnie, heard parts of the conversation. "Joe, that guy Raymond is a Nam Veteran. You need to cut him some slack."

Uncle Joe didn't like to be reprimanded, so he huffed a bit and retorted, "I'm not the one who called the man crazy. It was Matty Matassa – and Matty has been living there with him for…well, I don't know for how long, but for a while anyway, so he knows him better than just about anybody."

"But what brought that on?" asked Jack. "Everybody was getting along really well. I sure didn't see any problems when we were there talking and having breakfast. Hey, that breakfast was pretty good, huh?"

The five of us who had gone to the Bayou Manchac home agreed that, for the price, it was great. Heck, it was great even if we *had* had to pay for it. When we finished complimenting the cook at the home, we took turns guessing how much that same breakfast would cost at Frank's. We couldn't agree, so we asked Wendy for a menu. She was a little surprised because none of us had used a menu in years, having memorized the thing, and we always checked the chalkboard for specials as we walked in.

We found an omelet that was close to what we had, then priced the bacon, grits, toast, and orange juice – and coffee too. We came up with $21.49, not including tip. Dang! But we all agreed that none of us ordered that much food as a rule, unless someone else was picking up the tab. We usually got out of there for $12 or less. We also all had multiple cups of coffee every time, so that was worth something. Sometimes I had only coffee and a biscuit with strawberry jam – and with my metabolism, that was plenty.

Jack had not forgotten his question about why someone thought that Raymond Sedgewick was crazy. He asked again, this time looking directly at me. I said, "All that Raymond told me was that American Airlines encouraged him to retire because he and some of the other pilots reported seeing things in the air that they couldn't explain. Call them UFOs or UAPs or whatever, but the pilots who had seen these things wouldn't shut up about it and I guess it was bad for business or something."

Jack, confused by this, asked, "But what does that have to do with Matty calling him crazy?"

I decided to answer before Uncle Joe could jump in again and create further confusion. "Probably everybody at the home has heard about Raymond's experiences. He doesn't seem too shy about telling people. I only just met him five minutes before he practically told me his life history. It seems like Matty told Uncle Joe that Raymond thinks some of the residents there might be aliens." I tried to sound casual about this, but it was hard not to think that "crazy" might be properly descriptive.

"I'd like to talk to Raymond next time we go," stated Jack. "He's a veteran and he deserves respect, not people talking about him and smearing his character behind his back. When are we going again?"

"I'm glad you reminded me about that," I answered and pulled out my blank spreadsheet. I stood up and tapped on my coffee cup with a spoon, first making sure it wasn't full of coffee, and got everyone's attention. "Five of us went to the Bayou Manchac Retirement Home last Friday to visit with some of the men residing there. We had a really nice time and a very good breakfast." And here Uncle Joe broke in with "And free too!"

"I spoke with the manager, Jenny," I continued, "and she would like to have a few of us, maybe four, come every week. Those who don't go on any particular week will still gather here. I made up a spreadsheet for the next four Fridays that I'll pass around. Check your calendars and fill in your name on the Fridays you can go. Not everybody is here today, so if there are still some blank spaces, I'll send an email out to the group."

Then I added, "I already put my name in for next Friday. I think that for the first few weeks we ought to make sure that someone in the group has been there before, you know, to make introductions and such."

After about thirty minutes and three more cups of coffee, the spreadsheet made it around the table and back to me. For next Friday the group would consist of me, Jack, Kevin, and Slim. The spreadsheet for the next few Fridays was almost completely filled. Just wait until Darlene saw this. I'd get the last laugh. The only thing I was surprised about was that Uncle Joe didn't sign up for next week. This was good, though, because the idea was to get some new faces to go. I asked him about it on the way home.

"Me and your Aunt Millie have doctor appointments next Friday," he explained. "I told her not to make doctor appointments on Friday mornings, but she said that was the only time we could get the dermatologist we like. I got this rash on my leg – look here, look at this. You ever seen anything like that?"

We were stopped at the red light on Airline and Hwy 42, so I glanced down and was sorry I did, especially after my corned beef hash breakfast. "That's disgust…I mean, man, that looks bad. Yeah, you need to go and see about that. I can't believe you have to wait a week though. Aren't you worried about that rash spreading or getting infected or something?"

"No," he said, "the little pharmacist over at Walgreens, you know the cute one, she said that it looked like – what-do-you-call-it – starts with a 's' …"

"Psoriasis?" I suggested.

"Yeah, that's it," Uncle Joe confirmed. "Anyway, she recommended something to put on it until we see our doctor. Hey, you ought to see our dermatologist. She is a real looker, that girl. No wonder people have to wait so long to get an appointment. Millie got this one three weeks ago."

For the rest of the drive to Uncle Joe's house we compared our various doctors, numerous ailments, and the efficacy, or lack thereof, of our respective medications. We didn't have time to go into the interesting side effects of some of them before we got to the house. I said a quick hello and goodbye to Aunt Millie and headed home. Darlene was playing tennis with friends at the YMCA on Perkins in Baton Rouge, and would be having lunch with them afterward, so I was on my own. I did my weekly yard work, cleaned up, made a sandwich for lunch, and looked at the spreadsheet I created for visits to Bayou Manchac Retirement Home. There were only a few openings, so I sent out an email to the whole MOSS group and attached the spreadsheet as a pdf. I asked that if anyone wanted to fill in for the few seats remaining over the next month, to let me know.

Then I took a nap in my leather recliner. I can't watch TV in that recliner because I just can't stay awake. It's great for a 30 or 40 minute power nap, though. I slept just long enough to dream about getting beamed up to the Starship Enterprise and asking Chekov for directions to the bathroom when Darlene opened the garage door and woke me, yelling, "I won all three sets today!" She and her friends play three sets, swapping partners each time, so winning all three sets either meant that she was the best player that day or it was just luck. We always go with the "best player" explanation.

She liked to decompress a bit after playing, so she told me about her partners and the games, how she played, including the mistakes, and which partners were weak, which were strong, and so forth. Then she gave me a lengthy description of lunch at Parrain's Seafood on Perkins, showing me her leftovers – three fried shrimp, a piece of fried catfish, and some wilted sweet potato fries. I'd reheat all of that later in the air fryer.

It was our turn to host cocktail night, so Darlene made a list of stuff for me to pick up at Harvest Market while she cleaned up the house. Based on the length of the list, I asked her if she was trying to compete with Connie's Friday night cocktail spread and she laughed and said that competing with her spread was a lost cause. This effort was just enough to keep us from being embarrassed. Before leaving for the store, I checked our liquor and condiment supply and found that we were decidedly low on garlic-stuffed olives, so I added those to the list and headed out.

Darlene doesn't like to send me to the store alone because I have rarely, if ever, stuck to just what's on the list. She says that I have a "wandering eye," but it's not for women, it's for snacks. Harvest Market is a great local store. They know where to put stuff that will grab your attention as soon as you enter. Right there, as I walked in with a basket, was a display of something that I have a particular weakness for – Rice Krispie Treats. They are the Achilles Heel of my stomach, my Weight Watcher's Waterloo. As much as I like chocolate, you'd think that Rice Krispie Treats couldn't compete, but you'd be wrong. There's something about the sickly-sweet, sticky, crunchy marshmallow goodness that I can't pass up. I grabbed a box and began thinking about how I could hide them somewhere in the garage so Darlene wouldn't know that I had succumbed once again. Then I thought, *What's the use, she'll smell them on my breath anyway.* I'd have to just come clean. I'd tell her that they were on sale.

Chapter Six

Even though I had long since canceled the ad I placed in *The Crawfish* and *The Premium Post*, my email address was still out there and I was still getting snarky emails from locals to go along with the various spam emails such as *Never Clean Your Gutters Again!, A Reverse Mortgage Can Save Your Retirement,* and *Why Suffer From Erectile Dysfunction?* I don't know how they do it, but some of the spam emails were addressed to me and appeared to be <u>from</u> me. If I blocked them, I'd be blocking myself. I'd have to ask my grandson about how to fix that.

Emails related to the MOSS kept flowing in and, unless I changed my address, I guess they'd keep coming:

"Mr. Campachi, I heard that you were banned from the Grapevine because you drank too much and didn't pay your bill. We can help you, but you must want to be helped. Please contact me." – Harvey Plaisance, Westside Chapter of AA

"I'm sorry that the movie thing didn't work out, but I have a great idea for a movie in Donaldsonville. I don't want to share too much by email though. All I can say is that it's about a priest, a nun, and the ferry boat George Prince. Call me." – Lester Braud, local playwright.

"Do you still need people to join the MOSS thing? I want my pawpaw to join y'all to give him something to do. All he does is sit around in his underwear and pick at his toes, and my mama says she's gonna kill him if he farts at the dinner table one more time, and I like my pawpaw and don't want him to die." – Kenny Carboni, Pawpaw Ken's grandson

"The people you got to clean 'MOSS sucks' off of the gymnasium wall still haven't finished, and it's been months now. 'ucks' is still highly visible. Please have someone complete the removal as soon as possible." – Teri Crocket, Principal, ACHS

"Mr. Campachi, I'm sorry that you couldn't make the last HOA meeting. Elections were conducted, and you were unanimously elected as President for the coming year. Congratulations!" – Emily Fontaine, Past President, Oak Brook Subdivision

That last one was a bit of a surprise, as I thought that being a Board Member at Large on our HOA put me in a protected class of sorts. I guess I'd better read the by-laws.

Golf was rained out on Tuesday, so the four regulars just met for lunch at BurgerSmith. That's when Dustin asked if we were seriously going to start playing tennis. I had been putting off doing anything since we came up with four guys, so I promised I'd get us together and at least hit some balls around. After lunch I called Terry and T-Joe, checked with Dustin, and we were all free Thursday morning, so we decided to meet at the courts in Gonzales at 8:00 a.m. before it got too hot.

I borrowed a new can of balls from Darlene's bag, along with her spare racket, picked up Dustin, and headed to the Gonzales courts. Terry and T-Joe arrived just after we parked and the four of us put our water bottles and towels and such on the bench and decided that we ought to stretch before we did anything. I sure hope nobody saw us and took any photos, because four old guys trying to touch their toes was a sorry looking thing to behold. Besides that, spread among the four of us were five various and sundry braces – five that were visible, anyway. All of us had at least one and Terry had *two* knee braces.

After a while we decided that stretching was highly overrated, so we split up with Terry and me on one side and T-Joe and Dustin on the other. It took about one minute to realize that I should have brought four or five cans of balls, because we spent most of our time chasing the three balls we had.

It didn't take very long for us to work up a sweat and decide that we wouldn't even bother to try to play an actual game. We piddled around for a little longer, someone mentioned that the Starlight Café was right down the street, and that was the end of our tennis for the day, and it wasn't even 9:00 a.m. Over coffee and pastries at Starlight I suggested that pickleball was a lot of fun and a lot less running around and that maybe we ought to switch to that. Then I made the mistake of trying to explain the scoring system for pickleball and almost had a mutiny before we even started. I promised that it wasn't as hard to figure out as I was making it sound, so they agreed to give it a try. I'd reserve a court at Lamar Dixon for next week. There were even indoor courts there. T-Joe asked if they were air-conditioned, but I didn't know. In any case, they would be out of the sun. Then I passed around the bottle of Advil that Darlene suggested I bring and we all partook.

While we sat there recovering, Terry asked, "Who's going to the retirement home tomorrow?"

"Let's see, uh, Jack, Kevin, Slim, and I are on the schedule for tomorrow," I answered.

Terry followed up with, "What was all the talk last Friday about someone over there being crazy?"

"That's just my Uncle Joe talking to Matty Matassa about another resident," I said. "You have to take their comments with a grain of salt."

Dustin chimed in with, "It's all about aliens at the home and I don't mean from across the Mexican border. Matty Matassa says that this other resident Raymond is nuts because he thinks somebody at the home is from Mars or somewhere."

"Raymond never said anything about Mars or any other planet," I said defensively. "We just talked about UFOs and his career as a pilot and stuff like that. I'm telling you, Raymond Sedgewick is a regular guy."

T-Joe said that he was sorry he didn't sign up to go tomorrow. He was on the list for three weeks from now. I didn't know this, but he told us that he watches the Travel Channel and told us about a series called The Alaskan Triangle. T-Joe said that more people disappear in the Alaskan Triangle than anywhere else on earth and no one can figure out what's going on, but for sure it has to do with aliens.

None of the rest of us had ever heard of the Alaskan Triangle, only the Bermuda Triangle. I said that I would ask Raymond tomorrow if he knew anything about either one of the mystery triangles. He might have even flown through them for American or for FedEx. I wasn't a believer in any of this alien stuff. The Bible doesn't say anything about God creating life on any other planet, so I didn't buy into these government/alien conspiracy theories. I admitted that it was pretty interesting, but I believed that it was all explainable without involving extra-terrestrial life. Unless it's satanic. I wonder, *is hell considered extra-terrestrial?* I'll have to ask my pastor.

Chapter Seven

Jack was sitting on a bench outside of the Bayou Manchac Retirement Home when I drove up at 7:15 on Friday morning. Slim and Kevin arrived separately a few minutes later. All of us old guys are always early, my philosophy being "if you're on time, you're late." I put in the code and we went through the entrance into the foyer and signed the visitor log. Then we headed straight back to the dining room, where the same table with four male residents was waiting for us. It was the same four guys as last time - Raymond Sedgewick, Tuna Aguillard, Charlie Matherne; and Matty Matassa. The only difference I noticed was that Raymond had a cast on his right arm. I hoped he wouldn't tell Jack that it was from an alien encounter.

Jack and I introduced Slim and Kevin to the four residents and Jack made a point of sitting next to Raymond. I started a conversation with Matty. I remember his family from working with my grandpa Campachi in his retail produce business. For the first thirty minutes, though, we drank coffee and talked about Uncle Joe.

"He hasn't changed much since we were kids, except for getting old," Matty offered. "It's funny, our families were really competing against each other, but everybody got along and we helped each other out. I can remember us selling stuff to your grandpa if he ran out and needed something for a customer, like peaches or tomatoes or something."

Then we talked about how we used to go to the French Market in New Orleans at 4:00 or 5:00 in the morning to load up the trucks for the next few days for deliveries to the stores in Donaldsonville, Belle Rose, Paincourtville, and up and down the river road. I was just a kid, but I remembered going to Central Grocery to get olive oil – good, extra virgin olive oil from Italy – for my grandmother Campachi and getting a meatball sandwich at a little restaurant right in the market. Neither of us could remember the name of the restaurant but agreed that the meatball sandwiches were the best.

Matty, being a couple of years older than Uncle Joe, remembered Rosemary Rizzo fondly. He was one of the guys who tried to date her, but just as Uncle Joe had said, she wouldn't go out with the Donaldsonville boys. Matty thinks that her daddy didn't want her dating Italians, even though he was Italian himself. He wanted something better for Rosemary. Matty agreed with me that her eventual choice of a husband wasn't what you'd call "something better" – not by a long shot.

We were just finishing breakfast when Jack signaled to me to come over, so I excused myself and pulled up a chair next to Raymond and Jack. "What happened to your arm?" I asked Raymond.

"Oh, something stupid," he replied with disgust. "I was out in the garden area between buildings on a zoom call with some friends a couple of nights ago and tripped on a sprinkler head. It's just a fracture though. Could have been worse. It sure scared my friends on the call. They didn't know what the heck happened."

"Tell Tony what the call was about," prompted Jack.

"I have a regular zoom call with three of the guys I used to fly with for American Airlines," Raymond explained. "We talk every Wednesday night, and sometimes more often if there's something happening, about what we're all doing in retirement, what's going on at NASA and at Area 51, and any other chatter we've picked up about UAPs."

"That's great that you keep up with your friends," I said, not knowing what else to say about the UAP stuff. "That's one of the reasons I put this MOSS group together – to stay in touch with friends. Anything interesting going on, uh, with NASA and such?"

"Nothing new since the formation of the study team by NASA," Raymond replied. "I don't expect very much to be made public right away, but we hope that there's enough interest in Congress to keep things from being buried. My friends and I are keeping our Congressmen on their toes about it."

"Ray, tell Tony about this resident here that you and your group have some suspicions about," suggested Jack.

"Well, first of all, you have to understand that my friends and I have been collecting data, sightings, and theories about UAPs for years," Raymond began. "Based upon our collective knowledge and further research we've done, we have a pretty solid working theory about aliens living here on our planet."

"Listen to this, Tony," Jack said excitedly. "It makes my skin crawl."

Raymond cautioned both Jack and me to be quiet about this – and that it was just a theory. There hadn't been any solid proof of alien life here – no proof that Jack and his friends had anyway. He said, "We have reason to believe that aliens have, for some time now, inhabited the bodies of an unknown number of people on earth."

Oh man! Was Matty right about Raymond being nuts? I thought to myself. I sure hope I don't have to apologize to Uncle Joe again. He'd never let me forget it. I didn't know what to say to that, so I asked, "Where would these aliens be from? Mars?"

Raymond smiled at me like I was a kid in grade school and got 2 + 2 wrong. "I don't know why everyone thinks aliens have to be from Mars," Raymond chided. "They're not from our solar system for certain. We think that they are from somewhere else in the Milky Way galaxy, because coming from another galaxy is just too far-fetched, literally."

So, I thought, the only thing far-fetched about the aliens taking over bodies on earth is that it's stupid to think they're from Mars.

I decided that I'd better play along. What was the harm? "Why would aliens want to take over people on earth? I mean, for what purpose?"

"We don't really know," replied Raymond dejectedly. "If we did, we might be able to do something about it. We have theories, of course. By the stealth they appear to be using, it doesn't seem like a matter of trying to dominate us. If it were, they would be assuming the bodies of important people, not folks in a retirement home."

I thought to myself, *I wouldn't count out some of the elected people in Washington from being aliens. Heck, D.C. might be their home base.*

Raymond seemed to be sorry that he had mentioned that last thing about folks in a retirement home. He bent closer to us and motioned for us to do the same. "Our best theory is that they are dying out on their own world and are experimenting to see if they can tolerate existing here. In that case it would make sense that they would use people who were not, let's say, in the spotlight."

"How come our radar systems and military haven't spotted them coming here from outer space?" asked Jack. I thought that was a good question.

"That's a good question," replied Raymond. "We don't know for sure that our military hasn't spotted them. We think probably not, though. They may have some sort of stealth system that we can't detect."

"But where are their ships – Area 51?" asked Jack.

"We think they're somewhere off the coast of Alaska, in the Alaskan Triangle," Raymond suggested. "There have been a lot of sightings by locals all over Alaska, especially on the coast."

I told him that my brother T-Joe had told us something about the Alaskan Triangle and it was the first time any of us had heard about it.

"Check out the Travel Channel. It has several shows about the

Alaskan Triangle," Raymond advised. "There's one on tonight about UAPs and 'ghost ships.' You should watch it."

I figured it was time we got to the bottom of this thing, so I asked, "Do you really think that a resident here at Bayou Manchac Retirement Home has been, uh, taken over by an alien?"

Raymond sighed and said, "Please keep this to yourself. There's one male resident who shows at least some of the signs of being an alien, based upon the research my friends and I have collected."

Jack asked him, "What are the signs, Ray? How can you tell? Is it bumps on the forehead that might be antennae? Or maybe the aliens don't have navels. Is that it, Ray? They don't have navels?"

Raymond bent over laughing at this, causing Jack to blush right through his farmer's tan. "You watch too many Star Trek reruns!" Then more seriously, "We don't really know what they look like in their own bodies. When they take over a human body, you can't tell by looking at them – at least we haven't been able to figure out how. What we have figured out is that they have trouble, even in their human host bodies, tolerating certain things."

"Like what?" I inquired.

"Well, we think that they can have caffeine, but can't drink coffee, maybe something about the acid in coffee," Raymond began. "We also think that they have very low tolerance for garlic and shellfish. More interesting, though – they appear to select humans that have access to medical equipment, especially x-ray machines."

Jack asked, "But what about the guy here that you suspect…," then in a whisper, "…is an alien? He wouldn't be able to use an x-ray machine."

Raymond smiled. "As it happens, he was a dentist – and although he no longer practices, he still owns the business and his son-in-law runs it. He visits the office from time to time. We think that's when he gets his 'booster' of x-rays."

"What about these friends of yours that you're in cahoots with?" asked Jack. "Have they found people like that? I mean, people they think are aliens?"

Raymond nodded. "We have a few candidates that we're keeping tabs on, but right now Mr. Authement here is our best bet. We're working on an approach to attempt to prove that he is a host to an alien being."

Jack asked, "Why don't you just ask him?"

Raymond chuckled. "I have, in a round-a-bout way. Either he didn't have a clue as to what I was on about, or he's a great actor. I couldn't get anything out of him."

"So, what are you and your friends thinking of doing to prove what you suspect?" I asked.

"Keep this to yourself," Raymond cautioned. "We were thinking of somehow getting him to ingest coffee or garlic to see if it would force the alien to expose himself. But it's just too risky. If he died we'd have a hard time explaining ourselves."

It bothered me that he told us this so matter-of-factly. He and his friends were actually thinking about clandestinely giving a resident there – Mr. Authement – something that they knew might kill him.

It was time to leave, so we said our "goodbyes" and Raymond once again reminded me to watch the Travel Channel that night.

Chapter Eight

While I was trying to remember whose turn it was to host cocktail night, Darlene informed me that she and Connie had decided that we would go out for cocktail night because neither of them felt like cleaning house. Dustin and I knew better than to even so much as suggest a place to go because our suggestions were invariably met with either a scowl of contempt or a "so-and-so went there last week and said the food has really gone down in quality, and she thinks that they water down the drinks. Also, it's always too crowded."

Fortunately, the girls decided on Sno's, which is one of my absolute favorite places and not far from the house. We got there early enough to snag a table in the bar and quickly ordered our first round of drinks and a couple of appetizers. When Connie and Darlene happened to take a sip of their drinks at the same time and so stopped jabbering about the sale at Kohl's, I started to tell everyone about our breakfast gathering at Bayou Manchac Retirement Home.

"So, this guy I told y'all about, Raymond, he admitted to me that he and his buddies think that one of the residents there, a Mr. Authement, is an alien," I said. "Or at least he's possessed by an alien. I really thought that Uncle Joe must have misheard Matty Matassa last week, but he was right."

Both Connie and Darlene laughed at this and Connie asked, "Why in the world would this guy think that someone there is an alien? Do you think he just meant that the resident, who was it, Mr. Authement? Do you think that he meant that Mr. Authement is from another country?"

"Yeah, another country on another planet," I answered. "Not only another planet, but from somewhere outside of our solar system. Somewhere else in the Milky Way Galaxy."

"Raymond must have dementia," suggested Darlene. "People with dementia can dream up some really crazy stuff."

"I don't think so," offered Dustin. "I heard him talking last week and he seems really intelligent and rational."

"I'm sorry, but talking about spotting an alien in a retirement home doesn't sound rational to me," was Connie's analysis.

"No, it doesn't," I agreed, "but he has three other former airline pilots he talks to every week that believe the same thing. They've done some sort of study and have come up with some, let's say, characteristics that they believe are common to these people who are supposed to be possessed by aliens." I let this sink in while I took a big sip of my martini and ate one of the blue cheese stuffed olives.

"Okay, okay," smirked Darlene. "Quit holding us in suspense. What are these so-called characteristics?"

I pulled out my phone and opened the "Notes" icon where I had jotted down the things that Raymond had told to me and Jack. "There are mainly three things. Number one, they can't tolerate coffee. Raymond thinks it has to do with the acid. Number two, they can't have garlic or shellfish. Raymond doesn't know why."

Connie jumped in with, "Maybe they can't have garlic because they're alien vampires!" That got a good laugh from everyone.

"And number three," I continued, "For some reason they must have access to an x-ray machine periodically. Raymond and his buddies don't know why."

"That's just weird," suggested Darlene. "Do you mean to say that they found someone at the retirement home that doesn't even drink coffee? I can understand allergies to shellfish. I don't know about garlic, though. Tony's whole dago family practically lives on garlic."

"That might be true, but who eats a whole head of garlic at every crawfish boil?" I said as I looked accusingly at Darlene. She nodded in silent admission.

"Yeah, I'm with you on the coffee thing, though," replied Dustin. "I don't know any old folks that don't drink coffee. I do know a couple of people that can't eat shellfish, though."

"The only older person that I know who doesn't drink coffee is Ronald," I offered. "He drinks iced tea at Frank's every Friday morning."

"Hey, you know what?" asked Connie rhetorically. "We had Ronald over for dinner when he first moved here. Remember – y'all were there. It was before he met his wife, Jill. I fixed crawfish etouffee and I made a Sensation Salad with a lot of garlic. He couldn't eat anything! I felt so bad that I made him a sandwich."

"So what are you saying?" Dustin asked. "Ronald Burgoyne is an alien?"

"I don't know," replied Connie. "It's just funny, that's all."

"Holy cow!" I said with excitement. "Ronald owns a few of those urgent care places. They have x-ray machines, don't they?"

We all looked at each other for a moment, then started to laugh.

"Look," said Dustin, getting our attention. "Do any of us seriously believe in the possibility of alien life at all, much less aliens living among us right now?"

No one said anything for a minute. Then Darlene said "I think we ought to keep an open mind about it. I mean, it's a big universe. I guess it's possible."

"You have to admit that some weird stuff has gone on in Area 51," I added. "Nobody seems to be able to prove that there aren't any aliens."

"It's hard to prove a negative," offered Connie.

"I just mean that there seems to be a lot of stuff that just can't be explained unless you consider the possibility of aliens coming here," I responded.

"Yeah, but Ronald Burgoyne? Seriously?" asked Dustin. "Let's just call him and ask if he's from Venus."

"It wouldn't be Venus," I said lamely. "It would be from another solar system."

"Tony, I hate to say this," said Darlene, who obviously couldn't wait to say it, "but you are sounding like your Uncle Joe."

"That's a low blow, Darlene," I shot back. By this time, we had all had a couple of drinks and what some might call the "loose lip" syndrome.

"Hey, I have an idea," offered Connie. "Let's call Ronald, but just to ask him if he knows that guy at the Bayou Manchac home who's supposed to be an alien."

"But why?" I asked her.

"Well, shouldn't they know each other? I mean, if they're both aliens?" answered Connie.

"Hey, that's a good point," I said. "They must be coordinating with each other." I heard myself make that last statement and wondered just how many brain cells I had killed with two martinis.

"Y'all are nuts," was Dustin's only comment.

We all agreed that we had had enough to drink and shouldn't drive, so we decided to stay and have dinner and a lot of water. Dustin and I both ordered the pork chop, the best thing on the menu as far as we were concerned. Connie and Darlene both got the redfish special topped with crawfish etouffee. As we waited for our salads, I decided that I could text Ronald and mention that there was a guy at the home that he might know, by the name of Authement. The girls thought this was a good idea, but Dustin still thought we were nuts.

"Look," he said. "Just suppose that they are both aliens. Why would Ronald admit to knowing him? Wouldn't he naturally deny it?"

"Okay," I told him. "If he says 'No,' then either he doesn't know him or he's lying. If he says 'Yes,' then, uh…." I was struggling with logic after two martinis.

"Then he might be an alien, but it doesn't prove that he is," suggested Darlene.

We all sat there in deep and hopefully sobering silence, picking at our salads.

I had an idea. "What if I texted Ronald that I met Mr. Authement at Bayou Manchac Retirement Home and he said to make sure I told Ronald Burgoyne 'hello'? If he still denies knowing him, that would seem weird, right?"

Everyone pondered this for a minute. The girls thought it was a good idea. It didn't change Dustin's opinion on our lack of sanity, though.

I texted Ronald the following: "Ronald, I ran into an old friend of yours at the Bayou Manchac Retirement Home this morning – Mr. Authement. He said to tell you hello."

Our dinners arrived just as I hit "send."

We were well into the pork chops and fish when my phone dinged to let me know I had a text. It was Ronald responding. He texted "That must be Martin Authement. We played football together at Ville Platte High School. He's a couple of years older than me. I'll have to go see him. Thanks."

"I didn't know Ronald was from Ville Platte," noted Dustin.

"So what are two guys that grew up in Ville Platte doing living in Ascension Parish?" I thought out loud.

Connie suggested, "I remember Ronald saying at dinner that night that he was in the service – Air Force, I think. He probably moved around a lot."

Darlene added that a whole lot of people have moved into Ascension Parish since we came back in 2006.

"Okay, so we proved that they know each other and we found out that they're both from a little town north of Lafayette somewhere," I said. "Don't y'all find that a pretty wild coincidence?"

By the shrugs and head shakes it was clear that I was the only one suspicious about all of this. Then I had a bad thought.

"Hey, what if Ronald goes over to the retirement home and looks up Mr. Authement. He'll find out that I never even met the guy and that he didn't tell me that he knew Ronald."

"He'll probably just chalk it up to both of them being old and forgetful," suggested Dustin. "I wouldn't worry about it."

By this time we were done with dinner and told the waitress politely that no, we didn't want to hear about the fabulous dessert special and to please bring us one check which we would split. Whenever we went out for dinner on cocktail night, we still ended up at one house or the other for coffee and dessert. This night it was our house because I had recorded the Travel Channel while we were gone. This episode featured the Alaskan Triangle. When we got home, I started a pot of decaf while Darlene took out our dog Beau to pee. Darlene had picked up some blueberry scones from Harvest earlier, so she heated them a little in the microwave and served them with a scoop of Cool Whip. Then we sat down in front of the TV with four TV trays and I pulled up the recorded program.

We all thought that the program was kind of hokey, but the people in Alaska who were interviewed sounded sincere, like they really bought into this deal about aliens living under water just off of the coast. Some claimed to have seen lights under water, strange flying things at night, and heard inexplicable noises and so forth. The program had special effects of an imaginary alien base under water with ships coming and going, able to both fly and operate under water.

One of the visiting investigators went out to a suspected area where there had been strange sightings and she and two others donned scuba gear and explored the ocean floor. The thing is, they were diving in clearly shallow water and the alien bases were supposed to be miles under water, so I don't know what they were trying to prove – maybe to find some discarded spaceship equipment or something. The aliens must be a lot more careful about littering than we are because they didn't find a thing. It was, to say the least, anticlimactic.

Chapter Nine

As promised, I had reserved a pickle-ball court at Lamar Dixon for 10:00 a.m. on Thursday and let my foursome know. They were less than enthusiastic about it, but everyone agreed to show up. We all got there early, as is typical of us, and sat on folding chairs on the side of the indoor court putting on our various braces, stretching a bit, and watching a match finish up on the court we had reserved. I brought the two paddles and balls that Darlene and I had and Terry had gone to Dick's Sporting Goods and bought two paddles and balls, so we were set.

On the court a mixed doubles match was underway involving four very young players. When I say "very young" I mean that they were clearly less than half my age. They were having a very competitive game, moving on the court and striking the ball with ease. I had two immediate thoughts: 1) *Why weren't they at work?* and 2) *Our game will look nothing like the game they're playing, and I hope no one is around to watch us.*

When their match was over, they all shook hands across the net and one couple came over and apologized for making us wait, although they finished right on time. We sauntered onto the court and I explained the layout to everyone, what the lines designating the "kitchen" meant, and where the serve had to be hit to start each point. One of the young men who had just walked off of our court came over and asked if we were new to the game and did we need any help getting started or learning how to keep score. We all replied with some version of "No, no, no, we're good, we're good, thanks a lot, really, thanks, but we're good." He shrugged his shoulders, wished us luck, and headed for the door.

We practiced a bit and after a while everyone got the hang of getting a serve in play, where to stand if your partner was serving, when to come up to the kitchen line, and so forth. We finally got to the point where we felt like we could try to play a game and that was when the explanation of the scoring came in. Now understand that of the four of us, three had college degrees including one with a Masters, and the other had two years at ITI in Baton Rouge. We were, supposedly, no dummies. But the scoring almost got the best of us. By the time we were all comfortable with playing and scoring, our time on the court was over. Regardless of the issues we had, everyone agreed that it was fun and a far sight easier than tennis and the group was all for trying again next week.

We drove over to Don's for lunch since T-Joe wanted to go to Cabela's later to shop for bass lures. We were led to a booth, handed menus, and ordered drinks. I hadn't had a chance to talk to anyone about Raymond Sedgewick, Mr. Authement, and the suspicions some of us (mainly me) had about Ronald Burgoyne. I brought it up casually as we were waiting for our lunch. Dustin just shook his head.

After I had provided what I thought was a very objective, factual, unbiased explanation of why we should all be worried, very, very worried, Terry asked, "Are you trying to tell us that Ronald Burgoyne, the guy we've been going to breakfast with once a week for years, the same man who sponsors my grandson's baseball team and is Past-President of the Gonzales Rotary Club – that Ronald Burgoyne – is an alien?"

"I didn't say for sure that he's an alien," I replied weakly. "I'm just stating the facts. I mean, it could all be just a coincidence, I guess, that he doesn't drink coffee or eat garlic or crawfish. And the x-ray thing…" My voice trailed off as I furtively searched for the last hidden shrimp in my seafood salad.

T-Joe added to the discussion with, "I know a few people who are allergic to shellfish and not everybody likes coffee. I don't think that proves anything."

Then Dustin chimed in with, "How did Raymond and his airline buddies come up with this list of so-called alien characteristics in the first place?"

"I don't really know for sure," I admitted. "I'll have to ask him next time."

"Who's going over to the retirement home tomorrow?" asked Dustin.

I pulled out my phone and brought up the spreadsheet. I had to enlarge sections of it because the print was so small. "Here it is – looks like my Uncle Joe, Dr. Dart, Ronald, and Donnie."

"Hey, let's ask Uncle Joe to keep an eye on Ronald, see what happens when he meets that Mr. Authement," suggested T-Joe.

"But none of us has met Mr. Authement," I replied. "He hasn't come to sit with us yet. I got the impression that he and Raymond Sedgewick might not get along."

"Why do you think that?" inquired Terry.

"Raymond told me that he came right out and asked Mr. Authement if he was an alien and he said that he played dumb," I replied. "If somebody asked me that, I'd think that they were nuts and I'd avoid them."

"So how will Ronald meet with him if he isn't one of the guys who comes to breakfast?" asked T-Joe.

"I guess that he would just go to the desk and say that an old friend of Mr. Authement is here to visit with him," I surmised.

"But if they don't have breakfast with the other guys, how will Uncle Joe watch what they're doing?" asked T-Joe.

"I know what I'll do," I said. "I'll email Jenny Landry – she's the manager – and ask her to get Mr. Authement to come down for breakfast, that an old friend of his is visiting. That ought to work."

I sent the email to Jenny and then when we left Don's I called Uncle Joe from the truck.

"Well, if it isn't my favorite nephew!" he said when he answered.

"How did you know it was me?" I asked.

"Because I sensed it. I got ESPN. Also, we got caller-ID now so I don't have to listen to somebody wantin' to do a survey or know who I voted for," he responded.

"Hey, look, you're still going to Bayou Manchac tomorrow, right?" I asked.

"If the good Lord says the same," he answered. "I found some old pictures to show Matty and I'm bringing that book by Will LeBlanc about Donaldsonville. He ought to get a kick out of that."

"Look, I want to run something by you," I said, changing the subject. "There's a guy that lives there by the name of Authement.

Ronald says that he and Mr. Authement are old friends from Ville Platte."

"I didn't know Ronald was from Ville Platte," replied Uncle Joe.

"No, none of us knew," I said. "Anyway, Raymond Sedgewick and his airline buddies suspect that Mr. Authement is possessed by an alien."

"No kidding!" exclaimed Uncle Joe. "I told you Matty was right. That guy is nuts."

"And maybe he is," I conceded. "But look, if you get the chance, will you kind of listen to what Ronald and Mr. Authement talk about?"

"Yeah, I guess so," he said. "Why do you want me to do that?"

I didn't want to tell Uncle Joe my suspicions about Ronald yet, so I said, "I'll fill you in after your breakfast tomorrow. You got a ride?"

"Yeah, Donnie's picking me up," he said. "I'll call you when I get home."

"Great, thanks," I told him and we hung up.

Chapter Ten

Those of us who were not scheduled to visit the Bayou Manchac Retirement Home for a free breakfast the next morning met as usual at Frank's to keep the local economy going strong. Around the table joining me were Dustin, Kevin, Slim, Terry, Rodney, Jack, Alden, and T-Joe. Not our usual dozen, what with four of the guys elsewhere, but enough to keep Wendy busy.

I sat next to Dustin and whispered to him that I had asked Uncle Joe to try to listen in on whatever Ronald and Mr. Authement had to say to each other. Dustin just shook his head.

"You have always, ever since I've known you, had an overly active imagination," he accused.

"I don't think that's true at all," I rebutted. "I think that I simply have an inquisitive mind."

"Do you still think that Kennedy was shot from the grassy knoll?" he asked in a tone that I thought was just a bit sarcastic.

"I'm not the only one that thinks something was fishy about his assassination," I replied defensively. "Lots of people think so."

"What about the moon landing? Do you still believe that it was shot in Hollywood?" he asked, still somewhat snidely.

"I never said 'Hollywood,'" I replied emphatically.

"Oh, that's right, you said it was shot in Area 51, didn't you?" Dustin said, smiling now.

"I might have said 'Area 51,'" I admitted. "I thought it was reasonable at the time."

"I rest my case," was all Dustin said in response.

I turned around and started talking to Slim, who tended to be a lot less judgmental. "You need a haircut," was all he had to say to me.

"Can you take me today?" I asked.

"Come over right after breakfast," he suggested. "I don't have anyone else coming in until 9:30."

Slim has a one-chair little barber shop in the rear of his wife's Christian school building where she teaches a handful of kids in home-school fashion. Uncle Joe had introduced me to Slim several years ago, and I've gone to him ever since. Slim is a Vietnam vet and very patriotic. He can't stand some of the nonsense going on in the world today.

"I swear on the Bible, if I was coach of any of the NFL players who kneeled during the National Anthem, they'd never play another down," he said, with conviction, as he was trimming around my ears. I hoped that his emotion wouldn't result in my blood being spilled.

I decided I'd better change the subject. "Slim, when you went with us to the retirement home, did you happen to hear any of what was said between me, Jack, and Raymond Sedgewick?"

"Bits and pieces," he replied. "I was talking to Charlie Matherne and, for a guy his age, he's got pretty good hearing – or maybe he could read lips – because he was telling me that Raymond was talking to y'all about UFOs and aliens and such. He said that him and some of the other residents thought that Raymond was a few sandwiches short of a picnic."

"Did he happen to mention a Mr. Authement?" I asked.

"No, I don't think so," answered Slim. "Why? Who's Mr. Authement?"

"Oh, he's just another resident there," I said evasively.

Slim brushed off my shoulders, put a little powder on a brush, wiped it across the back of my neck, and took off the drape. I paid him, said I'd see him next week at the MOSS gathering, and left. Uncle Joe called just as I was pulling out of Slim's parking lot.

"Hey, Uncle Joe," I said. "How was your breakfast?"

"We had French toast and bacon," he replied. "It was real good, real good. Did you go to Frank's?"

"Yeah, the rest of us that didn't go to the retirement home showed up at Frank's. Did you see if Ronald met with Mr. Authement?"

"He met with somebody over at another table. I don't know who it was, but they talked real quiet the whole time. When I left at about

9:00 they were still huddled over the table. So what's going on? Why did you want me to check on Ronald and this other guy?"

I guessed that I'd better tell Uncle Joe something or he'd never leave me alone. "Here's the thing. Darlene and I and Dustin and Connie were having dinner the other night and we figured out that Ronald doesn't drink coffee, is allergic to shellfish and garlic, and has x-ray machines at his urgent care businesses."

As I finished telling him this, I realized that he must be completely confused.

"I'm confused," he replied, right on cue. "What are you talking about? I know he doesn't drink coffee. I think he had orange juice this morning with breakfast."

I explained that, according to Raymond Sedgewick, those are tell-tale signs of an alien possession.

"Oh no, nephew. Don't tell me that you are just as nuts as Raymond," was Uncle Joe's response to this revelation. "You know your daddy had to see a shrink more than once. It might run in your family."

I reminded him that he was family too, so then he said it might be from my mama's side. I was about to argue about that but realized that there was just enough truth in it that I'd better not say anything.

"So was Raymond at breakfast this morning?" I asked, changing the subject.

"Yeah, he sat with us. He was talking to Donnie and Dr. Dart. Say, what is Dr. Dart's given name?" Uncle Joe asked.

"I don't really know," I replied. "Everybody just calls him Doc. Hey, did you notice if the guy talking to Ronald said hello or talked to anybody else?"

"He said hello to the guys at our table as he was passing, but when Raymond walked up he grabbed Ronald by the arm and went off to another table across the room," he said. "I thought that was a little funny."

"That's because the guy with Ronald was Mr. Authement and that's who Raymond and his friends think is possessed by an alien," I explained. "And I think Mr. Authement knows what Raymond thinks and avoids him."

"Well, I don't blame the man," said Uncle Joe indignantly. "Now do you think Raymond is a wacko?"

"I don't know, maybe," I replied weakly. "I have to think about this some more."

"Well, while you're thinking about it, can you think of whether you know a good cheap plumber?" he asked me.

"Why?" I asked. "Are y'all having plumbing problems?"

"We can't get any hot water," he explained. "Millie wants me to call a plumber, but not the one we used last time because she saw his butt crack every time he looked under the sink. You know anybody?"

"I don't know any good plumbers, but I can come over and look," I offered. "Maybe it's just the pilot light; maybe it blew out."

"It's not the pilot light," was Uncle Joe's response.

"How do you know it's not the pilot light?" I asked. "Did you check it?"

"I don't have to check it. I know it's not the pilot light," he said with some exasperation in his voice.

"Look, I don't mind coming over to check it for you," I offered again. "Sometimes it's hard to tell if the pilot light is on or not."

"I know it's not the pilot light because it don't have a pilot light," he explained. "It's electric."

All I could say was, "Then I guess it's not the pilot light."

I heard him mumble something about education and no common sense. I think he was talking about the plumber.

"Let me ask you something," said Uncle Joe out of the blue. "Why do they call it a 'hot water heater'?"

"Call what a 'hot water heater'?" I replied, often confused by Uncle Joe's questions.

"A 'hot water heater', that's what," he answered.

"I don't know what you're talking about. Why does who call what a 'hot water heater'?" I shot back.

"Are you sure you graduated from LSU as a engineer? It's a simple question. Why do they call a 'hot water heater' a 'hot water heater'?" he repeated in exasperation.

"Who's they?" I asked, still not getting it.

"Never mind who 'they' is, for crying out loud." I swear, he sounded like he was about to either cry or hang up. "Why is a 'hot water heater' called a 'hot water heater'?"

"I don't know," I answered. "It's always been called a hot water heater. What else would you call it?"

"I'd call it a 'cold water heater'," he replied with conviction. "You heat cold water until it's hot, right? You don't heat hot water that's already hot. It's a stupid name."

I got it now. "Some people just call it a 'water heater'."

He shot back with, "Nobody I know just calls it a 'water heater'. They call it a 'hot water heater'."

He's right. I've only ever heard of it called a 'hot water heater'." Dang. I hate to admit Uncle Joe is right about something. "Maybe it's just a Southern thing, like neutral ground or hosepipe."

"What about 'hosepipe'?" he asked. "What else would you call a hosepipe?"

"Darlene says that I sound ignorant when I say 'hosepipe'. She says it's just a hose, or maybe a garden hose," I answered.

"She must be a Yankee. Only a Yankee would call a hosepipe a garden hose," was his conclusion.

"You know as well as I do that she was born and raised in New Orleans right off of Magazine Street," I said defensively. "She's no Yankee and neither were her parents."

"Then you better check who's she hanging out with, because she's picking up that Yankee talk from somewhere," was Uncle Joe's final word on the subject.

Chapter Eleven

When I got home Darlene told me that both daughters had called to check on us. It's weird, they almost always call at the same time, as though they coordinate it to freak us out. Our oldest, Elizabeth, called to tell us when her vacation would start. She's a teacher in Owensboro, Kentucky and spends a lot of her vacation time back with us in Louisiana – to visit and to eat as much seafood as she can handle. Our youngest, Edie (short for Edith, my grandmother's and Darlene's mom's name, which she hates, by the way) called to ask how I like the Ninja blender she had given me for Christmas because she had it in her mind that I should be eating healthier.

I felt a little guilty about not having used it much, so I decided to make a smoothie for lunch. This Ninja blender is great. It has a single-serve option that's perfect for a quick, no-mess fruit smoothie. Well, not a lot of mess anyway. Darlene came in from walking Beau as I was pulling ingredients out of the refrigerator and freezer.

"Edie will be happy that you're using that thing," she said. "What are you putting in it?"

"Oh, some fresh banana, frozen blueberries and strawberries, a little milk, you know, healthy stuff," I replied. "I found a Weight Watcher's recipe."

"What's that can that you just opened that you're hiding behind the toaster?" she asked suspiciously.

"That's the milk," I said.

"That's condensed milk," she noted. "I don't think that would be in a Weight Watcher's recipe."

"Well it ought to be," I replied defensively.

"Then I wouldn't say that you're going for healthy," was her reply.

I asked her if she wanted me to make her one also, but she was leaving to meet Connie for coffee.

I was just finishing my smoothie when I a got a text from Raymond Sedgewick. His three airline buddies were coming to visit him and would be here by mid-morning next Friday. He asked me to please come, that he'd like me to meet them. I checked my spreadsheet and scheduled to go to the Bayou Manchac Retirement Home next week were Dustin, Kevin, Terry, and Alden. I guess Jenny wouldn't mind if one extra guy showed up, especially since I was invited. I texted Raymond back that I'd be there for breakfast and that I would hang around to meet his buddies. I planned to get there early to talk to Raymond about my suspicions regarding Ronald – that he showed all the signs of being possessed by an alien.

I spent the rest of the day trying to figure out how to do a blog. Saying that you want to do a blog and actually doing it are two different things. I remember going to Barnes and Noble and other bookstores back in the day and seeing all of the books for dummies, like *Auto Repair for Dummies* and *Guitar for Dummies* and so forth. Well, sure enough, there are books for dummies who want to start a blog and you don't have to go to a bookstore, you can order it right online. That is, if you've already read *Ordering Stuff Online for Dummies*.

I did a search on "How to start a blog" and got all sorts of information. Apparently the first thing one does when deciding to start blogging (if that's the right term) is to pick a blog name that's descriptive. "A Blog for Old Farts With Nothing Else To Do" came to mind, but I thought that was a little too long and maybe too descriptive. I settled on "Old Fart Blog." I thought that would get some attention.

The next step is to get your blog online, for which you need web hosting and blogging software. Hmm. Apparently at this stage certain out-of-pocket costs come into play. After all of that you must, according to the directions, "choose a blog design template and tweak it." Hmm. I'm not sure what they mean by "tweak it." I know how to tweak some things that I can actually get my hands on, such as a lawnmower carburetor, but how do you tweak something online that you can't touch? After you figure that out, you can "share your thoughts with the world." And, apparently, if you're good at this blogging stuff, you can make money somehow. That part I don't get at all.

Yes, I'm an engineer, but I used a slide rule at LSU. Hand-held calculators came out when I was a senior and by then it was too late. I had to be dragged kicking and screaming into the computer age, so none of this stuff comes easy for me. Darlene can attest to the fact that I don't have a lot of patience. I don't like to read instructions in the first place and when I can't follow instructions in a book written for dummies, well, it's not going to go well. And soon I figured out that if I started this blog thing, I couldn't control who read it – and I guess that's the idea. Those who make money doing blogs want as many people as possible to read their stuff. I don't think that I have the energy to write stuff that people would want to read day in and day out. The thought of it exhausts me.

Then I thought maybe if I could write a blog about aliens from the stuff that Raymond was telling me, maybe that would be interesting. I figured maybe there weren't too many people blogging about stuff like that but, just to check, I searched online for "blogs about aliens" and immediately found one site that offered "70 Best UFO Blogs and Websites To Follow." Dang! No question that I was behind the times on this stuff. I started reading some of those blogs and wow, it was like the Twilight Zone. Before I knew it Darlene was yelling at me to come down for supper.

It's true that I lack patience, but I do have perseverance and it's rare that I completely give up on something without a fight. But the idea of blogging died very much like the idea of jogging, in a quick and unceremonious fashion.

Chapter Twelve

During Bible study before services on Sunday morning, I asked my pastor to give us his thoughts about the possibility of life on other planets. He said that the Bible is clear that God created earth for mankind and created man in His image and that the entire universe was created by Him during the creation week. The Bible does not even suggest that God placed life anywhere but on earth and, therefore, there is no life on other planets. I told him that I knew someone who believed that people on earth are being possessed by aliens from another solar system and that he was pretty convincing. After the laughter from the other Bible study attendees died down, he suggested that I might want to see him in his office after services for some one-on-one counseling. I quietly snuck out of the church and into the parking lot during the last hymn and headed home.

Local farmers were blessed with a pretty steady rain on Tuesday morning, which, for non-farmers, meant no golf, no outdoor pickleball, and no yard work. This would have been a great time to work on a blog for anyone who knew how to navigate the instructions for setting one up. The golf regulars met at BurgerSmith for lunch. I couldn't help but cast a wary eye on Ronald the whole time. I didn't think he noticed, though.

"Tony, why the heck are you looking at me like that?" Ronald asked. "Do I have something stuck in my teeth?"

"No, no, Ronald, sorry, I didn't realize I was staring or anything," I said. "Did you get new glasses?" I thought that I covered that up pretty well.

"No, these are the same glasses I've had for years," he replied.

"Oh, I thought they looked new," I ad libbed. I thought that he looked a little nervous, so maybe I was getting to him. I was really close to asking him what he thought about life on other planets when I noticed Dustin trying to get my attention.

Dustin looked at me from across the table and passed his finger under his throat in a slicing motion, which I took to mean either to shut up or to kill myself. For the rest of the lunch I tried hard not to stare at Ronald as we talked about how well we would have played today if we hadn't gotten rained out. We also hatched a plan to tell the BurgerSmith staff every Tuesday that we all got birdies, so everybody had to pay for each other's meals just to screw them up.

When Friday finally came, I showed up at the retirement home, much to the surprise of the other guys who had signed up. I just explained that I was there by special request from Raymond. During coffee and before breakfast was served, I quietly filled Raymond in on my suspicions about Ronald Burgoyne. He was fascinated and asked a lot of questions such as "How long have you known him?" and "Is he married?" and "Does he have any children?" and that sort of thing. I told him everything I knew and he asked if I would write it all down for him to share with his friends.

"I'm not real comfortable telling other people about this," I told him. "What if I'm wrong?"

"Tony, you don't have to worry – we will treat this as Top Secret and Confidential," he said, trying to ease my concerns. "You'll meet my buddies in a short while and I'm certain they will reassure you that we can be trusted."

"But what will you do with this information?" I asked.

"All we'll do is a little clandestine background check on him," he replied. "But it sounds to me like you have good reason to be suspicious of him."

We were then served with a very nice breakfast of grilled ham steak, scrambled eggs, and biscuits with white gravy. Although they wouldn't let us pay for breakfast, we had decided early on to put a few dollars into a kitty at the place to be used for the residents at Jenny's discretion.

At about 9:30 or so, after the rest of the MOSS guys had gone, an attendant came over to Raymond and let him know that he had visitors up front in the reception area. He and I hustled to the front to greet his friends. I hadn't had a chance to write down what I knew about Ronald Burgoyne, but Raymond said not to worry, that I could just tell them what I knew for now. Raymond's friends were clearly glad to see him and, as they couldn't shake hands because of his injury, they all gave him a gentle hug. Then Raymond introduced us.

"Boys, this is a new friend and confidant, Tony Campachi – did I say that right Tony?" he asked.

"Perfectly, better than some of my family can say it," I said jovially.

"Tony, this is Harold Pendergrass – just call him Harry – Justin Washington, and Robert Sanderson – he goes by Bob."

"Really nice to meet you all," I said as we shook hands. "Raymond has told me quite a lot about you."

"Really?" replied Justin. "I wouldn't think that he'd even claim knowing us!" he said laughing.

"Guys, Jenny said that we could meet in the Chapel," Raymond told us. "Nothing's scheduled there until this afternoon."

We all headed just down the hallway to the Chapel, a very nicely appointed space with cushioned chairs and wood tables. We pulled up chairs around one of the tables and sat. Raymond offered coffee or soft drinks, but everyone declined.

They all inquired about Raymond's general health and how his arm was doing and did he get along okay with using his left hand for eating and getting dressed and, most importantly, for going to the restroom. He laughed it all off and said that he was doing fine and if he needed help he just rang for someone. Besides, he would be getting the cast off in a couple of days.

Raymond's phone beeped, he looked at it, and told us, "I've got to go and take my medication. I'll be back in just a few minutes. Tony, why don't you tell the guys about your friend Ronald," and he excused himself and left the room.

After he closed the door, Harry asked me, "What's this about your friend?"

"Well, I told Raymond about him, and he has all of the characteristics y'all have figured out that someone possessed by an alien would have," I explained matter-of-factly.

"Oh, no!" exclaimed Bob. "Don't tell me that Ray is still telling people that he's found alien life here!"

"Uh, what?" was all I could say in reply.

"Ray has been on this kick for years now," offered Harry in the way of an explanation. "And apparently he tells people that we're in on it too."

"Wait a minute," I said, taken completely by surprise. "Do you mean to say that y'all haven't been all working together on this? What about all of the stuff you saw when y'all were flying for American? I mean the UAPs and stuff?"

They all looked at me quizzically. "We worked for American Airlines all right, but we were all mechanics," Justin said. "None of us were pilots."

"Wait – Raymond wasn't a pilot either?" I asked, confused. "He told me that he was a fighter pilot in Nam!"

Bob responded, "He was in Nam alright. He had some experience working on plane engines for his dad who was a crop duster, so they had him working on helicopters. He had an inner ear thing that affected his balance, so he couldn't be a pilot. It almost kept him out of the service."

"In fact, his problem with balance is probably why he fell and broke his arm," suggested Harry.

I was at a loss and they could tell. I just didn't know what to say, so I asked, "But y'all have zoom calls every week. What do you talk about?"

"Ray was on our bowling team," explained Justin. "We bowl on Wednesday nights and we get Ray on Zoom to say hello while we're all together."

I must have looked really confused because Bob said, "Look, Tony, don't feel too bad. Ray's done this before. He was into marijuana in Nam and he was also exposed to the chemicals that they used over there – stuff like 2-4-D and 2-4-5T. Some bad herbicides. You know, Agent Orange and stuff. That stuff affected a lot of the guys."

"But he even told me that, after he was let go from American Airlines, he flew for FedEx," I told them. I was exasperated by this time.

They all chuckled at that. Then Harry told me that Raymond drove a truck for FedEx for a while after he retired from American – and he had wanted to retire, he wasn't forced out.

"Look Tony," said Bob softly. "Ray is a great guy. We just humor him about this alien stuff. We think he really believes what he tells people. We don't think he's purposely lying. And it hasn't gotten him in too much trouble yet."

Then Justin added, "But that is why he's in a retirement home here in Louisiana and not back home. He was scaring people. His family thought that he'd stop with the alien nonsense if he was closer to his daughter. We're afraid that he might have to be committed one day if he keeps it up."

"I didn't know he had family here. He never mentioned it that I recall," I said. "You say that he has a daughter nearby?"

"Yes," answered Harry. "I think she lives here in Gonzales."

Just then Raymond came back into the room and we all got quiet.

"Hey, I didn't die!" he said. "I just went to get my medication. Why the long faces?"

We all grinned and laughed and Bob told him that if he had died, they'd be having drinks and celebrating, not sitting around crying about it.

"Well, that's more like it," Raymond said. "I hope you throw a big party in my honor."

Funny that he was talking about dying, because part of me wanted to kill him.

Chapter Thirteen

I went home feeling as though I had been punched in the gut. But I also felt somewhat relieved that one of my golfing-buddy friends was not possessed by an alien. Probably not. Then I briefly had this idea that maybe Raymond wasn't supposed to be telling me all of this alien stuff that he and his buddies had found and that they were lying to me to cover it up. Then I thought, *Don't be an idiot. You've been had.*

I knew that Darlene was playing tennis that morning and then going to lunch with the team, but I had to talk to someone, so I called Dustin and asked him to meet me at Philay's for lunch. He was happy to get out of the house, because Connie was on a cleaning tear and he was in the way. We agreed to meet at 11:30, before it got too busy.

We got there at the same time and snagged the last open table in the very back of the restaurant. I guess we should have come at 11:00. The place was packed with folks our age who probably got up and had coffee and breakfast at 6:00 a.m. and were starving by mid-morning. Philay's is open only Thursday through Sunday and has some of the best seafood dishes in town. We asked for iced teas and perused the menu, even though I almost always ordered the same thing – thin fried catfish filets with fries and lima bean with shrimp soup. After the waiter took our order, Dustin asked me why I wasn't at Frank's this morning.

"Uh, Raymond Sedgewick over at the retirement home asked me to come over to meet his friends today," I said a little loudly, because the back room was pretty noisy. "They were visiting from Missouri."

"Oh, are those the guys he flew with for American Airlines?" he asked.

"Uh, about that…." I stammered. "That's what I wanted to talk to you about. It turns out that, uh, and this is kind of funny, uh, maybe Raymond wasn't a pilot after all."

"What was that?" asked Dustin. "I didn't catch that – did you say that Raymond didn't fly for American?"

I smiled and said, "No, Raymond did work for American Airlines,

228

but he didn't fly for them or for anyone else either. Uh, he, uh, was never a pilot and neither were his friends."

Dustin looked perplexed. "But what about all of this alien stuff that you've been so excited about? You even believed that Ronald is an alien."

"Now, I wouldn't say 'excited' exactly, and I never came right out and accused Ronald of being an alien or anything," I said defensively. "At least not to his face."

"Are you telling me that Raymond made up all of this alien stuff just to mess with us?" Dustin asked.

"No, no, I don't think that he was messing with us," I replied. "His friends say that Raymond probably believes everything he told us. Apparently, he's been on this alien kick for some time."

"Well, if that doesn't take the cake," he said. "Wait until I tell Ronald what's been going on. He'll get a kick out of this."

"Oh no, no, don't say anything to Ronald," I urged. "He'll think I'm nuts."

"Well?" was all Dustin had to say about that.

That night at Dustin and Connie's I was forced to spill the beans on the whole alien caper, even though I had already told Darlene by that time and Dustin had filled Connie in also. They all just loved to see me embarrassing myself. I accused Connie and Darlene of being taken in by the alien story too, but they denied it and I was left holding the bag. It was a three-martini night and Darlene had to drive us home.

But the worst was yet to come. I stopped by Uncle Joe's and Aunt Millie's on Saturday to see if their water heater problem was fixed and figured I'd better tell Uncle Joe what I found out about Raymond and his alien adventures.

"I don't like to say 'I told you so'," he began, after I told him the gist of the story, "but I told you so."

He went on a while about how gullible I was and "didn't Matty Matassa tell me that Raymond was off his rocker," and "what did I learn at LSU after all if you would fall for something as nutty as aliens taking over someone's body?"

I took my licks and left as I heard Uncle Joe explaining to Aunt Millie about how some of my mother's side of the family were looney tunes. This was going to be fodder for Uncle Joe for years.

Chapter Fourteen

They say that women are the ones who gossip the most, but I'll argue that old men can hold their own in that contest. By the time the next Friday had rolled around, word of the fake alien news had spread. Those of us not scheduled to visit the Bayou Manchac Retirement Home (I might never go there again) showed up at Frank's. I had picked up Uncle Joe and we arrived earlier than usual because there was some lame excuse for the kids to be off of school and traffic was unusually light. I was glad that the trip was shorter because I caught flack from Uncle Joe the whole way.

Jack was the only one sitting at our table when we walked in and he just looked at me and laughed. "I can't believe you fell for that alien stuff," was his opening greeting. I wanted to remind him of how he was all excited talking to Raymond and asking about antennae and navels and such, but it wouldn't have done any good. I was the goat for sure.

The guys started trickling in, all ribbing me about my gullibility and wondering how I could suspect that one of them was from outer space. The only ones that hadn't shown up by 7:35 were Dustin and Ronald. I dreaded facing Ronald because I was sure that Dustin had told him about me thinking he was an alien. I was just getting a coffee refill from Wendy when Dustin walked in, followed closely by Ronald wearing a motorcycle helmet with the visor pulled down. Everyone at the table – and in the room in fact – stopped talking. Ronald walked up to me, stopped, gave me the Vulcan split-fingered "live long and prosper" sign, and said "Nanu Nanu." I told him that he was confusing Star Trek with Mork and Mindy, but nobody heard me over the laughter. At least he had a sense of humor about the whole thing, which made me feel better.

In spite of getting sidetracked by the alien nonsense, the guys all thought that visiting the male residents at the retirement home was a really good thing for us to do and that they thought that we should keep it up. Jenny surely agreed. She was really excited that we were willing to visit and spend quality time with "her guys" as she called them. She had all kinds of ideas about what other things we could do at the home, such as helping the residents put together bluebird houses from kits, helping to build raised vegetable and flower gardens, and other such things. I figured that it would be a good thing for us also.

One of the other ideas that I suggested to Jenny was something that my Rotary Club did at a nursing home a few years back. We had teams of two visit the residents – those who agreed to participate – and interview them about their lives, their family history, what it was like when they were kids, and so forth. She loved the idea and was anxious for us to get started.

I got the guys' attention and mentioned this project. Dustin, who was involved with the original nursing home interviews, thought we should do it, but also involve the Rotary Club and maybe the high school kids who were in the Interact Club that our Rotary Club sponsored. We all talked about this project for a while and the consensus was to start doing the interviews. Dustin and I agreed to take the lead and organize the thing. This sounded like another spreadsheet project to me.

While I had the floor, I said, "I'm thinking about writing a book about the MOSS group."

Jack asked, "What sort of book?"

"You know, about stuff we've done in the Parish to help out, like the solar panel thing, and the dog candy thing – stuff like that," I explained.

"Leave me out of it," was Uncle Joe's response. "I don't want to be associated with any of that. I got a reputation to protect."

"You're not going to write about the alien stuff, right?" was Jack's concern.

"I don't know," I said. "I might keep that part out. I don't want to embarrass anybody." *Especially me,* I thought.

"What makes you think that you can write a book?" asked Slim.

"It's almost impossible to not be able to write a book," I replied. "Just look at some of the books out there. Any fool can write a book," I replied.

"Well," offered Dr. Dart, "You are not just any fool, that's for sure."

I took that as a ringing endorsement.

THE END